NOVEL LAST NAMES

Books by Larry J. Hoefling

Chasing the Frontier: Scots-Irish in Early America

Pittsburg County

Nils Thor Granlund: The Swedish Showman Who Invented American Entertainment

Last of the True Irish: A novel

NOVEL LAST NAMES

Surname Meanings for the Creative Fiction Writer

LARRY J. HOEFLING

INLANDIA

NOVEL LAST NAMES: Surname Meanings for the Creative Fiction Writer is an original publication of Inlandia Press. This work has never before appeared in book form.

INLANDIA press
b.a. oklahoma

Cover Graphics by McHuston Graphics
Illustration: Quilp and wife, The Old Curiosity Shop, 1912 ed.
ISBN 978-0-9822313-1-9

First Trade Printing: January 2009

Manufactured in the United States of America

For Maria P. Fabiola Jasso de Hoefling

Mi esposa bella and a woman of many names.

Introduction

The name of the character can make all the difference. James Bond, Uriah Heep, Dirk Pitt, Silas Marner, Ebenezer Scrooge – all names intimately identified with their characters and seemingly inherent to the type of stories they inhabit.

Writers may select names arbitrarily, accidentally, or as a matter of deliberate planning, but the choice remains crucial to the completed work.

Should the name mean something?

It is safe to say that no writer wants a character named Bill Carpenter if his job involves a hammer, nails, and a toolbelt, but there is nothing wrong with taking a little surreptitious pleasure in naming the plastic surgeon Dr. Case, whose name in medieval times described the *maker of chests.*

The novelist's characters may require foreign surnames or names of ethnic origin, but the selection of a character's name does not have to be entirely random in nature. Cognate forms are versions of last names in a different language with the same meaning.

In early times there were no last names at all, as settlements were small and the duplication of given names could easily be avoided. Additional identification of medieval men only became necessary when the numbers of men named William, Stephen, et.al. became so great as to require differentiation. Last names have been around since medieval times in most cases, and although last names are now indispensible, most Americans have little knowledge as to the meaning or origin of their surname.

Each last name has a story but many of the specifics have been lost to time, and this collection of names is the result of a great many inquiries toward shedding light on that particular chapter of history.

There is no single collection containing every surname in the world, and this compilation is no exception. It represents research conducted over the course of many, many years, during which time the collection of references grew to include Anglo-Saxon dictionaries and materials providing insights into the origins of English language and Latin-based names.

Last Name Origins

The word *surname* arrived from Latin through Old French to Middle English, the prefix sur- meaning *over, above, or beyond,* and came into usage when there were enough people with the same first name to make things confusing. An identifier *over, above, or beyond* a person's given name became common in the years following the victory over the English in 1066 by William the Conqueror, who wanted a list of all his new subjects, which was compiled in what came to be called the *Domesday Book.*

In 1086, when William of Normandy commissioned the *Domesday Book* last names were not in existence, although some Irish clans traditionally used an ancestor's name as a means of identification. By the 15th Century, the majority of the populations of England and France regularly used last names as a means of identification.

When early settlements began to include non-family members, it became a simple matter of attaching a description to identify a specific person. William the carpenter was distinguished from William the miller by his trade. William the young was William Young or – if he shared his father's name – or William, William's son.

There are several distinct types of surnames.

Patronymic Surnames

Particularly when a distinctive man lived in a settlement or community, it was a simple matter to identify the sons by mentioning the father. Sometimes the identification was as simple as adding the name itself: John Thomas, William John. At times, a possessive form created the surname, as in William Steven's or William Steven's son, eventually forming Stevens and Stevenson, along with the variant spellings.

Different cultures used identifying words to indicate the lineage. Among the Gaelic-speaking Scots, the term *mac* meant "son of," as did *ap* among the Welsh, *fi* among the Italians, and *fitz* in the language of the Normans. In his settlement, John Mac

Donald was the son of Donald, John Ap Rice was the son of Rhys. The mercenaries who aided William the Conqueror received land in lieu of cash for their services, and many settled in Ireland and present-day United Kingdom. They can be identified by the prefix *fitz* in their surname, as in Fitzpatrick and Fitzhugh, used to specify the sons of Patrick and Hugh, respectively. Other languages added a suffix to a given name to form a patronymic surname, such as Michalski (son of Michael, Polish), and Romanov (son of Roman, Russia).

As each settlement might contain one or more persons bearing any particular given name, there was little exclusivity among them, resulting in the large number of those names in existence as surnames in later history. Persons bearing the given name Jones (John's, or John) existed in nearly every early settlement, given the popularity of the first name *John*. William Johnson of one settlement likely had no kinship at all with those bearing the "John's son" identifier in other areas.

There are not many surviving surnames based on the name of the mother, but some cultures used the matriarch of the family as a basis for identification, and those rare names fall under the classification of *matronymic surnames*.

Occupational Names

There are a great many surnames derived from the occupations of the first bearers of any name, and those names relate directly to the medieval trades. Each prosperous settlement or community would require the services of a smith or a carpenter, and John the Smith evolved into the simplified, John Smith. Some names reflected positions, rather than actual trades, such a Mayor. In most cases, names such as Abbott and Bishop identified a person in the service of that official, rather than the actual official.

The occupational names evolved in various languages and *cognate* forms are those with the same root expressed in a different language. The *zimmerman* in Germany performed the same work as the *carpenter* in England.

Place Names

It was an early tradition to use a specific place to identify a man, especially if that man was a recent arrival from some other location. William Paris might have relocated to England from that city. John England might have recently moved from there to Ireland or Wales, and although he might have been called John (who lived near the) Ford, in his native land, it would have little significance for his new neighbors who would more easily identify him as the newly relocated outsider.

Some of the significant locations were topographical, such a hills, fords (crossing places in a river or stream), marshes, trees, or lakes. John Underhill made his home at that location, and William Lee lived near the pasture or meadowland, which in the language of the Middle English was called a *lea*.

Nicknames

Throughout history, humans have used derivatives or pet forms of names to address contemporaries, and sometimes nicknames are adjectives based on physical traits or characteristics. Often, nicknames were cruel or unflattering, but with continued regular usage, they managed to become an identifying mark. In the cases of the exceptionally unkind descriptors, descendants altered the surnames to more acceptable forms.

Many descriptions have managed to survive the centuries, such as *sly as a fox*, and those sorts of verbal comparisons were common in medieval times. As a result, some surnames are nicknames based on a perceived trait of the bearer, and his peers might have considered William Fox a sly man. (The name Fox could also be derived from the picture on the business sign outside the public inn, as most persons at the time were illiterate and paintings of animals generally adorned exterior signage.) John Whitehead no doubt lost his original hair color, and William Grey might have been in the same situation, although he could have known for always wearing clothing of that color.

In a time when entertainment was simple and any pageantry at all was significant, men often came to be known by the role they portrayed in a seasonal play or pageant. John King might have played that part in the annual pageant with such authority that it became his identifier. Similar names are Angel and Easter.

Ornamental Names

Some cultures managed to exist without surnames until much later in history, and eventually took names at the direction of their government or other agency. Those names have little significance to the history of the ancestor first acquiring the name, other than as a depiction of the person's individual tastes.

When the Swedes were obliged to take last names, the government offered a list of acceptable terms for use as names or in combination with another term to form a compound surname. Lundquist, Americanized from Lundkvist, is literally translated as "grove twig." The pleasing sound of the elements formed the basis of their usage as names.

Arbitrary Names

In some rare cases, last names came into usage because of the arbitrary listing or notation by a clerk of a governing body or commission. Particularly in instances of names based in a foreign language, individuals found themselves at the mercy of the recording clerk, or alternately, in their interpretation of the clerk's entry.

The standardization of spelling came relatively late in history, and a court clerk with an extraordinary flourish might pen several examples of a letter in a row, just for fun. Later, when the bearer of a name saw it represented on a court document, it inferred a legal form. Names like Ffolkes and Ffrench came from such florid inscriptions or printing ligatures, that the early bearers of the name misunderstood to be the correct and legal version of the name.

Some arbitrary surnames are the result of confusion or lack of a literal translation. Some members of the Native American nations had their identities set by English-speaking government clerks or commissioners with an unkind streak or an inability to translate a word or phrase, resulting in such surnames as *Left Hand Woman*, *Man on Cloud*, and *Heap of Birds.*

Variations and Spellings

Since the standardization of English spelling did not come about until the mid to late nineteenth century, spelling variations among surnames are frequent and widespread. In addition, some variations evolved much in the same way that relatives refer to young Bill as Billy, and young John answers to Johnny. In the case of surnames, such pet forms constitute diminutive versions of the name.

Much of the logic of the changes has been lost with time, particularly in cases of nicknames or diminutive forms of names that are no longer used or fashionable. Some use Jack and Jackie as interchangeable versions of the given name John, as a more familiar or pet form of the name, and in that same fashion some surnames like Hobbe arrived through a pet form of the name Rob, which was a shortened form of Robert.

Less common are those medieval insults forged into an enduring - if unflattering - surname, in which a suffix with a derogatory inference was added, or the addition of a suffix to form a surname with offensive connotations. Such names are termed pejorative versions, coined as an insult in the manner achieved by adding the suffix –y- to the surname Dark, to construct a racial epithet.

Names with variant spellings come from the same origin in most cases, and names that have an adopted diminutive or pejorative version are variations of the root surname.

The Names

It should be noted that this collection of surnames came about in a wholly random fashion based on individual requests received over time, and does not constitute a list of most-common surnames in America, nor a list of any other collective title.

Without a doubt, hundreds of both common and unusual English language last names are missing from this collection, but their absence does not infer those names are rare or uncommon. Conversely, inclusion in the collection does not necessarily mean that the name is one commonly found or widely distributed.

Regarding the use of the word 'novel' in the title; which comes from a Middle English form of the Latin word *novellus* and meaning 'new' – it is not intended to suggest that these last names are recent acquisitions. Names have been handed down for generations and generations. A second meaning for the word 'novel' has come to suggest something original or striking in concept. Last names are certainly that.

A

Abercrombie is a Scottish place name from a so-named location in Fife which was earlier called *Ababcrumbach*. It is derived from the Brittonic *aber* = confluence, added to the name of a river, which was named from *crom* = crooked + the local suffix *-ach*. **Abercromby** is a variation.

Abbott: English Occupational name for the man who lived in the house of the Abbott, or sometimes as a nickname for the sanctimonious person.

Adam is an English, French, Catalan, Italian, German, Flemish/Dutch, Jewish (Ashkenazic), and Polish patronymic name derived from Hebrew *adama* = earth. **Aitken, Aiken, Aitkin** are forms generally found specifically in Scotland -- it's a diminutive form.

Adlparvar: from Arabic *Adl* = justice + *parvar* = one who nurtures (Persian).

Adolphus is derived from **Adolph,** which comes from the Germanic given name *Adalwulf*, and is composed of the elements *adal* = noble + *wulf* = wolf. Until the Second World War, Adolph was a common given name. Cognate forms include **Ahlf, Alf** (Low German); **Adolfi, Adinolfi** (Italian). **Adolfino** is an Italian diminutive form, and other patronymic versions include **Ahlfs, Alfs, Adolfsson** (the last being Swedish).

Aichelmeyer is a compound name that likely originated in the German Lowlands, where **Aichele** is a diminutive form of the name that means *oak* in English. Meyer is a German term for town official or steward, sometimes similar to Mayor. The name would literally be translated as "oak mayor" which doesn't make for a logical explanation. If there is Jewish heritage involved, it is likely one of the Ashkenazic ornamental names adopted when required by the government. They didn't make literal sense, but were taken because of their pleasing sound, in the same fashion as were the Swede's names. Examples: **Aichenblatt** (oak leaf), **Aichenbaum** (oak tree), **Eichelberg** (oak hill), **Eichenholz** (oak wood).

Alexander is a name common throughout the early British Isles taken from the English given name Alexander, which means "defender of men."

Alarcon is a Spanish place name derived from Alarcon in Cuenca and Cordoba.

Alarid: may be a version of the name Alard (Alar-i-d) which is a Patronymic name derived from the given name Adelard. From Old English *adal* =noble + *hard* =hardy. Another variation of the name is spelled **Allard.**

Albright is an English variation of the surname **Albert,** found among the English, Low German, French, Catalan, and Hungarian cultures, from a Germanic name *Albrecht,* from *adal* = noble + *behrt* = bright, famous. **Aubert** is another English variant; **Abert, Aber, Allebrach** (Low German); **Auber, Aubert, Aube, Aubey** (French).

Alford is an English place name that described an old crossing point in a stream or river, and three particular places (Surry, Somerset, and Lincolnshire). The man who emigrated from one of these locations would be known at his new residence as Alford, since people tended to point out the outsiders in their midst as an identification feature. The Surry location derived its name from Old English *eald* = old + *ford* = water crossing. The Somerset locale was named for the Old English female given name Ealddyd (from *eald* = old + *gyd* = battle). The Lincolnshire location is from *Ealh* = temple + *ford.* **Allford** is a variation.

Alger is an English patronymic name, from the given name Alger, which comes from several places -- Germanic, Norman, and Old English -- which kind of ran together. The second syllable - *ger* is derived from the Germanic element *geri/gari* =

spear. *Alfgeirr* (elf spear) was a Norse name which served as one source; *Aelfgar* is another version (French Norman). The first element of the name is generally assumed to be associated with *alb* = elf, *adal* = noble, or *ald* = old. Variations are **Algar, Auger, Elgar, Elger.**

Allam is likely a spelling variation of **Allem,** which is a variation of the French patronymic name **Alleaume,** from an Old French version of the Germanic given name *Adalhelm,* composed of the elements *adal* = noble + *helm* = protection, helmet. **Alliaume** and **Allem** are variations; **Ahlhelm** is a German cognate, **Alm** is the Frisian version, and **Adlam** is the English cognate.
Allard/Alard/Allert: English Patronymic Name...from the old name Adelard. It's components are adal = hardy + hard. Allart and Allert are variations of the name.
Alle is a Germanic name that meant "noble" and *Brand* is often used in Germanic compound names such as **Hildabrand**, and derived from the personal name Brando, which was a shortened form of several names that contained the element *brand* = sword < *brinnan* = to flash. **Allenbrand** is "noble sword" when taken at its literal sense.

Allyn is a spelling variation of the English and Scottish patronymic name **Allen**, an ancient Celtic name derived from Gaelic *ailin* = little rock. Variations are **Alan, Allan, Allegyne, Alline, Allin.** Patronymic forms include **Allenson, Allis, Allanson, Allison, Allinson, Hallison, FitzAlan, McAllan, McAline, McEllen, McElane, McKellan,** and **McKellen.**

Allender: English/Scottish patronymic name, from the Celtic name of antiquity – Alan, from Ailin = rock and sometimes derived from Allen as the name of a town or settlement.

Alston is an English patronymic name derived from the Middle English given name *Alstan,* which was a combination of several other names of the time composed of the elements *oedel* = nobel, *aelf* = elf, *eald* = old + *stan* = stone. There were several places named Alston (Lancashire, Devon, and Somerset) and the name may have described a man who came from there. **Alstone,** and **Allston** are variations.

Ameigh may be a diminutive cognate of the English name (from French-Norman) **Amis,** from the Old French nickname *Amis* = friend. Variations are **Amiss, Amies, Ames.** Cognates include **Ami, Amy, Lamy** (French); **Amico** (Italian). Diminutives include **Amiguet, Amiot, Amyot, Amiel** (French); **Amicelli, Amicino, Amighini, Amigh, Amigotti, Amietti** (Italian); **Amigo** (Catalan). Patronymic forms include **D'Amico, D'Amici,** and **De Amicis** in Italy, and in England -- **Amson** and **Amison.**

Anderson is the ninth most common surname in America, and owes that position to the popularity of the name Andrew in England, Scotland, and Scandinavian countries. Andrew (man) was the first of the disciples called by Jesus, and was a revered name due to its church influences through medieval times. St. Andrew is the patron saint of both Scotland and Russia and many given names were chosen to honor the saint. Patronymic surnames are names used to describe a man by using his father's name. In Norway, the name takes the form **Andresen, Anders,** and **Enders;** the Swedes in American eliminated the extra -S- they normally include to become Anderson. It was **Andersson** and **Anderssen** before they emigrated. The French form is **Andre,** with an accent mark above the ending letter. **Andrews** is largely found in Scotland, along with **McAndrew** -- the prefix Mc being another patronymic designation -- which is also found in Ireland. In Italy, the name is **D'Andrea,** in Poland, it is **Andrzejewski,** in the Ukraine, it is **Andrijenko,** and in Czechoslovakia, Andrew takes the form of **Ondrus.**

Andrade is a Portuguese patronymic name that is believed to be derived from the Greek given name Andras, from *andros* = man, male. It is also commonly found in Spain. There are several locations in Portugal by this name, which were likely named because of someone bearing this name.

Angell is a variation of the English and French nickname **Angel,** derived from Old French *angel* > Latin *angelus* > greek *angelos* = messenger. It was the nickname for the man of angelic quality, or occasionally, the nickname for the man who played the part of the angel in a local pageant. **Angeau** is a French variation. Cognates exist in many languages.

Anger is a French variation of the English (of Norman origin) and French patronymnic name **Ainger,** which comes from the Germanic given name Ansger, composed of the elements *ans* = god + *ger,gar* = spear. **Angier, Anger, Angear, Aunger** are English variations. **Anger, Anquier, Ansquer** are among the French versions.

Angulo is a form of the name **Angle,** a place name that described the man who lived on an odd-shaped piece of land. The form Angle is English, which is also found as **Nangle.** Angulo (actually **Ángulo** -- with the diacritical mark above the A) is the form of the name found originally in Spain.

Annesley is a English place name in Nottinghamshire, derived from Old English *an* = solitary + *leah* = wood, clearing. It described the man who came from the settlement at the "woods that stand alone."

Antecki is a variation of the name **Anthony,** one of the most common names, derived from Latin *Antonius,* an ancient Roman family name of unknown etymology. **Antaki** may be a variation as well.

Appel/Appelbaum: The German Place names Appel and Applebaum /Appelbaum described the man who lived by the apple tree, and **Appelt** is a likely variation.

Armitage is an English place name for the medieval man who lived near a hermitage, from Middle English and Old French *hermitage* > *hermite* = hermit, coming by way of Late Latin *eremita, eremos* = solitary. Variations are **Armytage, Hermitage.** Most if not all of those who bear the name are descended from a family that lived at Hermitage Bridge in Almondbury, near Huddersfield in England, during the 1200's. Enoch Armitage was born in 1677, and was the first of several family members to emigrate from Wooldale, Yorkshire, and brought the name to North America.

Arnold is an English patronymic name from a Norman given name comprised of the Germanic elements *arn* = eagle + *wald* = rule. Occasionally it is derived as a place name to describe the man from any of the so-named locations in England and derived from Old English *earn* = eagle + *halh* = nook, hollow. Variations are **Arnhold, Arnould, Arnout, Arnoil, Arnald, Arnaud, Arnall, Arnell, Arnull, Arnott, Arnatt, Arnull, Harnott, Harnett, Hornet,** and **Hornett.** Numerous cognate and diminutive forms also exist.

Arrington is derived two ways: first, as a variation of the surname **Harrington,** which - when of English (Cumberland) origin -- comes from Old English *Hoeferingtun* = "settlement associated with Hoefer." *Hoefer* is a nickname that meant "He-goat." When of Irish origin, Harrington is derived from Gaelic *O'hArrachtain* = "descendant of *Arrachtan* (powerful, mighty). When Arrington isn't a variation of Harrington, it is derived from a place in Cambridgeshire, which was named from Old English *Earningatun* = "settlement of the people of Earna." *Earna* was a nickname that meant "eagle."

Arthur is an English and French patronymic name, from the Celtic given name *Arthur,* which is of disputed etymology, but has been in continuous use since the Middle Ages, partly due to the King Arthur tales, based on a 6th century British leader. French variations are **Arthus, Artus,** and **Arthuys.** Cognates include **Arturo, Artusio, Artuso, Artusi** (Italian); **Artur** (Portuguese). **Arthurs, MacArthur, McArthur, McArtair, McAirter, McCairtair, McCarter** are patronymic forms.

Asbury is also an English place name, but of uncertain origin, although the second element is derived from Old English *burh* = fortified town. The first element may have been derived from Ash or a medieval given name. It was predominately found in the West Midlands area of England.

Ashe is a variation of Ash found primarily in Ireland. **Ash** is an English place name that described the man who lived by the ash tree, from Old English *oesc* = ash. It also described the man who emigrated from any of the several locations by that name.

Ashmore: is an English Place name that was derived from the Old English *oesc* = ash + *mor* = marsh...for a literal translation of ash-marsh. The man who lived near there often acquired that as his surname.

Asmussen is a variation of the surname **Erasmus** that is most commonly found among the Danish, Norwegians, and Lowland Germans. Erasmus is of German origin, from a given name that came from the Greek *erasmos* = loved. A St. Erasmus was a patron of sea-going men, but remained a somewhat obscure figure, which contributed to the obscurity of the name. Variations are **Rasmus, Asmus, Eras;** diminutive forms are **Rasem, Asam, Asum, Rassmann, Assmann, Raes, Raskin.** Patrnymic forms include **Asmesen, Asmes** (German); **Asmussen** (Low German); **Rasmussen, Asmussen** (Danish, Norwegian).

Atkins is a Patronymic name, derived from the early given name Adam (Hebrew *adama* = red earth or man), originating in England, France, Catalan, Italy, Germany, and Poland, as well as the Ashkenazic Jewish, Dutch and Flemish. Diminutive forms of Adam are **Adkin, Atkin, Aitkin, Adnett, Adnitt,** and **Ade.** Italian variants are **Adami, Dami;** Polish and Jewish versions include **Adamski.** The Hugarian cognate is **Adam,** in Provencal it is **Azam,** in Spain, **Adan.**

Atnip: English Place Name...The Medieval English said *atten* to mean "at the" creating names like ATWOOD meaning "at-the-woods." The Old English word *heope* (pronounced like hip) meant "rose-hip." *Atten* + *heope* or "at-the-roses" can easily be anglicized as Atnip.

Oak is an English place name that described the man who lived near a prominent oak tree or in an oak woods, from the Middle English word *oke* = oak. It may also have been a nickname for the man who was exceptionally strong, as the tree. Variations are **Oake, Oke, Oaks, Oakes, Oaker, Atrtock, Attoc, Attack, Atack, Aikman** (Scottish version).

Aton is derived from two Old English elements *æt* = at, near + *tun* = settlement, enclosure -- and described the man who lived near, or at, a recognized local settlement.

Austin is an English Patronymic name, derived from the given name *Aoustin* introduced into England by the Normans.

Avans is a patronymic version of the Welsh name **Evans,** which was originally drawn from the given name *Ifan,* Evan = John. Occasionally it is a variant of the Scottish surname **Ewan** which is an Anglicized form of the Gaelic personal name *Eogann.* Other patronymic forms are **Evans, Evens, Evance, Ifans, Iving, Heavans, Heavens, Bevan.**

Ayers is a patronymic version of the surname **Ayer,** an English Nickname for the man who was well known to be the heir to a title or fortune, from the Middle English word *eir, eyr* = heir. Variants include **Ayr, Ayre, Eyer, Eyre, Hayer, Heyer,** among others.

B

Baca is a Spanish cognate of the Italian nickname **Vacca,** which is derived from the Latin *vacca* = cow, and is the name given to the cowherd or gentle person. **Vacchi** is an Italian variant. **Vetch, Veitch** are Scottish cognates, while **Vaca** and **Vacas** are additional Spanish cognates of the name. Numerous diminutive forms exist including **Vachelli, Vachette, Vachey, Vachez, Vachon, Vachot, Vachoux, Vacquez,** and **Vacquin.**

Bagwell is an English place name derived from the Medieval given name Bacga + the Old English *wella* = well, spring -- and would have described the man who lived by a well owned by a man named Bacga, probably a notable location at the time.

Bailey is an English occupational name for a steward or official, from the Middle English *bailli* = carrier, porter. In Scotland, the bailli is the magistrate and bailiff is a form that has evolved elsewhere. Occasionally, the name is derived as an English Place name from a Middle English word derived from Old French *baille* = enclosure. In this form it originally meant the person living by the outer wall of the castle, but Old Bailey, a place in Lancashire which formed part of the outer wall of some medieval castle, also became the origin for surname for people from that location. There are numerous variations in many countries, including **Baillie** (Scotland), **Bayless, Bailess, Lebailly** (French), **Bally** (Swiss), **Baglione** (Italian), and **Bailloux** (Provencal).

Baker: As you might suspect, this name originated in the occupation of a medieval townsman, where many of the most frequently found surnames were derived. Baker is the 7th most frequently found occupational surname in America.

Bakeman was likely originally spelled as **Bakmann** -- at any rate, it is a cognate form of **Baker,** the occupational name for the owner of a communal oven who cooked the breads for the entire village, or for the man who baked goods in the village great house or castle. The maintainance of a community over operated in exchange for loaves of bread was a hereditary privilege during the feudal period in England. Variations are **Baiker, Bacher, Baxter.** Cognates (same word in another language) include **Backer, Becker, Beckermann** (German); **Bakker, DeBaecker, De Backer, De Becker, Bakmann, Beckers** (Flemish, Dutch); **Becker, Beckerman** (Jewish).

Baldwin is an English Patronymic name from the given name comprised of the Germanic elements *bald* = bold, brave + *wine* = friend. Baldwin was an extremely popular given name among the Normans and in Flanders during the Middle Ages. The first Christian king of Jerusalem was Baldwin, as was the count of Flanders who lead the Fourth Crusade and became the first Latin Emperor of Constantinople in 1204. Occasionally, Baldwin is an Irish surname adopted by bearers of the Gaelic name *O'Maolagain,* as a result of an association with an English term meaning bald, as a nickname. Congnative forms of the English version are **Baudouin** (French); **Baldovino, Balduini, Baldoin** (Italian); **Valdovinos** (Spanish); and **Baldewin, Ballwein, Bollwahn,** and **Bollwagen** (German).

Ballard: Many times nicknames stuck and became a surname. Some were cruel, some weren't too bad. Those that had particularly cruel names either changed the spelling or changed their names altogether. Ballard is the nickname that the English sometimes gave to those whose heads were short in the hair department. **Bald, Balch,** and **Ballard** are typical English Nicknames for the bald-headed man.

Barlow is an English place name taken from any of the so-named locations in Lancashire and West Yorkshire, derived from Old English *bere* = barley + *hlaw* = hill. The location by that name in Derbyshire is name from Old English *var* = boar + *leah* = clearing, meadow.

Barna/Barner: Hungarian Patronymic name from the given name Barnaby, who was St. Paul's companion and a common early given name.

Barnard is a French and English variation of the surname **Bernard,** which has origins among the English, French, Polish, and Czechs, and is derived from the Germanic given name *Bernhard,* from the elements *ber* = bear + *hard* = brave, hardy. The name was introduced to England by the conquering Normans in 1066 (that was the date William won the battle; the name might have been introduced a day or two later...) Variations are **Barnard** (English, French); **Beneard, Besnard, Benard** (French); **Biernat, Biernacki, Bernadzki** (Polish); **Ber, Bern, Beran** (Czech).

Barnes: English Place Name, from Barnes (in Surry or Aberdeenshire) so named because of the barns that were located there. There were also Barnes families who were known by the name of their father (English Patronymic Name) who was called Barn, a pet form of Barnabas – a name not used much these days – that means 'son of prophesy or consolation.' Some Barnes families are descended from Beorn, a given name that meant 'nobleman' and still others had a patronymic designation from Bairn, a name often given to a young child of a prominent family.

Barnett is a variation of **Barnet,** an English place name derived from Old English *bærnet* = place cleared by burning. There are a number of so-named locations by the name, and the man who emigrated from such a place was referenced at his new home by his place of origin.

Barnwell is an English place name from from Barnwell in Cambridgeshire, from Old English *beorna* = warriors' + *wella* = stream, or from Barnwell in Northamptonshire, from Old English *byrgen* = burial mound + *wella* = stream. **Barnewall** is a variation.

Barrett is an English patronymic name derived from the given name *Bernhard,* of Germanic origin, which was introduced by the Normans into England with William the Conqueror. Bernhard is derived from *ber* = bear + *hard* = hardy, and Barrett is a diminutive form. Barrett is occasionally derived from Middle English *barat* = trouble, strife, deception -- and was a nickname for the quarrelsome person. Also, it is occasionally an occupational name for the hatmaker, from Old French *barette* = cap, bonnet. Variations are **Barret, Barrat, Barratt, Barritt.** Cognate forms and diminutives are also abundant.

Barrington: English Place name, from several locations by that name, the one in Gloucester derived from Old English *Beorningtun* (settlement of Beorn), the Somerset location derived from Bara's Settlement. Occasionally Barrington is an Anglicized form of *O'Bearain,* descendant of Bearan (spear).

Barron: English Nickname that called attention to noble birth or exalted rank.

Bartol is a cognate of **Bartholomew,** from the medieval given name from Aramaic *bar-Talmay* (son of Talmay) whose name meant 'having many furrows' in the sense of having much land. **Bartlam** is an English variation of Bartholomew. Cognates include **Bartelmy, Barthelmy, Barthelemy, Berthelemy, Berthelmy,** (French); **Bartholomieu, Bartomieu, Berthomieu, Bertomieu, Berthome, Berthomier** (Provencal); **Bartolommeo, Bartolomeo, Bortolomei, Tolomei, Tomme, Tommei, Tolomio, Meo** (Italian); **Bartolome** (Spain); **Bartomeu, Bertomeu** (Catalan); **Bartolomeu** (Portugal); **Bartholomaus, Bartoloma, Bartolomaus** (German); **Barthelme, Barthelmes, Meus, Mebius, Mebus, Mebis, Mobius, Miebes** (Low German); **Bartolomivis, Mewe, Mewis, Meeus, Mees, Meys, Mebes** (Flemish, Dutch); **Bartosch** (German, Slav origin); **Barta, Bartak, Bartos, Barton** (Czech); **Bartlomiej** (Polish); **Barta, Bartal** (Hungarian). Diminutive forms include **Bartlett, Bartleet, Bart, Bartle, Barty, Bartie** (English); **Berthelemot, Bertelemot, Bartholin,**

Bartol, Bartolin, Bertolin, Bartel, Barthelet, Bartelet, Berthel, Barthot, Bartot, Bertot, Berthot, Barthod, Bartod (French); **Bartolomeotti, Bartolomucci, Bartolini, Bartoli, Bartalini, Bartali, Bartoletti, Bartaletti, Bartolozzi, Bartalucci, Bartelli, Barocci, Bartolotti, Bortolini, Bortolutti, Bortoluzzi, Tolussi, Tolomelli, Tolumello,Tolotti, Tolossi, Tolussi** (Italian); **Bart, Barth, Barthel, Bartel, Bartl** (German); **Baert, Bartolijn, Bartoleyn** (Flemish, Dutch); **Bartke, Bartek, Bachura, Bacha, Bachnik** (German, Slav origin); **Gartosek, Bartusek, Bartunek** (Czech); **Bartlomiejczyk, Bartoszek, Bartosik** (Polish); **Bartok, Bertok** (Hungarian). Patronymic forms also exist in several languages.

Bass/Basso: English/Italian Nickname...Surnames were often taken from nicknames given to the progenitor of a family -- in the case of Bass, the English used the word as a nickname for a small or thin person, along with **Block, Grubb, Littell, Short, Smalley,** etc. In Italy, the same nickname is **Basso.**

Bauer is a German status name for a peasant or a nickname for the "neighbor, fellow citizen."

Baumann is a variation of the German and Jewish nickname Bauer, which meant 'neighbor' or 'fellow citizen.' It was derive from German *bauer,* from *bur* = occupant of a small dwelling. **Pauer, Gebuhr, Bauman** are other variations. Cognates are **Burmann, Bur, Buhrmann, Burmann, Bouwer** (Low German); **Boerma, Boersma, Bouman** (Frisian); **De Boer, Boere, Boerman, Bouwer, Bouwman, Bouwmeester,** (Dutch); **Bohr** (Danish); **Por** (Hungarian).

Bays is a patronymic form of the English and French nickname **Bay,** which described the man with the chestnut or auburn hair, derived from Old French and Middle English *bay, bai* = reddish-brown. **Bai** is a French variation. **Bayo** is a Spanish cognate and **Baaij, Bay** are found among the Dutch. **Bayet** is a diminutive French form, and diminutive forms found in Provencal include

Bayol, Bajol, Bajolet, Bayoux. Bays and **Bayes** are patronymic forms meaning "son of Bay."

Beachum is a variation of the English (Norman) and French name **Beauchamp,** a place name from several so-named French locales, from Old French *beu, bel* = fair + *champs* = field, plain. **Beacham, Beachamp, Beehcam, Beacom, Belchamp** are other forms.

Beard was a fairly common English Nickname, for the man who wore a beard, and a number of surnames were derived from it. The suffix - *den* or - *don* is from an Old English element for dune, or hill. **Bearden** in that context would be "Beard's Hill" a fairly good description for a medieval location, from which many surnames drew their meaning.

Bearce, Bearse: the old English word *bearu, beara,* meant "grove, wood" and there are nearly forty places in SW England named from that root in variations such as **Beare, Beere,** etc. The man who hailed from that location and moved to another town was often described by his former place of residence. The addition of the -S most often designates a patronymic form. If a man named John moved to a town, where there were several men named John already, he might be described as "John, of Beare." His son would be described as Beare's, or Beare's son. Most of surnames of this style are related to the Old English *bearu/beara* = grove. Spellings became standardized after the American Civil War, a fact sometimes overlooked in modern times. There is an Anglo-Saxon vocabulary word *bearce* that means "barking."

Beattie/Beaty/Beatty/Beatie/Beatey: Scottish and Northern Irish Patronymic name derived from the name Bartholomew. Bate was a pet form of that given name, and sons of Bate might be known as Beattie, Beatty, or Beatey.

In medieval times (when surnames were adopted), there were several given names that were commonly found among both men and women, a practice continued into modern times. **Bebbe** was one such name. **Bebb** is a patronymic surname of Anglo-Saxon origin, as a variation of the given name **Bebbe,** which would also occur as a surname in that spelling. **Bebbing** is a diminutive form, and the location in Cheshire, England called *Bebbington* is derived from the combination of Bebbe/Bebbing + Old English *tun* = settlement, which described a medieval settlement headed by Bebbe or Bebbing.

Bechtel is a German patronymic name that described the descendant of Betto, a name that was a pet form of several German names that began with Bercht, which meant "bright, famous." Berhtolf and Berhtari are examples of names that would have been reduced to Betto in a familiar or pet form.

Beck/Beckman/Bachman: German Place Name...There were many names for the 'one who dwells by the stream' and in Germany they included as Beck/Beckman/Bachman.

Beddow is a Welsh patronymic name that was derived from the personal name Bedo, which was a form of Meredydd with elements that meant "splendor, lord." Variations are **Beddoe, Bedo, Eddo** (achieved through *Ap'Bedo,* meaning "son of Bedo") with patronymic forms including **Beddowes, Beddows, Beddoes, Beddis, Eddowees, Edess.**

Beebe: a variation of Beeby, the English Place name for the man from a so-named settlement in Leicestershire, which was named from Old English *beo* = bee + Old Norse *byr* = settlement, village.

Bekker is a variation of the German Occupational name **Becher,** the occupation of the man who created wooden vessels such as cups, mugs, and pitchers. It is derived from Middle High German *becher,* from Greek *bikos* = pot, pitcher. Occasionally it referred to the German man who worked with pitch, a substance used in waterproofing such items; and also, Becher originates sometimes as a Jewish name of uncertain origin or an English

Place name as a variant of **Beech.** The **Bender** was a common term for the German maker of casks and barrels, and he often came to be known by his trade name.

Bennett/Bennet: English Patronymic name from the name Bennet, which means 'blessed' – a popular name during the middle ages. It has variations in several languages, and spellings. American singer Tony Bennett uses two versions -- his artworks are signed Anthony **Benedetto,** his name before being American-ized. He was `blessed' – Bennet – with a great voice!

Bentley: is an English Place name that is a combined form of the Old English word *leah,* which meant 'clearing in the woods.' The bent-leah was the 'clearing in the woods with the bent grass,' and Bentley was the man who lived there.

Benz/Benzer: In early times when advertising was in its infancy, (before television and the proliferation of literacy -- and the subsequent decline due to the aforementioned...) innkeepers had pictures placed on their hanging outdoor signs for identification. The bear was one of the popular depictions. Benz is a German place name derived from the place of the 'bear sign' with Benzer as a derivative.

Berger is polygenetic, in that it comes from more than one origin. As a variation of the German surname **Berg**, it describes the man who lived on or by a hill or mountain. **Bergman** is another variation. Berger is also derived as a French cognate form of the English surname **Barker,** when it is used in the sense of the shepherd and derived from Anglo Norman French *bercher.* During the Middle Ages, -er was pronounced as -ar and bercher became barker -- it was sometime later that educators began reteaching the proper pronunciation of common words. Barker is also the occupational name of the tanner of leather, derived from Middle English *barken* = to tan, stemming from the use of tree bark in the tanning process. **Berger, Bergey, Berget** are French cognates of the shepherd version, while **Berguier,**

Bergier have their origins in Provencal. **Bergeret, Bergerot, Bergeron, Bergeroneau, Bergerioiux** are diminutive forms.

Berheiser is a German place name derived from the Old High German *ber* = bear + *heiser* = house, which described a public house or inn that displayed the sign of the bear outside. The innkeep was often known by the name of the animal who picture appeared on the sign outside his door.

Bernier is a French cognate of the English (of Norman origin) patronymic name Berner, comprised of the Germanic elements *bern* = bear + *hari* = army. **Benier, Besnier** are other French cognates. **Berneret, Bernerette, Berneron, Bernerin, Bernelin** are French diminutive forms.

Berthet is a diminutive form of the French (also found as English, and rarely German) Patronymic surname **Bert,** from the Germanic given name *Berto,* which occurred mainly in compound names with *berht* (bright, famous) as the first element. It is found in Italy as **Berti.** Other diminutive forms are **Bertie** (English); **Berton, Berthoneau, Bertet, Berthellin, Berthelot, Bertellin, Bertelot, Bertillon, Berthilet** (French); **Bertorelli, Bertelli, Bertinetti, Bertinotti, Bertuccelli, Bertuccioli, Bertozzi, Bertuzzi, Bertocchini, Bertoccini, Pertini, Pertotti** (Italian); **Berthelin, Bertolin** (Catalan); **Bertl** (German); **Bethke, Bethmann** (Low German).

Best is an English and French occupational name for the man who took care of the animals (the beasts, Old French *beste*) or as an unflattering nickname for the man who had a beastly temperament or appearance. **Beste** is a variation. When of German origin, Best is a place name for the man who lived by the river Beste, or who hailed from any of the several villages called Besten. When of Beatles origin, it designates the drummer before Ringo, *Pete Best.*

Bettencourt: French Place name to describe someone from Bettencourt, France. There are several spelling variations of the place name. Bettencourt was originally or Germanic origin; Betto's court, with Betto a variant of the personal name Bert with the suffix court, which means farmyard. It is prevalent in Portugal where it was first recorded in the 1300's.

Bialas is the Polish nickname for the fair haired man, from the Polish word *bial* = white, blond + *as* = masculine suffix. **Biela** is a variation. Cognate forms include **Bily, Bilan** (Ukraine); **Bil, Bily, Belohlavek** (Czech). Diminutive forms include **Bealasik, Bialczyk, Bialek, Belik, Bilek, Bilko, Belyak, Bialik, Bielak, Bialovchik.**

Biedenweg, an unusual German place name, means "by the way" as a location of where someone lived -- 'way' meaning course or path. An Old Middle German given name was *Budde,* which evolved into several surnames. Budde's Way, or the path to Budde's settlement or enclosure, might have been taken as a surname for someone who lived along that trail -- as **Buddeweg** or **Budweg.**

Biel is derived from the Slavic element *byel* = white. There are several Eastern European cities named Byale from this same element.

Bielski is a Polish and Jewish (Ashkenazic) place name for the man from one of the so-named locations in Eastern Europe, from Slavic *byel* = white + *-ski* (surname suffix). Occasionally it was a nickname for a fair-haired person, from Polish *bial* = white. **Bielecki, Bialecki, Bielinski, Bielawski, Bilski** are Polish variations, **Bilski, Bialski, Bielecki, Bielicki, Biletzki, Bielinski, Bielinsky, Bielensky, Bialinski** are Jewish forms.

Billings: English Place name for the man who was one of "Billa's people" or who is from Billinge (which is derived from an Old English term for sword) in Lancashire.

Bingley is an English place name, as determined by the suffix -*ley,* from Old English *leah* = clearing, meadow. The prefix is generally a descriptive term for the clearing, and in this case, it may be derived from Old English *byne* = cultivated. The man who came from the so-named town in Yorkshire would be known by that description at his new location, as would the man whose dwelling was near a similar cultivated clearing in the woods.

Bish is a variation of the English place name **Bush,** for the man who lived near a thicket, from Middle English *bushe* = bush. **Bish, Bysh, Bysshe** are variations. Cognates include **Busch, Buscher, Bosche, Bosch, Boschmann, Zumbusch,** and others.

Bixby is an English place name from "Bekki's homestead" in Lincolnshire.

Blackburn: Scottish Patronymic/Place name...Blackburn is somewhat of an oddity in that many Scottish families with the name originated from the town of Blackburn, which was named for an original settler. He likely got the name because of where he formerly lived -- black-burn being the reference to a 'dark stream.'

Blain: is a Scottish Patronymic name derived from Blane, or Blaan -- given names that honored St. Blane, a Scottish Saint.

Blair is a Scottish and Northern Irish (Ulster) place name from any of the several so-named locations, derived from Gaelic *blár* = plain, field (often in the sense of battlefield).

Blaise is a French patronymic name from the Medieval given name *Blaise,* derived from Latin *Blassius,* which originally was a nickname for a person with difficulty speaking or a limp, from Latin *blaesus* = stammering and Greek *blaisos* = bowlegged. One of the early Christian martyrs bore the name, which lent to its popularity as a given name despite the original meaning of the name. **Blais** is a variation. There are numerous cognate forms of the name in several languages.

Blalock and **Blaylock** are English Nicknames for the man who had the black hair, or the Bla'ck locks.

Blankenship is an English place name from the location in Northumberland called *Blenkinsopp,* meaning "top valley."

Blau is a German nickname, from Old High German *blao* = blue, and was given in several senses -- the person who almost always wore blue clothing, the man with blue eyes, or the man with the pale or bluish complexion (generally not a sign of good health). **Blauer, Blauert** are German variations. **Plabst, Plab** are found in Bavaria. Blauer is also a Jewish variation. Cognate forms also exist in several languages include **Blue** (English); **De Blauw, Blauw, Blauwaert** (Flemish); **Blaauw** (Dutch).

Bleau is likely a variant cognate of the German nickname Blau, from German *blau* = blue, which described the man who tended to wear blue, had blue eyes, or a pale complexion -- something distinctive enough that the neighbors knew who was being discussed when "blue" was used as a description beyond the given name. A number of Blau surnames are Jewish Ashkenazic ornamental names, taken when surnames were ordered by the government. Variations of Blau are **Blauer, Blauert, Plab, Plabst.** Cognate forms include **De Blauw, Blaauw, Blauwaert** (Flemish); **Blaauw, Blauw** (Dutch); **Bleu, LeBleu, Blauf** (French); **Blue** (Anglicized). The Jewish ornamental name generally had a suffix, such as **Blaufeder** (blue feather).

Blevins is a patronymic form of the Welsh name **Blevin,** from the given name *Bleiddyn* which meant "Wolf Cub" from *blaidd* = wolf + *-yn* (a diminutive suffix). Blaidd was often used among the early Welsh to describe a hero. **Blethyn** is a variation. **Blevins, Pleavins, Plevin, Pleven, Pleaden** are patronymic forms (those beginning with P are derived from **ap'Blevin,** meaning "son of Blevin).

Blood was taken from Old English *blod* = blood, but as a surname, its significance isn't clear. It may have been a nickname for the man with the red hair, or the name for the physician -- they used that term to describe the man who 'let blood.' The suffix -worth is from Old English *word* = settlement. The name **Bloodsworth** is literally 'Blood's settlement.'

Blount/Blunt: English descriptive name...derived from the Old French word *blund* -- which meant 'blond, or yellow-haired.'

Boarder is the English place name for the man who lived in a house built of wood planks, from OE *bord* = board, plank of wood. Boardman is a variation (chiefly Lancashire) along with **Bordier, Border, Board, Boord.** There are numerous cognate and diminutive forms as well.

Boatright is an English occupational name, in the same sense as shipwright or wheelright, and is a compound comprised of the Old English elements *bat* = boat + *wyrhta* = worker, builder. A wright is a person who builds, generally with wood -- but the term is usually found as a compound.

Boeuf is a French Nickname for a powerfully built man, from the Old French *boeuf* = bull. Variants are Leboeuf, Boey, and Boez. Cognates are Boff, Leboff (England), La Bau, Boe, Boi, Lo Voi (Italian), and others.

Bohannon is likely derived as an Anglicized version of the Gaelic *O Buadhachain,* which meant "descendant of Buadachan" whose name meant "victorious." **Boohan, Bohane, O'Boughan, O'Bougan, O'Boghan, Boghan** are variations.

Bohm: and its variants are German Nicknames derived from the terms used to identify a person from Bohemia. From Old German *Baii* + *heim* =home. Variations include **Bahem, Boehme,** and **Boehm,** among others.

Bois is a French place name for the man who lived or worked in the woods, derived from Old French *bois* = wood. Variations are **Dubois, Desbois, Bost, Dubos, Dubost.** Cognate forms include **Boyce** (English); **Bosc** (Provencal); **Bosque** (Spain); **Bosch Bosque, Boscos, Bosca** (Catalan); **DelBosco, Boschi, Busco** (Italian). Diminutive forms are also found.

Bolek is a Polish diminutive version of the patronymic namy **Boleslawski,** from the given name *Boleslaw,* from the Slavic elements *bole* = greater + *slav* = glory + *ski* = surname suffix. **Bolecek** is a Czech version. **Boleslawski, Boleslavski,** and **Boleslavsky** are Jewish cognates derived as adoptions of the non-Jewish surname.

Bolin is a variation of **Boman,** a Swedish place name that described the man who lived in a settlement that was some ways distant from a larger settlement, and comes from the Swedish word *bo* = dwelling, farm + *man* = man. The terms were derived from Old Norse *bú* + *maðr.* The Swedes were among the last to adopt surnames, and in many cases this name was taken as an ornamental surname (chosen for its pleasing sound, rather than having any actual basis in fact) when surnames were adopted. Variations are **Bohman, Bohlin, Bolin.** Similar ornamental compounds are **Boberg** (farm hill), **Bogren** (farm branch), **Bolinder** (farm with lime tree), **Boqvist** (farm twig), **Boström** (farm river).

Bonner is a variation of **Bonar,** the English and Scottish nickname derived from Middle English *bonere* = gentle, courteous, handsome > from Old French *bonnaire* > from the phrase *de bonne aire* = of good bearing. **Bonnar, Boner** are other variations. **Bonnaire** is a French cognate -- **Bonaro** is the Italian version.

Booth is an English Place name for the man who lived in a small hut or *bothy* from the Middle English word *bothe,* and usually designated a cowman or shepherd. It has Scandinavian origins and denoted the various kinds of temporary shelter, and is more common in Northern England and Scotland. Variations include **Boothe, Boothman, Boden, Bodin.**

Borel is a variation of **Bourrel,** a French nickname derived from a diminutive form of **Boure,** which had different meanings in different contexts, but could be understood as cushion, harness, headdress, collar. The nickname would apply to the habitual wearer of one of these items. It could also be given as an occupational name for the maker of one of these items. **Bourreau, Borel, Borrel** are variations. **Burrel, Burrell, Borrel, Borrell, Birrell** (English) and **Borrelli** (Italian) are cognates.

Boulton is a variation of the English place name **Bolton,** and described the man from one of the several so-named locations in Northern England. It is comprised of the Old English elements *bodl* = dwelling, house + *tun* = enclosure, settlement.

Bounds is a patronymic form of the name Bound, meaning "son of Bound" and **Bound** is a variation of the English, Swedish, Norwegian name **Bond,** derived from Old Norse *bonde* = farmer. It designated a peasant farmer, and was also used as a given name, which lead to many Scandinavian surnames. After the Norman conquest, the word bond/bound took a dive in status, and came to be understood as "bound servitude" or "free landholder bound by loyalty to the landlord" but originally, and among Scandinavians, it meant simply "farmer." Variations are **Bonde, Bound, Boundey, Bundey, Bundy. Bönde, Bonne** are Norwegian and Danish cognates. **Bunde** is the Low German form. **Bounds, Bonds** are English patronymic forms while Bondesen and **Bonnesen** are found among the Scandinavians.

Bowen is a Welsh Patronymic name from the given name Owen. In early times, when they said "son of" they said it *ap* or *ab.* For example, William ap'John, was William the-son-of John. In the case of Owen, it was William ap'Owen -- which when said the least bit quickly, immediately becomes, William *Bowen.* Occasionally, Bowen is an Anglicized form of the Gaelic *O'Buadhachain* (descendant of Buadachain).

Bower: English Place name for the person who lived in a small cottage or occasionally, an occupational name for the house servant, derived from Old English *bur* = cottage, inner room. Variants include **Bowers, Bour, Bowerer, Boorer, Bowering,** and others. Dutch versions include **Van Buren, Van Buuren,** and **Van den Bueren.**

Bowman is a name that is quite literal; it's the English Occupational name for the archer, from Old English *boga* = bow + *mann* = man, although occasionally it is an Anglicized form of the German and Dutch surname **Baumann** -- consult your heritage for the correct version. Variants of Bowman are **Boman,** and **Beauman.** The cognate form in Dutch and Flemish is **Boogman.**

Box is an English name that has several origins: it may have named the man who lived by the box thicket, or who emigrated from any of the several English locations called Box. Box wood is a hard wood used in medieval times to make tools, and Box may have described the toolmaker or woodworker. **Boxer** is a variation. Cognate forms in other languages include **Bouis, Buis, Bouix, Dubouis, Dubuis, Buisse** (French); **Boix** (Catalan).

Boydston is an English place name, derived from the Irish and Scottish name Boyd + Old English *tun* = settlement, enclosure.**Boyd** is of uncertain etymology, although sometimes listed as describing a man with yellow hair, or derived from the island of Bute in the Firth of Clyde, from Gaelic *Bod.* **Boyde, Boyda** are variations.

Boyes is a patronymic from a Low German and Danish given name -- **Boye** -- derived from Germanic given name Boio, which is of uncertain origin. Botha was a common medieval name and Boio may be another form. Variations of Boye are **Boje, Boie, Bohe.** Cognate formare are **Bov, Bovo, Bovio, Bovi** (Italian). **Boyke, Boyk, Boykin** are diminutive forms.

Boysen, Boyens, Bojens, Boeing, Boysen, Boisen, Bojesen, Boesen are other patronymic forms.
Boylan refers to the man who came from *Boyland* derived from Old English references to "Boia's grove" in Norfolk.

Boynton is an English place name, as identified by the suffix -*tun* = settlement, enclosure, a variation of **Bovington,** a place name from the Old English Bofingtun = settlement of Bofa, or a variation of **Boyton,** derived from the several locations so-named that meant "Boia's settlement." Additionally, it could identify another settlement named for another man whose name was similar to Boia or Bofa.

Brackett is a diminutive form of the English and German occupational name **Brack,** which was the name that described the master of hunting dogs, from the Middle High German word *bracke,* and the Old French word *brachet* which formed the English cognate. **Prack** is a German variation. **Brackner** is an English variation. Cognate forms include **Brac, Bracq, Braque, Braconnier, Braquennier, Bracco, Bracchi, Braccaro.** Other diminutive forms include **Bracket, Brachet, Braquet, Braconnet, Braconnot.**

Bradford: English Place Name...Settlers near a crossing point on a watercourse often adopted 'ford' as their surname. A wide crossing was a 'broad-ford' and those living there - Bradford. Incidentally, Bradford was one of the 50 surnames of people arriving on the Mayflower in 1620.

Bradley is an English and Scottish place name, from the Old English elements *brăd* = broad + *leah* = wood, clearing. Places called "broad clearing" or Bradley exist throughout Scotland and England. Occasionally, Bradley is derived as an Anglicized Irish version of the Gaelic patronymic name *Ó Brolchâin,* which meant "descendant of Brolach." Variations are **Bradly, Bratly, Bratley, Broadely, Broadly.**

Brake: English place name -- which derived from the way they described bushes or a thicket in medieval times. The person who lived by the 'bracken' thicket or bushes sometimes acquired the surname Brake.

Brandis is derived from **Brand,** the English, French, and German patronymic name from the given name Brando, *brand* = sword. Also, the place in Germany cleared by fire was called *brant,* giving cause for the surname for the man who lived near there. **Braund, Brant, Brandon, Brandt** are variations. **Brandi, Brando, Branno, Branni, Prando, Prandi** are Italian cognate forms. Occasionally Brandis is derived from **Brandejs,** the Czech place name from the town of *Brandys* on the Elbe, north of Prague. **Brandes, Brandeis** are other forms of that one.

Brantley is an English place name that described the man from "Brand's woods" or "Brand's clearing." It is comprised of the elements *Brand* (a given name of Germanic origin that means 'sword') + *leah* = woods, clearing. The man who lived at Brand's leah was identified by that location by others who referred to him, which evolved into **Brandley** and Brantley. The form with the -t was more common in the West Midlands area of England.

Brandon is an English place name, from any of the several locations so named which derived there names from Old English *brom* = broom + *dun* = hill. The man who emigrated from one location to another was often known by the place of his origin.

Brashears is a patronymic version of the English occupational name **Brasher,** which was brought to England by the Normans during the Conquest. Brasher is derived from Old French *brasser* = to brew. Occasionally, it originates as an occupational name for the worker in brass, from Old English *broesian* = to cast in brass. Variants are **Braisher, Bracer, Brasseur, Brasier, Braizier, Brazier.** A French cognate is **LeBrasseur.**

The name **Bray** is an English place name and described the man who either lived in the so-named settlement in Berkshire, or the settlement with the same name in Devon. The settlement in Berkshire was named from Old French *bray* = marsh, and the Devon location got its name from the Cornish term *bre* = hill. When a man moved to a new location, he was often described by his new neighbors by his place of origin, to differentiate him from others in the town with the same given name.

Bredon, Breden, Breedon of English origin. It is derived from places (in Leicestershire and Worcestershire) that are comprised of the Old English elements *bre* =hill + *dun* =low hill.

Breedlove may be a combination of the Old English *brad* = broad, wide + AngloNormanFrench *louve* = she-wolf. The term *louve* was widely used as a flattering nickname for a brave man or warrior, in the context of the fierceness of the she-wolf in protecting her young. Breedlove in that sense would be an English nickname describing the warrior of broad stature.

Brett is the ethnic name for a Breton, from the Old French word *bret.* The Bretons were Celtic-speaking folks who were driven from SW England to NW France in the 6th century by the Anglo-Saxon invaders. Some returned in the 11th century with William the Conqueror. As an English surname it is most commonly found in E. Anglia where many Bretons settled after the Conquest. Variations are **Britt, Breton, Bretton, Brittain, Bret, Lebret, Breton, Bretonnier, Bretegnier, Bretagne,** and **Bretange.** There are numerous cognative versions as well.

Breuls is a patronymic derivation from Old French *breuil* = marshy woodland, which later came to mean enclosed woodland, then later to mean cleared woodland, and both senses are used as definitions for the surname. Variations of the French place name are **Breuilh, Bruel, Dubreuil, Dubrule.**

Briant is a French cognate of the English patronymic name **Bryan,** from a Celtic given name Brian containing the element *bre* = hill and used in the transferred sense of "eminence." Bretons with the name accompanied William the Conqueror in his invasion of England, then went on to invade and settle in Ireland, mingling with the native Irish. Variations are **Brian, Brien, Bryant, Briant;** Cognates include **Briant, Briand, Briend** (French). **Briandet** is a diminutive French form. **Bryans, McBrien, Mac Briain, O'Brian, O'Bryan** are patronymic forms.

Briggs: A North English and Scottish variant of **Bridge,** derived from the Old Norse *bryggja.* Bridge is an English Place name for the man who lived near a bridge, or an English Occupational name for the keeper of the bridge. Building and maintaining bridges was one of three main feudal occupations, the cost of which was occasionally offset by a toll charged to cross, and the keeper of the toll often acquired the surname. Variations are **Bridges, Brigg, Briggs, Burge, Bridger, Bridgeman, Brigman.** German cognitives include: **Bruckmann, Bruckman, Bruck, Bruckner, Bruckner, Pruckner** (Austria), **Brugge, Brugger, Anderbrugge, Toderbrugge, Terbruggen** (at the bridge). **Van Bruggen** is Flemish, and **Van der Brug** is Dutch. Other versions exist in additional countries.

Brink is a Low German, Dutch, and Danish place name for the man who lived by a pasture, and derived from Middle Low German *brinc* = meadow, pasture -- especially a raised meadow surrounded by a marsh or fen. Variations are **Brinck, Brinken, Brinckman, Brinkman, Tenbrinck, Tombrinck, Zumbrink, Beimbrinke** (German), **Brink, Tenbrink, Van den Brink, Van de Brinck, Van de Brink, Brinckman, Brinkman** (Dutch), **Brinck, Brinch** (Danish).

Bronowitz/Bronisz: Polish Patronymic Name... owitz and owicz are typical patronymic endings applied to a given name in several languages of Slavic origin. Bronowitz would be the 'son of Bron.' Bron, by the way, meant 'defender.' The surname Bronisz is taken directly from that given name.

Brown: is one of the more common surnames, as you might expect. Among the light-skinned English anyone with a darker complexion, brown hair, tendancy toward brown clothing, etc. were often described that way, and it stuck as a surname. There are a number of derivatives in many countries.

Browning is an English patronymic name from the Old English given name *Bruning,* which was originally a patronymic form of the name *Brun,* a nickname that referenced something brown, like brown hair, brown complexion, or brown clothing. The son of Brun was sometimes called Bruning, which occasionally evolved into Browning (as did the vocabulary word brun > brown) **Brauning** is the German cognate. **Bruning** (with an umlaut -u) is the Low German form. **Bruning** is the Dutch form. **Bruynincks** is the Flemish patronymic form.

Brumley is an English place name comprised of the Old English elements that meant "broom field" or "broom clearing" and described the man who lived in that area.

Bruner and **Brunner** are versions of the German patronymic name that was derived from the given name *Brunheri,* with elements that meant "brown, army."

Bruno: Brown is one of the more common surnames - it is the most common of the surnames derived from nicknames. Bruno is the form the name takes in Italy and occasionally in Germany.

Bryant is a variation of the English surname **Bryan,** from the Celtic given name Brian, containing the element *bre* = hill, used in the transferred sense of 'eminence.' Bearers of this name accompanied William the Conqueror in the invasion of England in 1066, and went on to invade and settle in Ireland in the 12th century. Variations are **Brian, Brien, Bryant, Briant, Briand, Briant, Briend; Briandet** is a French diminutive. **Bryans** is a patronymic form, as is **McBrien,** and **O'Brian, O'Bryan.**

Buford is an English place name that described the crossing point of a river or stream, derived from the Old English word *ford* = crossing, ford -- along with the identifying location, in this case, likely "Bofa's ford." Bofa was a common medieval name of uncertain origin, and many locales were described by the man who lived nearby.

Buhl is a German nickname for a relative of an important man, who is not the head of the household, from Middle High German *buole* =kinsman. It is also occasionally known as a nickname for a lover, in the same context the word "paramour" is used.

Bulmer is an English Place name from a place in Essex that was recorded in the Domesday Book as *Bulenemera.* It is derived from the Old English elements *bulena* (the plural of *bula* = bull) + *mere* = lake, for a literal meaning of 'lake of the bulls.'

Burcham is a spelling variation of the English place name *Bircham,* which described the man from any of the so-named locations in Norfolk which derived their name from Ole English *bræc* = land newly plowed + *ham* = homestead.

Burckhardt/Borrows/Burg/Burge/Burks/Burr/Burris: German Place Name...The principal surnames that refer to a fortified castle, an imposing structure, or the peasant who lived nearby were Borrows, Burg, Burge, Burks, Burr, and Burris -- which all came from the Old English word *burg* which meant fort. Borg is generally the designation used in Sweden, Norway, and Germany. Burckhardt was an especially well fortified castle in Germany at the time surnames were being adopted.

Burdge is likely derived from Old English *brycg* = bridge, the English place name for the man who lived near the bridge, or the occupational name for the bridgekeeper. The business of building and maintaining bridges was one of the three primary obligations of the feudal system members, along with bearing arms, and building/reinforcing the fortifications. In the dialects of Somerset, Dorset, and other S. English locations there was a switch of the -u- and -r- for several words that were adopted as surnames.

Burgdorfer is a German place name -- a compound name derived from the elements (Middle High German) *burc* = fortified town + *dorfer* (a German cognate of Old Norse) *þorp* = hamlet, village.

Burgess: English Descriptive Name...taken by men of free birth, but not noble birth, who held substantial land for which they paid very little rent, and had no obligation to render services to the lord or king. Franklin and Freeman were names originating under the same circumstances.

The Old High German word *burc* = town added to the Old High German *grav* = count, magistrate created the compound status name *burc-grav* = town magistrate. Before you get all high-falootin' on us, in Medieval times it wasn't such a grand job, but eventually the name **Graf** (which survives as a German vocabulary word for magistrate) came to denote aristocracy, similar to Count, like Count Dracula, or Count Chocula.

Burlingame/Burling/Burlingham: Burling and Burlingame are corruptions of Burlingham, which was the 'settlement of Baerla's people,' and an English Place name.

Burney: English Place name from Bernay, Normandy which had its name originations in the Gaulish given name Brenno, or from Berney in Norfolk (recorded in the Domesday Book as Ralph de Bernai, a Norman who received land grants there). Occasionally, Burney is an Anglicized form of the given name Biorna, a Gaelic version of the Old Norse Bjarni (bearcub, warrior). Variations are **Berney, Burnie, McBurney, McBirney,** and **Mac Biorna.**

Burnham: an English Place name from various locations; Burnham Beeches in Buckinghamshire, various villages in

Norfolk, and Burnham-on-Crouch in Essex. The name Burnham is derived from Old English *burna* = stream + *ham* = homestead. A man from one of the Burnham settlements might have that name as his identifying surname.

Burns: English Place name. The man who lived in the lone cottage by the small stream was called Burn, or **Burns.** The -S- was often added to names as an aid to pronunciation. Other names with the same origin are **Brooke, Bourne, Beck,** and **Beckett.**

Bernstein: German/Jewish Acquired name...Many German-Jewish names were simply the result of a desire for something pleasant-sounding when Jews in Europe were obliged to take surnames in the early 1800's. Those who picked such names usually were compelled to pay a hefty tariff to the government officials for the privilege -- Amber (Bernstein) is a color with positive connotations and it also served as a descriptive name for some early day settlements, which may have been located in an area noted by that color. Elsdon C. Smith, in his work *American Surnames,* suggests that Bernstein was generally adopted because of its pleasing sound.

Birrell is a English cognate of the French name **Bourrel,** derived from a diminutive version of **Boure,** which was used in several senses in Old French, including "cushion," "harness," "headdress," and "crest." The name would have identified the maker or seller of any of these items. Occasionally, Bourrel was the man who served as the judicial torturer, from Old French *bourreau* < *bourrer* = to maltreat, torture (it is literally translated as "wool carder." Variations are **Bourreau, Borel, Borrel.** Cognates include **Burrell, Burrel, Borrel, Borrell, Birrell** (English); **Borelli, Borrelli** (Italian).

Bleich is a German term that means "pale" and is a cognate form of the English name **Blake,** which was a nickname for the wan or pale man, from Old English *blac* = wan, pale. The English name Blake, however, is a combined name for *blac* =

wan, and *blaec/blac* = black...and it is impossible to tell without evidence which form of the name applies in any individual case.

Breiling is a diminutive form of a cognate for the German place name **Brühl,** which described the man who lived on land that was cleared for use by burning, from Old French *brusle* = burnt in connection with a German verb. **Breuel, Bruhler** are variations. Cognate forms include **Brogelmann, Brogel, Briel, Breil, Breilmann, Tombreul** (Low German); **Breuls, Breul, Van der Brule, Broghel, Breughel, Van Breugel, Van Breukelen** (Flemish, Dutch); **Bryl, Bryla** (Polish).

Buchanan is a Scottish place name for a location near Loch Lomond (by the bonnie, bonnie banks of Loch Lomond....) which was named for the Gaelic elements *buth* = house + *chanain* = "of the canon." The man who removed from there to another settlement was sometimes described by his place of origin.

Burris: The medieval castle was an imposing structure and was often used as a reference point for those who lived nearby. The English word *burg* meant fort, and the principal names describing the English man who lived near one were: **Burg, Burge, Borrows, Burks, Burr, Burris.** It's an English Place name.

Burton is an English place name derived from the Old English elements *burh* = fort + *tun* = enclosure, settlement. There are numerous locations in England called Burton and the man who emigrated from such a place would have been known to his new neighbors by his place of origin -- to distinguish him from locals bearing the same given name.

Butler is an English and Irish Occupational name for the wine steward, who was the chief servant of a medieval household, from Anglo-Norman French *butuiller* = bottle. In the households of nobility, the title denoted an officer of rank and responsibility.

Button is an English cognate of the French patronymic **Bouton,** a variation of the name **Boudon** from the given name

Bodo = messenger. It is occasionally derived as a nickname for the man with a prominent boil or wart, from Old French *boton* = knob, lump. It was also sometimes found as a name for the maker of buttons, with the same OF origin, in the sense of knob = button. **Boutonnier** is a variation of Bouton (the buttonmaker). **Button, Botten, Butner** are English cognates.

Buxton is an English place name from Buxton in Derbyshire which was called *Buchestanes* in Medieval times, meaning bowing stones, derived from Old English *búgan* = to bow + *stanes* = stones. There were logan stones in the vicinity (boulders that rocked at the touch). **Buckston, Buckstone** are variations.

Byers is an English and Scottish place name for the man who lived by a cattleshed, from Old English *byre* = cattleshed, or as a place name for the man who hailed from a so-named location such as Byers Green (County Durham), or Byers (near Edinburgh). **Byres, Biers** are variations.

Byrne is an Irish name that was Anglicized from *O'Broin,* which meant "descendant of *Bran* " whose name meant "raven." **O'Byrne, O'Beirne, O'Berne, Berne, Beirne, Byrnes** are variations.

C

Cain: English nickname, derived from the Middle English word *cane* = reed or cane, and described the tall, thin man.

Calhoun is the Americanized version of **Colhoun,** found chiefly in Northern Ireland, derived from **Colquhoun** -- a Scottish place name for the location in former County Aberdeen first recorded as *Colqhoun* in 1246. It is derived from Gaelic *coil/cuil* = nook, corner + *cumhann* = narrow. It is pronounced ke'-hu:n. Swedish names that were descended from a Walter Colquhoun are **Cahund, Caun, Gaun, Gahn,** and **Kharun.**

Callicott: is a variation of Caldicott, an English Place name from any number of settlements originally spelled Caldecote, from Old English ceald = cold + cot = cottage or dwelling. Some suggest the name was in reference to unattended shelters for travelers, although in the Domesday Book (1086) many of these places had achieved some status. Variants are **Caldicot, Caldecott, Caldecourt, Callicot, Callcott, Calcut, Caulcutt, Caulkett, Cawcutt, Corcut, Corkett, Corkitt, Coldicott, Coliccot, Collacott, Collecott, Collicutt, Colcott, Colcutt, Colkett, Clocott, Chaldcot,** and **Chalcot.**

Calvert is an English occupational name for the man who tended cattle, from Old English *calf* = calf + *hierde* = herdsman. **Calverd, Calvard** are variations.
Camden: English Place name derived from the Old English elements *campas* = enclosure + *denu* = valley. Cambden is a variation.

Camp: is an English Place name that along with **Field, Prindle,** and **Viles** were references to the man whose home was the house in the open field (as opposed to the forest or some other recognizable feature).

Campbell is a Scottish nickname derived from Gaelic *cam* = crooked, bent + *beul* = mouth. Gillespie O Duibhne was the first to have borne the nickname, and founded clan Campbell at the beginning of the 13th century. **Cambell, Camble** are variations.

Cantello is a variation of **Cantellow,** an English place name of Norman origin. It described the man whose place of origin was one of the various similarly named locations in what is now called France, such as *Canteleu* (Seine-Maritime) or *Canteloup* (Calvados), which were named from Old Norman French *cante* = to sing + *lou/leu* = wolf. It was a name for the place where wolves were heard howling regularly. Variations are **Cantello, Cantelo, Cantlow.**

Cantrell is a diminutive form of the English and Scottish name **Cant,** the occupational name for the singer in a chantry, or a nickname for the man who loved to sing, from Old Norman French *cant* = song. Variations are **Cauant, Chant, Canter, Chanter, Cantor, Canty, Cantie.**

Cantwell is a placename that derived it's name from Old English personal name *Cant* + *wella* = stream, spring.

The placename **Capshaw** is derived from Old English *cæppe* = cap + *scæga* = copse, thicket -- and described the man who lived near the thicket on the headland.

Carberry: Scottish Place name in the parish of Inveresk, Lothian which was first recorded as Crebarrin.

Cardinalli is a version of the Italian surname **Cardinali,** which equates to the English and French name **Cardinal** -- a nickname derived from the name of a church dignitary. It was originally an adjective that meant 'vital' or 'crucial.' It may also have been derived as a name for the man who worked in the household of the Cardinal, but usually was given as a nickname for the person who always wore red, or who acted in a princely manner - like the Cardinal.

Cargile is a variation of the Scottish place name *Cargill,* from the so-named location near Stanley on the Tay, and derived from Old Welsh *kaer* = fort + *geall* = pledge, tryst, which is believed to have commemorated some now-lost event. Walter de Kergyl is the earliest bearer of the name, known through his signature on a document in 1260.

Carlisle is an English Place name for the town in Cumberland derived from the British *ker* =fort + Romano-British settlement named *Luguvalium.* How kerLuguvalium becomes Carlisle is yet another story. Variations of this name include **Carlyle, Carlile,** and **Carlill.**

Carnegie is a Scottish place name from a place near Carmyllie in what was then the county of Angus (now Tayside), which got its name from *cathair an eige* (Gaelic for "fort at the gap"). **Carnegy** is a variation.

Carpenter: At the time surnames were adopted, the average man built his own cottage and did not require the skill of the Carpenter, who usually was hired by those who were of some means, and required products only a craftsman could provide. It's an English Occupational name.

Carr: was a term used in old Scotland to describe 'low, wet ground' and the person who lived by that area was often identified by it. Carson is a Scottish Place name that describes the man who lived by the carr -- the low, wet ground.

Carrera: French Place Name from the Latin carraria = cart. It was the name used to refer to the man who `lived on the vehicle road' or busy thoroughfare where many carts traveled.

Carpinito: Spanish/Italian surnames are notorious for the number of spelling variants and pet forms. **Carpineto** is an Italian version of a French Place name for the dweller by a conspicuous 'witch elm' tree, or near a group of such trees, from

Old French *charme,* derived from the Latin *carpinus.* Variants include **Charmes, Charne, Carne, Decharme, Duecharme, Ducharne,** and cognizant forms in addition to **Carpinito/Carpineto** (which are diminutive forms) are: **Carpe, Ducarpe** (Provencal), **Carp, Carpin, Carpini, Carpino, Carpine, Carpene,** and **Carpano,** among others (Italian).

Carruthers is a Scottish place name, for the so-named location near Ecclefechan in Dumfries. It was first noted in 1334 with the spelling *Carrothres,* and again in 1350 as *Caer Ruther* (from Briton *ker* = fort + a personal name meaning "red + king, ruler"). Variations are **Carothers, Carrothers, Crothers, Carradice, Carrodus, Cardis, Cardus, Crowdace, Cruddace, Cruddas,** and **Caruth.**

Carter is an English Occupational name for the transporter of goods by cart or wagon from Anglo-Norman French caretier, a derivative of Old French *caret* which originally implied 'carrier.' Occasionally it is a form of **McArthur.** Variants include **Charter** and cognates include **Carreter, Carretier, Cartier, Charretier, Chartier, Chareter, Charater, Carratier, Carratie** and **Carretero.**

Carl is a variation of **Charles,** a French, Welsh and English surname, from the Germanic given name Carl = man. **Carlson** is a patronymic version denoting the "son of Carl." **Karl,** the German cognate form, was not in use as a given name during the Middle Ages, and is rare or unknown as a German surname since it was restricted to nobility. English variations of Charles are **Karl, Karle, Carle, Carl.** French forms are **Charle, Charlon, Carle, Chasles, Chasle.** Cognate forms are **Carlo, Caroli, Carlesi, Carlisi, Carlesso** (Italian); **Carlos** (Spain); **Carles** (Catalan); **Kerl, Kehrl, Keerl** (Low German); **Karl** (Jewish Ashkenazic); **Karel, Kares** (Czech); **Karoly, Karolyi** (Hungarian). Patronymic forms include **Charleston** (t-added); McCarlish (Scottish); **De Carlo, De Carli, Di Carlo, De Carolis** (Italian); **Carlens** (Flemish/Dutch); **Karlsen, Carlsen**

(Norwegian); **Karlsson, Carlsson** (Swedish); **Karlowicz, Karolak, Karolczak** (Polish).

Carrin is a variation of the French occupational name **Charron,** from Old French *charron* = cart, and described the man who made carts. It is also derived from **Caron,** which was a given name among the Gauls from the element *car* = to love. Both versions developed variations that include **Carron, Caron, Charron, Charon. Charrondier, Charrandier** are cart maker variations.

Cartwright: is an English Occupational name. One of the primary specialized crafts along with CARPENTER was that of the Cartwright, who fashioned the wheeled carts that traversed the early roads.

Carlin, an Irish name Anglicized from Gaelic *O Cearbhallain,* meaning "descendant of Cearbhallan" a diminutive form of the given name *Cearbhall,* from *cearbh* = hacking.

Carlyon is a Cornish place name that described the man from any of the several so-named places in Cornwall and derived from Briton *ker* = fort + the plural of *legh* = slab.

Carroll is an Irish patronymic name, Anglicized from the Gaelic *Cearbhall,* a given name of uncertain origin, but likely derived from *cearbh* = hacking...which probably described the use of a weapon or tool, as opposed to a violent cougher. Just kidding.

Case is an English occupational name for the maker of boxes and chests, from Anglo-Norman-French *casse* = case, container, derived from Latin *capsa* > *capere* = to hold, contain. When of Provencal origin, it is a variant of the name Casa. Among the Italians, Case was the maker or seller of cheese. **Cash** and **Cashman** are variations of the English version. **Kas** is a Dutch cognate. **Cassirer** and **Kassierer** are Jewish (Ashkenazic) cognates.

Casey is an Irish patronymic name, Anglicized from the Gaelic *O Cathasaigh,* meaning "descendant of *Cathasach"* whose name meant "vigilant, noisy." **O'Casey** is a variation.

Cash: is an English Place name that was given to the man who lived near the Cash -- or oak -- tree.

Castellana is an Italian cognate of the English (derived from the Normans) name **Castellan,** the occupational name for the governor or constable of the castle, or the prison warden. It is taken from Anglo-Norman-French *castelain* > Latin *castellanus.* **Castellain, Castelein, Castling, Chatelain** are variations of Castellan. Cognates include **Chastel, Chastelain, Catelain, Castelain** (French); **Castelan, Castelin** (Provencal); **Castellani, Castellano** (Italian); **Castella** (Catalan); **Castelhano, Castelao** (Portugal); **Casteleyn, Castelijn** (Flemish, Dutch).

Caswell: English Place name that identified the man who lived near a spring or stream. In his case the water was identified by the watercress nearby: Ole English *cressa* -- Cressawell, which evolved into Caswell.

Cates is an English Patronymic name from the Old Norse nickname Kati, which meant 'boy' and speculation that it was derived from the nickname Kate (from Catherine) should be tempered with the knowledge that the Kate nickname wasn't used for Catherine until after the Middle Ages, when Cates was already established as a surname.

Cayhill is an English place name derived from Old English *ca* = jackdaw (a European blackbird) + *hyll* = hill, and would describe the man who lived at the hill where the jackdaws were found.

Cesario is a form of **Cesare,** found among the Italians and taken from the given name *Cesare,* from the Roman family Caesar, a cognate form of the name Charles. Variations are **Cesaro, Cesari, Cesar.**

Chamberlin: is a variation of **Chamberlain,** an English Occupational name that originally was the job held by the one who was in charge of the private chambers of the master of the house, and later was a title of high rank. Variations include **Chamberlaine, Chamberlayne, Chamberlen,** and **Champerlen.**

Chance is an English nickname for the inveterate gambler or for the man who survived a disaster through a remarkable bit of luck. It is derived from Anglo Norman French *cheaunce* = good fortune. **Cance, Chaunce** are variations.

Chandler: The Chandler worked with wax, and in addition to making candles, he fashioned wax objects or icons that were used in church offerings. Chandler is an English Occupational name.

Chapman is an English occupational name for the merchant or trader, derived from Old English *ceapmann* < *ceap* = barter + *mann* = man. **Chipman, Chapaper, Chipper, Cheeper,** are variations. Cognates include **Chapelle, Capell** (French); **Capela** (Provencal); **Capella, Capelle** (Italian); **Capilla** (Spain); **Capela** (Portugal); **Capel, Van Keppel, Van Keppel** (Dutch); **Van de Capelle** (Flemish).

Charbonneau is a variation of the surname **Carbonell,** found among the English, French, and in Catalan as a nickname for the man with dark hair or a swarthy complexion. the term carbon was used in Anglo-Norman-French, Old French, and Old Catalan to mean charcoal. English variations are **Charbonell, Shrapnel;** in France it is also found as **Carbonnel, Carboneau, Charbonel, Charbonneaux, Cherbonneau** and **Charbonnet;** in Catalan, a variation is **Carbo.** Italian cognates include **Carbone, Carbonelli, Carbonetti,** and **Carbonini.**

Karle is a variation of **Charles,** a French, Welsh and English surname, from the Germanic given name Carl = man. **Karl,** the German cognate form, was not in use as a given name during the Middle Ages, and is rare or unknown as a German surname since it was restricted to nobility. English variations of Charles are **Karl, Karle, Carle.** French forms are **Charle, Charlon, Carle, Chasles, Chasle.** Cognate forms are **Carlo, Caroli, Carlesi, Carlisi, Carlesso** (Italian); **Carlos** (Spain); **Carles** (Catalan); **Kerl, Kehrl, Keerl** (Low German); **Karl** (Jewish Ashkenazic); **Karel, Kares** (Czech); **Karoly, Karolyi** (Hungarian). Patronymic forms include **Charleston** (t-added); **McCarlish** (Scottish); **De Carlo, De Carli, Di Carlo, De Carolis** (Italian); **Carlens** (Flemish/Dutch); **Karlsen, Carlsen** (Norwegian); **Karlsson, Carlsson** (Swedish); **Karlowicz, Karolak, Karolczak** (Polish).

Chatham is an English place name for the so-name location in Kent or Chatham Green in Essex, which appear in the Domesday book as Ceteham and Cetham. The Breton elemenet *ceto* = forest + Old English *ham* = homestead. The man who came from the place called Chatham often ended up with that as an identifying surname.

Cheesman ~ In the Tower of Record of London, there is a deed from Alan and Alicia Chesmongre, dated AD 1286, granting the land upon which the College and Priory of Hastings, Sussex, England were built. A cheese mongre sold cheese ~ Chees(e)man (the cheese merchant).

Keesee is a variation of **Keese,** which is a Low German cognate of the occupational name known as **Cheeseman** in English-speaking countries, which described the maker or seller of cheese. The English word is derived from Old English *cyse* = cheese + *mann* = man. **Cheesman, Cheseman, Chesman, Cheasman, Chiesman, Chisman, Chessman, Chismon, Cheese, Chiese, Cheesewright, Cheeseright, Cheswright, Cheeswright, Cherrett, Cherritt** are variations of the English form. Other cognate forms are **Käsmann, Käser, Keser, Käs, Käse** (German); **Kaasman, Kaas, Keesman** (Low German); **Caesman** (Flemish); **Kaes, Kaas, Kaaskooper** (Dutch); **Keizman, Keyzman** (Jewish); **Chasier, Casier, Chazier,**

Chesier, Chezier, Chazerand (French); **Casari, Casaro, Caseri, Caser, Casieri, Casiero, Case** (Italian); **Queyeiro, Queyos** (Portuguese).

Cherrier is likely a variation or cognate of the French occupational name **Cerisier,** the name given the man who lived near a cherry tree or own a cherry orchard, from Old French *cerisier* = cherry tree. **Cherry** is an English cognate of the name, which also appears in several other languages.

Chrystal is a variation of the Scottish patronymic name **Cristal,** derived as a pet form of the name Christopher (bearer of Christ). Other variations are **Crystall, Chrystall, Crystol, Kristall.**

The old English term *cyrice* meant church, and *hyll* evolved into our modern word "hill." Cyrice-hyll was the name of several places in medieval England, including Devon, Oxfordshire, Somerset, and Worcestershire. The man who originally lived at one of those locales name **Churchill,** but later moved to another was known to his new neighbors by describing where he was from -- as opposed to someone with the same first name who was a local lad.

During the Middle Ages, the common pronunciation of -er was -ar, so the man who sold items was the marchant, and the man who kept the books was the **Clark. Clerc** was the origin, and designated a member of the clergy, hence *cleric.* At the time, the primary members of the literate class were the clergy, which in minor orders were allow to marry and have families. The term clerk came to designate any literate man. **Clarke, Clerk, Clerke** are variations. Cognates include **Cler, Clercq, Leclerc, Leclercq, Lecler, Leclert, Leclair, Cloarec, Cloerec** (French); **Clergue** (Provencal); **Chierici, Clerici, Chierego** (Italian); **Clerc, De Clerck, De Clercq, De Klerk** (Flemish, Dutch). Diminutive forms also exist in several languages.

Claxton is similarly derived, from a combination of the Old English given name *Clacc* + *tun* = settlement, enclosure. It described the settlement of the man known by the name of Clacc.

Clayton: is an English Place name that incorporates the most common ending found among English names -ton. In Old English, tun was the word for town, and it was used with other descriptions to pinpoint settlements. Clayton, or Clay-town, was the settlement on the soil of clay.

Clevenger is likely an English occupational name for the wood splitter, from the Old English elements *cloefan* = to split, cut + *-er* as an agent suffix. (See also Clover). I realize that doesn't account for the "g" but there are many names which had intrusive consonents added as an aid to pronunciation or by association. For example, the similar name **Cleverly** is derived from Old English *clif* = cliff + *leah* = wood, clearing...which created *Clevely,* but is generally found as Cleverly by association with the more commonly found word "clever."

Clifton is an English Place name, as determined by the suffix - *ton* - which originated in the Old English term *tun* meaning "settlement" or "enclosure." The Old English word *clif* meant "slope" which makes Clifton a "settlement on the slope," and a man who lived there might be described that way. There are towns all through England by the name of Clifton.

Cline: see Klein.

Clingan, Clingen: A not uncommon Galloway surname, from **(Mac)Clingan,** q.v. William Clingane in Ladieland, 1658 (Dumfries). Edward Clingzean in Castletoun, 1680 (Kirkcudbright). Alexander Clingane in Kirkcudbright signed the Test, 1684 (RPC., 3. ser. x, p. 248). Clingen 1684.

Clover is a variation of the English occupational name **Cleaver,** which described the man who kept a butcher shop, or split wood using a wedge and hammer. It is derived from Old English *cleofan* = split, cut. **Cleever** is another variation.

Cobb: English Patronymic name that is derived from Jacob 'the supplanter' or 'may God protect' (depending on whom is asked...) Cobb is a pet form of the name Jacob.

Cochran is a spelling variation of **Cochrane,** a Scottish place name found in the Paisley district, near Glasgow. It may have gotten its name from Old Welch *coch* = red, but the earliest known spelling was recorded this way: *Couran* (which sort of shoots a hole in the *coch* = red theory. It may be that the Couran was a phonetic spelling from a dialtectic pronunciation.) **Cochren, Colqueran** are other spelling variations. Cochrane is the name of the Earls of Dundonald, taken by William Blair when he married into the Cochrane family. Cochrane has its own distinctive highland kilt, although some Cochranes are descended from ancestors who married into the McDonald clan which wears the Clan Donald tartan.

Coggins: Irish/Welsh place name derived from a spot near Cardiff, which is a Welsh word for bowl, and likely described the terrain at the time.

Coghill is a Scottish version of the Danish name Kogel for the maker of hoods, or someone who wore one regularly.

There is a group of villages in Somerset that were named for the British river Cocker, from a word that meant 'crooked.' The Old Irish word *cucar* = crooked, awkward -- the river was named for a similar word from the Breton/Old Welsh languages. The man who originated in one of the villages so-named was called **Coker. Cockerham** is another name derived from a village along the river, with that location named with the elements Cocker + (Old English) *ham* = homestead.

Coldren is a variation of the English, French, and Jewish (Seradic) occupational name which described the maker of large cooking vessals, from Old French *cauderon* = cauldron < Latin *caldarium* = hot bath. Variations include **Cauldron, Cowdron,**

Coldron (English); **Chaudron, Codron** (French); **Kalderon** (Jewish). Cognate forms include **Calderon, Calero, Caldera** (Spain); **Caldeira** (Portugal); **Caldairoux, Caldairou, Caldayroux, Caldeyroux** (Provencal); **Calderone, Calterone, Caldroni, Caldaro** (Italian). Diminutive forms are **Chaudret, Chaudrelle, Jodrellec, Calderonello.**

Coleman is an English and Scottish patronymic name from the Old Irish given name *Colman,* from Columbun (from Latin *Columba* = dove). The Irish missionary to Europe, St. Columban (540-615) made the name popular. The name is sometimes derived as an Anglicized version of the Gaelic *O Clumbhain* (descendant of Clumhan).As an occupational name, Coleman was the man who gathered charcoal, from Old English *col* = coal + *mann* = man -- and somewhat rarely, the name for the personal servant of the man named **Cole.**

Collard is derived in a round-about way from the given name Nicholas. In several European languages where the accent tends toward the second syllable in Ni-chol-as, the first syllable is eventually lost due to lazy pronunciation. It's called aphetic loss, for example, when the word esquire becomes squire over time. Collard was derived as a pejorative form of **Coll.** Other variations are **Colle** (French), **Cola** and **Colao** (Italian), **Colle** (Dutch), **Col** and **Colla** (Flemish).

Colley/Coley/Collie: English Nickname from W. Midlands derived from the Old English word *colig* which meant `dark' and was sometimes used to describe a swarthy or darker skinned man.

Collins/Cole/Coles: English Patronymic Name...Nicholas was an extremely popular name in early times -- in the 4th century, Nicholas was the patron saint of children. Many names were derived from Nicholas, such as **Nichols, Nickles, Nickleson, McNichols. Collins** derived from the ending of Nicholas.

Collison became a surname in a round-about way. **Nicholas** was a common and popular name during the Middle Ages. A pet form of the name evolved as **Coll,** and was often found as a given name. **Collin** evolved as a pet or diminutive form of Coll. **Collison** is a variation of **Collinson,** meaning the "son of Collin." **Collis, Collyns,** are other forms.

Comerford is an English place name composed of the Old English elements *camb* = comb + *-er* = agent suffix + *ford* = ford, crossing. The primary method of untangling wool was a process called carding, and combing was alternative method that caused the wool fibers to lie parallel to one another, producing smooth cloth without nap. The crossing point of the river or stream was the ford, and the crossing near the comber was the comber-ford or Comerford.

Compton is an English Place name taken by the man from any of the English towns of that name, which were named from the Old English word *cumb* = short, straight valley + *tun* = enclosure. *Cumb-tun* would literally be "enclosure in the short straight valley" with an enclosure being a protective fort or stockade-type barrier within which several families resided.

Connolly is an Irish patronymic name, Anglicized from the Gaelic *O Conghalaigh,* which meant 'descendant of *Conghalach,* whose name meant 'valiant.' Variations are **O'Connolly, O'Connally, Connelly, Conneely, Conally, O'Conely, Conley.**

Conway: Welsh Place Name from Conwy, a town in N. Wales named for the Conwy River, which was named from an Old Brit term that meant `reedy.' It is also sometimes derived from the Scottish place *Conway* in Beauly Parish and was recorded in 1215 as Coneway. Conway when descended from Ireland usually an Anglicized version of *Mac Commidhe,* a name which meant `head smashing.'

Cook is the English occupational name for the cook, the man who sold cooked meats, or the keeper of an eating house. It is derived from Old English *coc* = cook. **Cooke** and **Coke** are variations.

Coomer/Coomber: English Place Name...Coomer is a variation of **Coomber** from the Old English *cumb,* which was a short, straight, valley.

Many surnames were Americanized when the recent arrivals wanted to blend in with their established neighbors, and **Coons, Coonce,** and others are examples of spelling that was less reflective of their origin. **Konrad** is a German given name composed of the elements *kuoni* = daring, brave + *rad* = counsel. It was extremely popular during the Middle Ages, and as a result led to a number of surnames and variations. **Kunrad, Kuhnert, Kunert, Kundert, Kuhnhardt Kuhnt, Kundt, Kurth** are variations. Cognates include **Konert, Kohnert, Kohrt, Kordt, Kort** (Low German); **Koenraad** (Dutch), **Kunrad, Konrad** (Czech); **Kondrat** (Polish); **Corradi, Corrado, Cunradi, Cunrado** (Italian). Diminutive forms include **Kuhn, Kuhne, Kuhndel, Kiehnelt, Kaindl, Kainz, Kunz** (from which Coon and Coonce were derived, among others), **Kuntz, Kienzelmann, Kunze** (German); **Cohr, Keuneke, Keunemann, Keuntje, Kohneke, Konneke, Kunneke, Kohnemann,** and others (Low German); **Koene, Keune** (Dutch); **Kuna, Kunes, Kunc** (Czech); **Kondratenkko, Kondratyuk** (Ukrainian). There are other versions of this name as well.

Coop: There are several variations of Coop, the English Occupational name that describes the maker of wooden barrels. **Cupp, Coope,** and **Cooper** are the most common.

Cooper is the primary spelling of the English version of the Occupational surname for the barrelmaker or repairer of wooden vessals. The widespread adoption of this surname is testimony to the fact that the cooper was one of the valued specialist trades in the Middle Ages all through Europe. English variants include **Copper, Coupar, Cupper, Kooper, Coope, Coupe,** and **Cooperman** (among others --always) and cognates are **Kiefer** (German), **Kupper** (Low German), **Kupker** (Frisian), **De Cuyper, Cuyp** (Flemish), **Kuijper, Kuiper, Kuijpers, Kuypers, Cuijpers, Cuypers** (Dutch).

Colson/Coulson/Collson: An English patronymic name that originates from a very popular Middle Ages given name - Nicholas. Cole was a pet form of Nicholas used in England (primarily) and Coulson is a Scottish/Irish variation on a pet form of Nicholas.

Coe is an English nickname from the jackdaw, from a local pronunciation of **Kay,** and originated primarily in the Suffolk and Essex areas. **Coo** is a variation.

Condon is an Irish patronymic name, Anglicized from the Gaelic given name *Condun,* which was itself changed to Gaelic from Anglo Norman "de Caunteton" a place reference to Caunton in Nottinghamshire derived from the Old English given name Calunod (where d is the old English character thorne) comprised of calu = bald + nod (again, the thorne character) = daring. **Congden** is a variation.

Connor is an Irish patronymic surname, Anglicized from the Gaelic *O'Conchobhair,* which means "descendant of Conchobhar" whose name was composed of the elements "cu" = hound + "cobhar" = desiring. In an Irish legend, Conchobhar was an Ulster king who adopted Cuchulain. Variations include **O'Connor, Connors.**

Conner is derived from Middle English *connere, cunnere* = inspector, from *cunnen* = to examine, from Old English *cunnan* = to know. It was the occupation of the man who inspected for standards, including weights and measures.

Copeland: originates in Cumberland county England and cope-land is "bought land," a way that the man living there was referenced in early times.

Coppe is the Middle English word derived from Old English *copp* = summit, which was drawn in a transferred sense from *copp* = head. It described the man who lived near the top of the hill, or as a nickname for the man with a large head. **Copp** is the most commonly found form of the surname.

Corder: is an English Occupational name for the maker of string, and occasionally as a nickname for the maker of ties.

Cordes is an English cognate of the French occupational name for the maker of cord or string, or sometimes it derived as a nickname for the man who always wore decorative ties or ribbons. It comes from the Old French *corde* = string, from Latin *chorda* > Greek *khorde*. **Cordier, Cordie, Lecordier** are variants of the French occupational name. **Coard, Cord, Cords, Coxrder,** and **Cordier** are English cognates. The name is found in Spanish speaking countries as **Cuerda.**

Corlies is likely a variation of the English place name **Corley,** which was derived from the so-named place in Warwickshire, which was recorded in the Domesday book as *Cornelie*. It is derived from the Old Englsh elements *corna* > *crona* = crane + *leah* = woods, clearing. When of Irish origin, Corley is occasionally a variation of **Curley,** an Anglicized version of the Gaelic *Mac Toirdhealbhaigh*.

Cornwell is an English regional name from the County of Cornwall, named for an Old English tribal name *Cornwealas*, from *Kernow* -- the name the Cornish people used to describe themselves, possibly meaning "horn, headland" + *wealas* = strangers, foreigners. Occasionally, Cornwell is a place name from Cornwell in Oxfordshire, from Old English corn < *cron*, *cran* = crane + *wella* = spring, stream. **Cornwall** and **Curnow** are variations.

Cosby is an English place name for the man who came from the so-named location in Leicestershire, derived from *Cossa* (an Old English given name) + Old Norse *byr* = farm, settlement.

Cotgreave is an English place name derived from the Old English elements *cot* = cottage + *groefe* = brushwood, thicket. It described the man who lived in the cottage by the brushy thicket. **Greave** is a place name that is often derived from the place in Lancashire by that name, and was used to describe the man who moved from that place. **Greve, Greaves, Greves, Greeves** are variations of Greave.

Cotter is a commonly found surname for the man who lived in the cottage by service rather than rent during the medieval feudal system, which is derived from OE *cot* = cottage.

Coster is generally an English occupational name for the grower or the seller of a large type of apple called the costard, which was a ribbed sort of fruit, and derived its name from that fact from the Latin term *costa* = rib, side. When of known Dutch ancestry, the name Coster is a cognate form of the name **Küster,** the Middle High German occupational name for the church sexton.

Cotter: English Occupational name from Middle English cotter a status term during the feudal times which described the tenant farmer or serf who planted only five to ten acres and lived in a cottage on the farm and payed for his place by service rather than rent. There are several variations for the name of this modest farmer, including **Cottier, Cotman, Kotter, Kother, Kotter, Kother, Kather, Cotterel, Cotterell, Cottrell, Cotterill, Cothererill, Cotterel, Cottereau,** and **Cottarel.**

Cottle: English Occupational name which described the tenant farmer or serf who planted only five to ten acres and lived in a cottage on the farm. There are several variations for the name of this modest farmer.

Cotton: Cotton originated from the village naysayer, who always said "I don't COTTON to that idea!" *Just kidding.* It also doesn't have anything to do with the fluffy white stuff. Cot was a shortened form of cottage, and was used as the ending of many English surnames such as Wolcott, etc. and in a diminutive form with the suffix -on the English Place name Cotton was derived. The man who came to be known by that name lived near the small cottage, or at the cottages.

The name **Couch** is primarily a Cornish name that served as a nickname for the red-haired man, from *cough* = red. As an English occupational name, it described the medieval man whose work was creating beds or bedding, from Old French *couche* = bed.

Couldridge: Just as the name 'Colegate' designates a 'cool gap in the mountain range,' the name Couldridge is an English Place name that designates a 'ridge of mountains where it is cold.' Spellings of names were not standardized until the 1800's and -o- and -ou- were often mixed with the same intent.

Coupar, when not a variant of Cooper, is a Scottish Place name from Cupar in Fife, likely of Pictish origin, with an unknown meaning. There are also locations Cuper Angus, and Cupar Maculty, but no known surnames are derived from these. The first known bearer of the place name in Scotland was *Solomone de Cupir,* who was a witness to a charter in 1245.

Cowell: English Place Name...In Merry Old England they stayed out 'til the *cu* 's came home, and pastured the *milque cu* on the hyll. Cu-hyll -- or cowhill -- was a reference to the places in Lancashire and Gloucester where cattle grazed on hillsides. Some people from that area took it as a surname.

Cox is an English Patronymic name taken from the suffix applied to a good many given names to create a pet form of the name. In medieval times, the term cock was used to denote the young man who strutted proudly like a rooster, and it came to designate any young man. Hancock and Alcock are examples of names which had the term attached as a suffix, which eventually came into its own as a given name or nickname. Cox is a patronymic version of Cock.

Crabtree is an English place name that described the man who lived by a prominent crabapple tree, derived from Middle English *crabbe* (which was of Old Norse origin). **Crabbe** is another version of the name.

Craddock/Cradduck: Welsh nickname from the Old Welsh term caradog, which meant `amiable.'

Craft: is a variant of Croft, an English Place name for the man who lived by an arable enclosure, normally adjoining a house. It is derived from Old English *croft,* with variations **Crofts, Craft** (s), **Cruft** (s), and **Crofter.** Occasionally it is a place name from Crofts in Leicestershire, which got its name from the Old English *croeft* = craft or skill, and likely referenced a mill located there.

Craighead is a Scottish place name that described the man who lived at the 'head-end' of the crag, or rocky outcropping. It is derived from Gaelic *cræg* = steep rock, which was 'borrowed' into Middle English as 'cragg.'

Crane is an English nickname from the bird, derived from Old English *cranuc* = crane, heron (heron wasn't a separate word until the 1300's). It described the tall, thin man with the long legs. German cognates include **Karnch, Kranich, Krohn;** the Low German form is **Krahn;** Dutch = **Kraan;** Flemish = **De Craen.** German diminutive forms are **Kränkel, Krenkel.**

Crawford is an English, Irish, or Scottish name that described the man who emigrated from the medieval locale called Crawford (there were several such places -- Dorset and Lancashire, England, for example, and Strathclyde, Scotland as another). The locations got their name from Old English *crawa* =

crow + *ford* = ford, river crossing. Variations are **Crauford, Crawfurd, Craufurd, Crawforth.**

Crawley is an English place name that described the man who lived near the woods where the crows were, or at the clearing in that woods, from Old English *crawa* = crow + *leah* = wood, clearing.

Crews is a patronymic form of the English place name **Crew,** from *Crewe* in Cheshire, which derived its name from Old Welsh *criu* = weir, ford. It was in reference to a wicker fence that was erected across the river Dee to catch fish. The man who removed from Crewe to another location was usually referenced by his place of origin by his new neighbors.

Crim: English Place Name...Those who took the name Crim kept their dwelling near a small pond or pool.

Crisp: English Nickname for the man with curly hair, from an Old English term. Variations include **Crispe, Chrisp, Cripps, Crippes,** and others.

Crumlick may be an Americanized spelling of the Flemish perjorative nickname **Crommelinck,** which described a crippled man, or man with a bent back. The English cognate form is **Crome** from Old English *crumb* = bent, crooked. Occasionally, Crome is an occupational name for the maker of hooks, from the Middle English word *cromb* = hook, crook. Croom is a place in East Yorkshire, and another locale called Croome in Worcestershire -- the man from those locations would sometimes be called Crome. Variations of Crome are **Cromb, Crumb, Crump, Cramp, Crimp.** Cognate forms include **Krump, Krumpp** (German); **Krom** (Dutch); **De Crom, Crommelinck** (Flemish). Diminutive forms also exist in several languages.

Cromie is a variation of **Crombie,** a Scottish place name from the so-named location in the former county of Aberdeenshire, now in the Grampian region, but derived from the same Brittonic elements as *Abercrombie.* Cromie is found in Northern Ireland primarily. Other variations are **Crumbie, Crummie, Crummey, Crummay.**

Cronin is an Anglicized version of the Gaelic name *O'Croinin,* which meant "descendant of Croinin" whose name was a diminutive form of *cron* = swarthy. **Crone** is a variation.

Cross: English Place name for the man who lived near the stone cross set up by the roadside or marketplace, from Old Norse *kross.* Variations are **Cruse, Cruise, Crouch, Crutch, Crutcher, Crossley, Norcross.** Cognitives include **De(la)Croix, Croix,** (French); **Croux, Lacroux, Lacrouts, De(la)croux** (Provencal); **Croce, DellaCroce, Croci** (Italian); **Cruz** (Spanish); **Kreutzer, Kreuziger** (German); **Vercruysse** (Flemish), **Krzyzaniak** (Polish), and **Van der Kruijs** (Dutch).

Crouse is a variation of the name **Cruise,** an English nickname derived from Middle English *crouse* = bold, fierce. *Cruse, Crewes, Crews, Cruwys* are variations.
Crowder is a variation of the English occupational name **Crowther,** for the man who made his living playing the musical instrument called the *crowd* (Middle English *croude,* the Welsh called it the *crwth*). It was a popular stringed instrument of the Middle Ages. Other variations are **Crother, Crewther; Crothers** is a patronymic form.

Crowell: is an English Place name from Oxfordshire and denoted the man who lived by the "crow's stream."

Crowley: is an Irish Patronymic name, and it means 'grandson of *Cruadhlaoch,*' whose name means 'tough hero.'

Crozier is an English and French occupational name for the man who carried the cross or bishop's crook during a church processional, from Old French *croisier* < *crois* = cross. Variations are **Crosier, Croser, Croisier, Croizier.** Cognates are **Crousier, Crouzier, Crousie** (Provencal).

Cuddihy is an variation of the Irish name **Cody,** Anglicized from the Gaelic *Ó Cuidighthigh,* which meant 'descendant of Cuidightheach' whose name meant "helpful person." Variations are **Coady, O'Codihie, O'Kuddyhy, O'Cuddie, Cuddihy, Cidihy, Cuddehy, Quiddihy.**

Cumb is the Old English word for valley and that -ie is found as a diminutive suffix on occasion, and as such, Cumbie could mean 'little valley.' Place names were derived in such a fashion to describe a man by the location where he lived.

Cunningham: Scottish/ Irish Place/ Patronymic Name...Cunningham is a polygenetic name (it has more than one source) Cunningham is a Scottish place name that described the man from the location near Kilmarnock and first recorded in 1153 as *Cunegan,* a word with Breton origins. The spelling with -*ham* added has its earliest known mention in 1180. When of Irish origin, Cunningham is the Anglicized form of *O' Cuinneagain,* meaning 'descendant of *Cuuinneagan'* a personal name derived as a diminutive form of *Conn* = leader, chief. **Cuninghame, Cuningham, Cunninghame, Coningham, Conyngham** are variations of the Scot version. **Conaghan, Cunnigan, Cunihan, Cunnahan, Kennigan, Kinnegan, Kinaghan, Kinnighan,** and **Kinihan** are variations of the Irish form.

Curry: English place name in Somerset named for the river Curry.

Cusack is an Irish place name from Cussac in Guienne, derived from the personal name *Cussius* + *-acum* (a local suffix). The name is present in Ireland, but apparently died out in England. A Gaelic version is **de Ciosóg.**

Cushing is a variation of the English and French nickname **Cousin,** from Middle English and Old French cousin, which during the Middle Ages had the meaning of "relative, kinsman." As a surname, it would have designated the relative of someone well-known or famous in the neighborhood. **Cousen, Cosin, Cussen, Cuzen, Cushing, Cushion, Cushen, Cusheon** are variations. **Cousi, Couzi, Couzy** are Provencal cognates; **Cugini** is the Italian version; **Cousyn Couzyn** are found among the Flemish/Dutch.

D

Dagwell is an English place name derived from Old English *dygel* > diegol = secret, deep + *wella* = spring, stream -- and described the man who lived by the deep spring or stream.

Dale is an English place name for the man who lived in the valley, from Middle English *dale* = dale, valley, from Old English *doel* and Old Norse *dalr.* It is also a name that described the man who emigrated from any of the several locations by that name. **Daile, Dales, Deal** are variations. Cognates include **Tal, Thal, Thaller, Thaler, Thalmann** (German); **Dahl, Dahler, Dallmann, Dalman, Tendahl** (Low German); **Van den Dael, Van den Daele, Va Daalen, Daelman, Daalman** (Flemish); **Van Dael, Dahl, Dall** (Dutch); **Dahlen, Dahlin. Dahlman** is a Swedish version, and numerous ornamental names of the Swedes use *Dahl* as a compound element.

Dalton is an English place name, from any of the so-named locations in Cumbria, Durhamshire, Lancashire, Yorkshire, and others -- derived from Old English *dœl* = valley + *tun* = settlement, enclosure. **Daulton, Daughton, Dawton, Daton** are variations.

Dancy is a variation of **Dansie,** the English place name (Norman origin) with the fused preposition de, from Anizy in Calvados, which was recorded in 1155 as *Anisie.* The man from there was **de'Anisie,** which was fused into Dansie. **Dansey, Dancy, Dancey, Dauncey, Densey, Densie, Denzey, Dinzey** are variations.

Danehl is a German variation of the English, French, Portuguese, German, Polish, and Jewish surname **Daniel,** derived from the Hebrew given name Daniel, which means "God is my judge." It was an extremely popular name during medieval times and as a result has numerous variations as a surname. English variants include **Daniell, Danniel, Danniell,**

Danell, Dannel, Dennell, Denial; French versions are **Deniel, Daniau, Deniau, Deniaud;** German versions include **Denigel, Dangel, Dangl, Dannöhl, Denehl, Dennehl, Danneil;** Jewish variations are **Danielli, Danieli, Daniely, Danielski, Danielsky.** Cognates include **Danis, Dany** (Provencal); **Ianieli, Danielli, Daniele, Daniello, Danello, Danielli** (Italian); **Danihel, Danhel.**

Dailey is a variation of **Daly,** which is the primary Anglicized form of the Gaelic *O Dalaigh,* which meant 'descendant of *Dalach'* whose name was derived from *dal* = meeting, assembly. **O'Daly, Daley, Daily, Dailey, Dally, Dalley** are variations.

Daniel/Daniell/Daniels: English, French, Portuguese, German, Polish and Jewish Patronymic name, from the Hebrew given name Daniel (meaning *God is my judge).* Variations are too numerous to list, but will be added as queries concern them.

Darby: English Place name taken from a Middle Ages term that described "where the wild animals are" and the man who lived nearby could easily be described by that surname.

Darcy most commonly is an English place name of Norman origin, with a fused preposition de' attached to Arcy, a town in La Manche. The man who originated in Arcy was identified by his new neighborsby his former place of residence.

When of Irish origin, Darcy is an Anglicized form of the Gaelic *O' Dorchaidhe,* which means "descendant of the dark one," from the gaelic word *dorcha* = dark, gloomy. However, there are Darcy families in Ireland who are of Norman descent, as the name was introduced to the island early on, by Sir William D'Arcy and Sir John D'Arcy (circa 1330). **Darcey, D'Arcy** are variations of the English form; **O'Doroghie, O'Dorghie, O'Dorchie, O'Dorcey, Darky** are variations of the Irish form.

Dare is a variation of the English patronymic name **Dear,** from the Middle English given name Dere < Old English *Deora* =

beloved. Occasionally, Dear was a nickname from Old English *deor* = wild animal or the adjective form that meant "wild, fierce." By Middle English, the adjective wasn't used much and the word evolved to modern English's deer. Variations are **Dare, Deare, Deere, Deer, Dearman, Dorman, Durman.** Cognates are **Teuer, Tayer, Taier, Tajer, Teuerstein, Teyerstein** (Jewish); **Thier, Dier** (German); **De Diere** (French); **Duursma** (Frisian); **Dyhr** (Danish).

Daugherty is another Anglicized version of the Scottish and Irish Patronymic name *O' Dochartaigh* "descendant of *Dochartach* " which was a nickname meaning 'unlucky' or 'hurtful.' The most common form of the name as Anglicized from the Gaelic is **Doherty. Docharty** is the common Scottish variation.

Davenport: English Place Name...Many of the surnames that originated in England came from places where the progenitor lived... The name Davenport was first used in England's county Cheshire, where the Dane river flowed. Davenport was the 'town on the Dane River' and became the name of some who made their homes there.

David/Davis/Davies: was the patron saint of Wales, and the name was popular throughout early Britain...as a result, there a many surnames derived from the given name David, including Davis, and Davies as the Welsh equivalent.

Davidson is a patronymic form of the Welsh, Scottish, English, French, Portuguese, Jewish, and Czechoslovakian name **David,** from Hebrew David = beloved. Variations are **Daud, Doud** (English); **Davitt, Devitt, Daid, Dade, Taaffe** (Irish); **Dewi, Dafydd, Daffey, Taffie, Taffee** (Welsh); **Davy** (French); **Davidai, Davida, Davidy, Davidman, Dawidman** (Jewish). Other patronymic forms are **Davids, Davidge, Davage, Davies, Davis, Davys, Davson, Davidson, Davisson, Davison** (English, Scottish); **McDavitt, McDevitt, McCavitt, McKevitt, McDade, McDaid, McCaet** (Irish); **McDavid** (Scottish); **Davidescue** (Romanian); **Davidsen** (Low German);

Davids (Dutch); **Davidsen** (Danish); **Davidsson** (Swedish). There are also several dozen Jewish patronymic forms.

Davies: English Patronymic name derived as a diminutive form of the given name David.

Day is an English and Irish name that originates in several forms: as an English variation of **David** -- a common pet form of the name; as a patronymic name derived from the Middle English given name *Daye* from Old English *dæg* = day or the given name *Dægberht;* as an Irish patronymic name Anglicized from *Ó Deághaidh,* meaning "descendant of *Deághadh* " whose name meant "good luck." **Daye, Dey, D'Eye, Daykin, Dakin, Deyes, Dayson, Deason, Dayman** are other forms of the name.

Dazey: is a variant spelling of **Deasy,** an Irish Patronymic name from the Gaelic *Deiseach,* a nickname for a member of 'Dei's community.'

Dean is an English place name for the man who lived in the valley, from the Middle English *dene* = valley. **Deen, Dane, Deane, Deaner,** and **Denner** are variations. See next entry.

The Old French word *d(e)in,* was derived from the Latin term *decanus,* which meant leader of ten men (from decem = ten). Dein evolved into Middle English as *deen,* which is now represented as dean. As a surname, **Dean** is an English nickname that described someone who was thought to resemble a dean, who in medieval times was the leader of a religious chapter at the cathedral -- or occasionally, the term dean was used to describe a servant of that official. **Deen, Dane, Dain, Deane, Deaner, Denner, Adeane, Atherden, A'Deane** are variations. The nickname was also used in other countries and languages, and cognate forms include **Doyen, Ledoyen** (French); **Dega, Degan, Degas** (Provencal); **Degan, De Gan** (misdivided); **Dechandt, Dechant** (German); **De Deken** (Flemish, Dutch).

Decrow or **DeCreau** -- the prefix *De* is generally found among Dutch as meaning "the" as an attachment to nicknames or occupational names. **DeCroes** is the Dutch nickname for the curly-headed man, and is a cognate of the German nickname **Kraus.** Other Dutch versions are **Croes, Croese, Kroese, Kroeze.**

Deeley is an English surname commonly found in the Birmingham area that is believed to be a variant of **Daly,** which is an Irish patronymic name Anglicized from the Gaelic *O' Dalaigh,* meaning 'descendant of *Dalaigh,* whose name meant 'meeting, assembly.'

Degenstein is literally translated as "sword stone" from German *degen* = sword, rapier + *stein* = stone. **Degenschein,** also found as **Degenszejn, Degenszajn,** is translated literally as "sword shine."

DeHart is likely a spelling variation of **DeHerdt,** a Flemish cognate of the surname **Hart,** which is a nickname meaning "stag" from Old English *heorot,* which the medieval timers used to describe someone they thought resembled the male deer in some fashion.

DeLeMaitre would be translated as "of the master" or "from the master." **Maitre** is a French cognate of Master, the English nickname for the man who behaved in a masterful manner, or was skilled at a trade. The term Master (or Maitre) also was applied to some freeholders of land who had others who tilled for them, rather than doing it themselves. **Meystre** is a variation of Master. Cognates include **Maistre, Maitre, Lemaistre, LeMaitre, Maitrier** (French); **Mestre, Mistre, Mestrier** (Provencal); **Maestri, Maestro, Maistri, Maistro** (Venetia); **Magistri, Magistro, Mastro, Marro, Mascio, Lo Mastro** (Italian); **Maestre, Maeso** (Spain); **Meister** (German). There are numerous diminutive and patronymic forms as well.

Denman is an English place name which described the man who lived in a valley. It comes from the Middle English term *dene* = valley. When Denman is of known Jewish ancestry the above doesn't apply, but the exact meaning isn't clear.

Dent: English Place Name...it comes from 'Dent' hill in Yorkshire, England. The first to use it as a surname lived in that area.

Derriman is a variation of the English name **Dearman,** which is itself a variation of the English patronymic name **Dear,** from the Middle English given name *Dere* < Old English *Deora,* a nickname that meant "beloved." Dearman and Derriman are literally translated as "dear man" or "beloved man." Other variations are **Dare, Deare, Deer, Deere, Dorman, Durman.**

Deutsch is the ethnic name applied to people in a mixed population area who spoke German rather than Slavic. The Middle High German word was *tiusch,* from Old High German *diutsik* < d *iot, deot* = people, race. Variations are **Deusch, Deutscher, Dutsch, Dutz, Daeutschmann, Deutschlander, Deutschman, Deitschman, Dayczman, Deichman, Taitz, Teitzman.**

Deveraux is a spelling variation of **Devereux,** the English (Norman) place name which resulted from the fused preposition -de- added to the location Evreux, which is located in Eure, Normandy. The name would have been recorded as in this example: John *de'Evreux,* which meant, John-from Evreux. Other variations are **Devereaux, Deveraux, Devereu, Deveroux, Deverose.**

DeWeil is a place name that described a man from a location called *Weil,* with De as a common prefix meaning "from" or "of." **Weil** is a German place name from any of the so-named locations in Baden, Wurttemberg, or Bavaria, originating from the Latin *villa* = country house, estate. **Weill, Weile** are German variations, **Weill, Weiler, Weiller** are variations found among those of Jewish heritage.

Dewhurst is an English place name, from a so-named location in Lancashire, from the adjective *dewy* + the Middle English word *hyrst* = wooded hill. **Dewhirst** and **Jewhurst** are variations.

Dibley: is an English Patronymic name, based on a corruption of the name Theobald (folk, bold), which when said often and quickly enough, became Dibald and formed the basis for the surnames **Dibble** and **Dibley.**

Dickenson is an English patronymic name derived from a diminutive form of the English and Scottish surname **Dick,** which was a pet form of the name Richard. Any of several who bore the name became known as **Dicken,** and the son of the man with that name was Dicken's son, or Dickenson.

There was a Medieval given name *Dillo,* derived from Old English *dilegian* = destroy, spoil -- that may have been shortened to creating a pet form of the name **Dill,** or it may have been derived from Old English *dyle* = dill, medicinal herb -- for the man who grew or used dill in a medicinal fashion.

The name **Dimmick** (also spelled **Dimick, Dimmock, Dimock, Demick, Dymoke** (the original spelling), and **Dimmuck,** is derived from a village on the Welsh Border called Dymoke; from Welsh *Ty mocce,* meaning pigsty. The earliest person bearing this name is Thomas de Dymoke, who is listed in Domesday book. One of the earliest badges borne by a Dymoke shows the head of a pig, so it is probable that at least in the middle ages the family was cognizant of the name's origin.

Dinse is a German cognate of the English surname **Dennis,** which is patronymic from the medieval given name Dennis, from the Latin *Dionysius* and the Greek *Dionysios,* which meant 'follower of Dionysos.' The big-D was the eastern god introduced to the classic list late in the game. St. Denis was an

early martyr (3rd Century) who became the patron saint of France and the namesake of many medieval Christians. Variations are **Denniss, Denis, Denness, Dinis** (English); **Denis, Denys** (French); **Dionisio, Dionis, Dionisi, Doniso, Donisi, Denisi** (Italian); **Denys, Dinnies, Dinse** (Low German); **Denys** (Polish); **Divis, Divina** (Czech); and **Denes, Dienes, Gyenes** (Hungarian), among many others.
Dinsmore is from Dinmore a place in Herefordshire that meant "great hill" and as such is an English place name that described the man from there.

Disney: is an English Place named derived from a French place - *Isigny* - which was Isinius' estate in France. Many who followed William the Conqueror into England became known by the French towns from which they emigrated. Micky Mouse is said to have been from there.

Dixon/Dickson/Dickinson/Dickey/Dix/Dickens: English Patronymic Name...The love of the English for Richard the Lion-Hearted in the late 1100's caused a rash of names in his honor, in addition to three often-used nicknames that derived from Richard: Rick, Hick, and Dick. The son of a man given the latter of the nicknames was "Dick's son" which evolved into Dixon, Dickson, Dickens, Dix, and Dickinson. In colonial America, Dick's River (in Kentucky, for example) was spelled Dix as often as Dick's until it was standardized, sometimes as late as the 19th century.

Dlugokenski is a variation or cognate form of the Russian patronymnic name **Dolgov,** from the nickname *Dolgi* = long, tall. Occasionally Dolgov is derived from *Dolg* = debt, duty -- another nickname apparently acquired over a feudal obligation. Cognate forms include **Dlugosz** (Polish); **Dlouhy** (Czech); **Dlug, Dlugacz, Dlugatch, Dlugatz** (Jewish Ashkenazic). Patronymic cognates are **Dolgin, Dlugin, Dlugovitsky** (Jewish Ashkenazic). A place name derived from the long, tall version is **Dlugoszewski** (Polish).

Dobrovolny is the Czechoslovakian version of the name found in Russia as **Dobrovolski,** and in Poland as **Dobrowolski.** The name is derived from *dobry* = good + *volya* = will + *-ski* (surname suffix). Some sources say the name is ornamental, similar to the type names assumed by Orthodox priests, and in the cases of the Polish and Slavic versions, attributed to Dobrowole (a Polish village as a place name) or as a nickname for peasants who had been freed from serfdom. Another source says the Czech version is a nickname for someone who voluntarily accepted serfdom.

Doherty is an Irish and Scottish Patronymic name from the Gaelic *O'Dochartaigh,* meaning 'descendant of *Dochartach* ', whose name meant unlucky or hurtful. Variants are **O'Doherty, O'Dougherty, Dougharty, Doghartie, Dogerty, Daugherty, Doggart, Dockert,** and **Docharty,** among others.

Donahue is an Irish patronymic name Anglicized from the Gaelic *O Donnchadha,* which means "descendant of *Donnchadh,*" whose name was comprised of the elements *donn* = brown + *cath* = battle. **Donohue** is the most common spelling, while other variations include **O'Donohue, O'Donoghue, O'Donohoe, O'Donochowe, O'Donaghie, O'Dunaghy, Donoghue, Donaghue, Donohoe, Donaghie, Donachie,** among others.

Donaldson is a Scottish and Irish Patronymic name form of the surname **Donald** that comes from the given name *Domhnall* and is comprised of the Gaelic elements *dubno* = world + *val* = might, rule. Variants are **Donnell, Doull, Doole,** and patronymic versions include **Donaldson, McDonald, McConnell, O'Donnell, O'Donill,** and **O'Daniel** (when derived from Gaelic *O'Domhnaill*).

Donathan has roots in the Irish given name *Donndubhan* (brown *Dubhan*)and was Anglicized as many of the longer Irish names commonly were. They're called Patronymic when the surname is derived from the father's name.

Donovan: is an Irish Patronymic name from the Gaelic *O Donndubhain,* which means descendant of *Donndubhan,* from the roots *Donn* = brown + *dubh* = black.

Dorey is derived from **Doré,** a French nickname from Old French *doré* = golden, which described either the goldsmith, or someone with bright, golden-colored hair. Cognates are **Dorat, Daurat** (Provencal); **Doree, Dorey** (English); **Dorado** (Spanish); **Dourado** (Portugal).

Double is a variation of the English (Norman) nickname **Dobel,** derived from Old French *doubel* = twin < Late Latin *duplex* = two-fold. Occasionally, it is of German origin as a variation of the name **Tobel.** Variations of the English form include **Dobell, Doubell, Double, Doble, Doubble. Dobler, Dobelmann** are variations of the German version.

Doughty is the English nickname for a powerful or brave man, often a champion jouster, and derived from Middle English *doughty* > Old English *dohtig, dyhtig* = valiant, strong. **Douty, Dowty, Dufty** are variations.

Douglass is a variation of **Douglas,** the Scottish place name for any of the so-named locations on a river named with *dubh* = dark + *glais* = stream. There are several locations in Scotland and Ireland with the name, but most with the surname originated in the area some 20 miles south of Glasgow.

Dove is a polygenetic surname that is derived from these various sources: 1) as a nickname for a mild or gentle person, 2) as an occupational name for a keeper of doves, 3) as a patronymic name from the Middle English period when Dove was a given name for either sex, 4) as a translation of the Gaelic *Mac Calmain,* an Irish patronymic name, 5) as a variation of the Scottish name **Duff** (Black), 6) as a Low German nickname for a deaf man. It is difficult to determine exactly which origin applies in any given case, although extensive family history research may provide clues.

Dowd/Dowda/Duddy: Irish Patronymic Name for *O'Dubhda*, a common name in Kerry County, where the term *dubh* = dark.

Dredge is a variation of the English occupational name **Drage,** which described the confectioner -- although it may have also have been adopted as an affectionate nickname. It is derived from Middle English *dragie* = sugar-coated spice > Greek *tragemata* = spices.

Driscoll/O'Driscoll: Irish name Driscoll was the one given to the man who served as an interpreter -- the prefix -O- means 'of, son of, or grandson of' -- so, O'Driscoll is the descendant of the Irish interpreter.

Drummond is a Scottish place name to describe the man who lived near the ridge, from the Gaelic *druim* = ridge. Gilbert de Drummyn is the earliest known bearer of the name, and signed a document as the chaplain to Alwyn, Earl of Levenax circa 1199.

Drury is an English and French nickname derived from Old French *druerie* = love, friendship. It was introduced to England with followers of William the Conqueror, and during the Middle Ages it also carried the meaning of "love affair" or "sweetheart." Variants are **Drewery, Druery.**

Duckett is an English nickname from a diminutive form of Middle English *douke* = duck, or from ME *douke* + *heved* = head. Occasionally it is derived as an English nickname from Old French *ducquet* = owl > from *duc* = guide, leader. I don't know what inspired men to nickname another 'duck' -- maybe he was a good swimmer! Variations are **Ducket, Duckit, Duckitt.**

Duckworth: English Place name from Duckworth in Lancashire which was derived from the Old English given name *Ducca* + OE *word* = enclosure, translating literally to Ducca's word or Ducca's Enclosure.

Duff is a Scots and Irish nickname Anglicized from the Gaelic *dubh* = dark, black and which was widely used as a nickname for the swarthy man or the man of dark temperament. It was also found as a given name. **Dow** and **Dove** are sometimes variations of this name, which was translated in Wales as **Dee,** among the Cornish as **Dew,** the Bretons called it **Le Duigo** or **Duigo.** The patronymic form is **McDuff** among the Scots and Irish.

Duguid is a Scottish nickname for a do-gooder or a well-intentioned person, from Northern Middle English *du* = do + *guid* = good. The earliest known bearer of the name is John Dugude, who was in Perth in 1379 and went to Prussia with the King's service in 1382. It is most commonly found in the Aberdeen area.

Duke is an English nickname for someone who gave himself airs and graces, from Middle English *duke* (from Latin *dux* = leader), or an Occupational name for a servant employed in a ducal household. Occasionally, it is a surname taken as a Patronymic version of a shortened form of the given name Marmaduke, which is of Irish origin, said to be derived from ' *mael Maedoc* ' which meant 'devotee of Maedoc' a name borne by several Irish saints. Cognates are **Duc, Leduc** (French); **Duca, Duchi, Lo Duca** (Italian); **Deuque** (Portuguese); and **Duch** (Catalan).

Dull: It depends on whether you are of Scottish descent, or English descent concerning Dull. If you are a Dull Scot, you hail from Dull (a plain) which is a village and parish in Perthshire. If your ancestors originated in England, the name is a nickname that is not as unflattering as some that wound up as surnames.

Dunaway: English Place Name...which refers to one who lived 'on the road to the hill.'

Duncan is a Scottish and Irish name that is the most commonly found version of the Gaelic name *Duinnchinn,* which would have pronounced similarly to Doon-keen. **Duinnchinn** is a nickname comprised of the Gaelic elements *donn* = dark, brown + *ceann* = head -- which described the brown-headed man. Other variants are **Duncanson** and **Dunkinson,** which are patronymnic versions.

Dungen is the general spelling with an umlaht (dots) over the U, and is a German Place name as a variant of **Dung,** the surname given to the man who lived on a pieces of raised dry land amidst marshy surroundings. **Dunk, Donk,** and **Dunkmann** are other versions.

Dunn is a Scottish and Irish name from the Gaelic *donn* = dark, brown... a nickname for the man with dark hair or a dark complexion. It is also derived as an English nickname with the same meaning, from Old English *dunn* = dark-colored. Occasionally, it is found as a Scottish place name from Dun the former county of Angus, from Gaelic *dun* = fort. Variations are **Dun, Dunne, Don, Donne, Donn. Dwynn** is a Welsh cognate.

Dutton is an English place name from the so-named locations in Cheshire and Lancashire which received their names from Old English *Dudda* (a given name) + *tun* = enclosure, settlement. It described the man who came from that locale.

Dvorak, which actually has diacritic marks over the R and A, is a Czechoslovakian occupation or status name for the man who worked at the main house or manor, rather than working on the land. It is derived from Czech *dvur* = manor, court and the surname is the fourth most common in Czechoslovakia. **Dworak, Dwornik** are Polish cognates. **Dvoracek** is a Czech diminutive form. **Dworczak, Dworczyk** are Polish diminutives. **Dvorsky, Dworakowski, Dworzynski** are place names derived from Dvorak.

Dye is an English matronymic name from a pet form of the female given name *Dennis.* (You don't run across too many women named Dennis anymore -- and Dennis Rodman doesn't count!...Just kidding, Dennis!) It is most commonly found in Norfolk and Yorkshire. **Dyett, Dyet, Dyott** are variations.

Dyer is an English occupational name for the man who dyed cloth, derived from Middle English *dyer* < Old English *deag* = dye. When of Irish heritage, Dyer is a variation of **Dwyer,** an Anglicized form of *O Duibhuidhir,* meaning "descendant of Duibhuidhir" whose name was composed of *dubh* = dark, black + *odhar* = sallow, tawny. **Dyster, Dexter** are variations, patronymic forms are **Dyers, Dyerson.**

Dykes is a variation of the English place name **Ditch,** which described the man who lived by a ditch or dyke, from Middle English *diche* < Old English *dic* = earthwork. In medieval times, the ditch was a form of defensive fortification to protect a settlement. **Deetch, Dikes, Dike, Deekes, Deek, Deakes, Deex, Ditcher, Deetcher, Deeker, Dicker, Decker, Diss, Dickman, Digman** are variations. **Dieckmann, Dieck, Zumdieck, Tendyck, Tomdieck** are Low German cognate forms. **Van Dijck, Van Dijk, Van Dyck, Van Dyk, Van Dijken, Van Dyken, Dijkman, Dykman** are Flemish cognate forms. **Deickstra, Dijkstra, Dykstra, Dijkema, Dykema** are Frisian forms.

E

Earhart is an Americanized version of **Erhart** and **Erhardt,** the German patronymic name from the elements *era* = honor + *hard* = brave. The name has also been known to be adopted by Ashkenazic Jews. **Erard** is the French version. This definition was originally missing over the Bermuda Triangle, but someone name Amelia kindly returned it.

Earley is a variation of the English place name **Early,** from places so-name (Berkshire, Sussex, Lancashire, etc) whose names were derived from Old English *earn* = eagle + *leah* = wood, clearing. Sometimes Early was a nickname for the 'manly man' from Old English *eorlic* = manly, noble; and among the Irish, Early was an Anglicized version of the Gaelic name *O Mochain* or several other similar patronymic names. **Erleigh, Erly,** and **Erley** are other variants.

Earnest is a spelling variant of the German and Dutch nickname **Ernst,** from the given name Ernust, meaning 'seriousness, firmness' or occasionally from Middle High German *ernest* = seriousness, battle. Variations are **Ernest, Ernster;** cognates are **Ernstig** (Flemish/Dutch), **Nesti** (Italian); Ernsting is a patronymic form.

There are a couple of origins for the name **Easter.** Generally, it is a Place name of English origin that described the man who lived East of the main settlement, as in:

"You mean John the Baker?"
"No, John the Easter."
"Ah, is he in town?"

There were a couple of English villages by that name, and someone from there might have acquired it as a surname. People who moved to a new area were often described by their home town. Also, in the Middle Ages, the festival of Easter was quite the event, and when someone had a clear connection with that event, a regular participant in the pageant, or someone baptized on Easter, they were sometimes known by that name. **Easterling** is a variation of the English name. Cognates in Germany were **Osterer, Ostermann, Oster, Auster, Austermann, Austerling.** Some Swedes derived their ornamental names with the element as a prefix, as in **Osterberg, Osterholm, Ostergren,** and **Osterlund.**

Eastland is an English place name that described the man who lived at the eastern territory or countryside. The Middle Ages usage of the word land had a more specialized meaning and was used in several contexts. The compound name is comprised of Old English elements *éast* = East + *land* = land (didn't really need to break that one down, I guess, since both OE words survived to modern English). The use of East in this context generally meant "away from the village", "in the countryside."

Easton is an English and Scottish place name, from any of the so-named places (Devon, Isle of Wight, etc) generally derived Old English *east* = east + *tun* = enclosure, settlement, although some of the Easton forebears derive their name from settlements named for *Aelfric* or *Aœlric.* The surname is generally derived as a description for them man who was from a settlement called Easton, regardless of which one it was or how it arrived at its name.

The Swedes were among the last Europeans to adopt surnames -- and did so at the urging of their government, who created a list of many words that they approved as parts of names to be adopted. The Swedish word *-eng-* means "meadow" and is used in a number of surnames adopted during the 1800's. The suffix -*lof-* means "leaf." Literally translated, **Englof** means "meadow leaf." Most of the Swedish surnames are strictly ornamental, and were created according to their pleasing sound. Here are a number of **Eng** names and their meanings: **Engvall** (meadow slope), **Engstrand** (meadow shore), **Engblom** (meadow flower), **Engberg** (meadow hill), **Engholm** (meadow island).

Edgar is an English Patronymic name from the Old English given name *Eadgar,* composed of the elements *ead* = prosperity, fortune + *gar* = spear. Variations are **Eagar, Eagger, Egar, Egarr, Eger, Edger, Adger, Agar, Ager, Adair, Odgar,** and **Ogier.**

Edwards: is an English Patronymic name from the Middle English given name Edward from the Old English eadward, derived from *ead* =prosperity + *weard* =guard.

Eggebrecht, from the given name comprised of the elements *agil* = edge, point (sword) + *behrt* = bright, famous. **Eggert** and **Egbert** are Low German cognates. **Ebbrecht, Ebrecht, Ehebrecht, Eckerecht, Eckbrett, Ehlebracht,** and **Eilebrecht** are variations.

Eiland may be a variation of the German nickname **Elend,** from Middle High German *ellende* = banished, miserable, luckless. It was used as a nickname rather than a literal description of a person. **Ellend, Ehlend** are other variations.

Elie is a French cognate of the English patronymic name **Ellis,** derived from a medieval given name Elis, a vernacular form of **Elijah** (from Greek **Elias** > Hebrew **Eliyahu** = Jehovah is God). Variations are **Elliss, Elis, Ellice, Elys, Heelis, Hellis, Helis, Elias.** Cognates include **Elie, Helie, Elias** (French); **Elias, Elia** (Italian); **Elías** (Spain); **Elias** (Portugal); **Elies, Leyes** (German); **Iliasz** (Polish); **Elijah, Eliyahu, Elijahu** (Jewish). **Ellison, Ellisson, Elliston, Bellis** (Welsh), **D'Elia, D'Elias** (Italian) **Eliet, Eliez, Elion, Alliot, Heliot, Heliot, Helin** (French), **Ilyenko, Ilchenko, Ilchuk** (Ukrainian) are patronymic forms.

Elliott: and its spelling variations are all based on the popular Middle Ages given name Elijah (My God is Yahveh). Among the many surnames that were adopted as English Patronymic names from Elijah were **Ellis, Ellison, Elias,** and **Elliott.**

Ellison is a patronymic form of the English name **Ellis,** from the medieval given name *Elis,* a vernacular form of **Elijah. Ellisson, Elliston** are other variations.

Elwell is an English place name derived from a so-named location in Dorset that was comprised of the Old English elements *hæl* = omen + *wella* = spring, stream, and likely in reference to pagan river worship. Occasionally the name is derived from two minor locations evolving from Old English *ellern* = elder tree + *wella* = spring, stream.

Elwood is a variation of **Ellwood,** the English place name from a location in Gloucestershire which got its name from Old English *ellern* = elder tree + *wudu* = woods. The man who moved from the village called Ellwood to a new location was often referred to by his place of origin. Occasionally, Ellwood is drawn from the Old English personal name AElfweald "elf rule." Variations are **Elwood, Allwood.**

Embery: is a variant of the surname Amery which is an English Patronymic name. The name was brought to the British Isles with the Normans, many of whom were referenced by the towns they emigrated from, or by the Norman given names of their fathers. Amery is derived from Old French *amal* =bravery + *ric* =power, and derivatives include **Amory, Emery, Emary, Emberry, Embrey,** and **Imbrey,** among others.

Ernst is a German and Dutch name from the Germanic nickname *Ernust* = seriousness or firmness, and occasionally, a Jewish (Ashkenazic) name from modern German *ernst* = earnest, serious. Variations are **Ernest, Ernster, Ernstig** (Flemish and Dutch cognate), and **Nesti** (Italian).

Erwin: and its counterparts **Ervin/Irvin/Irwin** are German Patronymic names from the Old German given name *Eorwine* which means "sea, friend." On occasion the name can be traced to Scottish roots and the places called Irvine and Irving, which meant 'green river.' If you are of Scottish descent, then the second is a strong possibility.

Espinosa is a collective place name originating in Spain, Catalan and Portugal, derived from **Espinos, Espinho** -- their cognate form of the French surname **Épine,** which described the man who lived by a prominent thorn-bush or an area overgrown with thorn bushes, and was derived from OF *espine* > Latin *spina.* Variations of the French name are **Lépine, Delépine;** other cognates include **Espin, Espine** (Provencal); **Spino, Spini** (Italian); **LaSpina** (S. Italy); **Spinas** (Sardinia); **Espin, Espinos, Espino, Espina** (Spain); **Espi, Espina** (Catalan); **Espinhho, Espinha** (Portugal). Diminutive forms are **Espinel, Espinet** (French); **Spinelli, Spiniello, Spinello, Spinella, Spinetti, Spinozzi** (Italian); **Espinola** (Spain); **Espinola, Spinola** (Portugal). Other collective forms are **Espinay, Épinay, Épinoy, Lepinay** (French); **Espinal, Espinar, Espinosa** (Spain); **Espinos, Espinosa** (Catalan); **Espinheira, Espinosa** (Portugal).

Estes is a variation of the Italian place name **Este,** from a so-named place in Venitia that was originally named in Latin - *Ateste.* It is a commonly found name in Padua and Venice, and a prominent noble family bears the name. **D'Este** is another variation.

Evans is a patronmic form of the Welsh surname **Evan,** from the given name *Ifan* or *Evan,* which was the Welch equivalent of John. Occasionally, when of Scottish derivation it is a variation of **Ewan,** an Anglicized form of the Gaelic given name *Eogann,* a form of the Latin name Eugene. **Heavan,** and **Heaven** are variations of the Welsh form, **Even** is a Breton cognate. Patronymic forms include **Evens, Evance, Ifans, Ivings, Avans, Heavans,** and **Heavens.**

Everett is one of the many variations of the English name *Everard,* which came from a Germanic given name comprised of the elements *ever* = wild boar + *hard* = brave, strong, hardy. The name may be of Norman origin or as a variation of the name Eoforheard. **Evered, Everid, Everett, Everitt, Everatt** are variations. There are numerous cognate forms as well.

Everson is an English matronymic name from the rare medieval female given name Eve, which is derived from Hebrew Chava, from *chaya* = to live. The name is that of the first woman, and may have been acquired by someone who played the part in a medieval pageant. **Eva** is a variation. **Eaves, Everson, Eveson, Evason, Evision, Evetts, Evitts** are all patronymic or diminutive versions.

Ewers is a patronymic form of the English name **Ewer,** which is an occupational name that described the man who transported or served water, from Middle English *ewer* > Old French *evier* > Latin *aquarius, aqua* = water. **Lewer** is a variation -- from L'ewer.

Eyles is an English place name from Anglo-Norman-French *isle, idle* = island, from Old French *isel* and Latin *insula.* The island of reference is likely to have been located in the North of France due to the origination of the surname. **Isle** is the most commonly found version, while **Iles** (primarily in Gloucester) **Illes, Idle,** and **Lisle** are variations.

F

Fach is a diminutive form of the German (of Slavic origin) surname **Wenzel,** from the given name Wenzel, a diminutive form of **Wenze,** which was borrowed from Slavic/Old Czech **Veceslav.** Other diminutive forms are **Wenz, Wach, Wache, Fache, Feche, Fech.**

Fagan is an Irish name found in Gaelic form as *O'Faodhagain.* That is a little confusing because generally that form means "descendant of *Faodhagain* " but that name isn't among the known Gaelic given names. It may be that Faodhagain is a Gaelic version of a Norman name that was later Anglicized to Fagan.

Fairfull/Fair/Fairchild: English Nickname....Both 'fair' and 'full' have their origins in Middle English words; *full* - the meaning of which has passed to us unchanged, and *fere,* which meant comrade, friend, or 'friendly one.' The earliest meaning of fair was beautiful, so Fairfull would be "filled with beauty" or if derived from 'fere,' - "full of friendliness." Not all nicknames that survived as surnames were as flattering!

Falgout is likely a Catalan or Provecal cognate of the French surname **Foucault,** from a given name of Germanic origin with the elements *folk* = people + *wald* = rule. The Catalan cognate of the name **Fougere** (the man who lived by a fern-overgrown area) is **Falguera,** and the Provencal cognate of the same name is **Falquiere.**

Falla/Fallas is an English (by way of the Normans) place name that describes the man who hailed from Falaise in Calvados, which happens to have been the birthplace of William the Conqueror. He brought many with him, and others followed shortly after, who became known by their place of emigration.

Farlow may be a variation of the English place name **Farley,** which comes from Old English *fearn* = fern + *leah* = wood, clearing, or it could be a literal translation for the man who lived by the "low fern."

Farkas is a Hungarian nickname derived from *farkas* = wolf; such nicknames were applied by acquaintenances or neighbors who believed they saw traits of the nickname in the man they applied it to. When of Jewish heritage, Farkas is a Hungarian translation of the Yiddish given name **Volf** = Wolf, or a simple ornamental name. **Farkash, Farkache** are variant spellings.

Farquharson: Scottish Nickname from Gaelic *fearchar* (Celtic elements mean man+dear) to signify a beloved person. Descended from Farquhar Macintosh, a grandson of laird of Macintosh who was at Braemar before 1382.

Farmer probably isn't what you expect...it is an English occupational name derived from Middle English *fermer* > Late Latin *firmarius,* and referred to the man who collected taxes and revenues and paid a fixed amount in exchange for that practice (Latin *firmus* = fixed). Secondarily, it denoted a man who paid a fixed rent for the purpose of cultivation. The word farmer in the context in which we know it today wasn't in use until the 1600's.

Farrell is an Irish patronymic name Anglicized from the Gaelic *Ó Fearghail,* meaning 'descendant of *Fearghal* " whose name was composed of *fear* = man + *gal* = valour. **O'Farrell, O'Ferrall, Farrel, Ferrell, O'Farrelly, O'Ferrally, Farley, Frawley** are all variations.

Faulker: English and Scottish occupational name for the man who kept falcons for the use of the lord of the manor, and occasionally the name for the man who operated the siege gun known as a falcon. Variations are **Falconer, Falconar, Faulkener, Falkiner, Faulknor.** German cognates are **Faulconnier, Fauconnier;** in Provencal the name is **Falconnier,** in Italy it is **Falconieri;** and in Germany it is

Falckner, Falkner, Felkner, while the Flemish version is **De Valkener.** William Faulkner -- the novelist -- was descended from Scottish settlers from Inverness who were named Falconer -- their name was altered to Falkner, and then William added the -U- himself later.

Favreau is a variation of the French occupational name **Fevre,** which described the iron-worker or smith, derived from Old French *fevre* > Latin *faber* = craftsman. Variations are **Febvre, Feubre, Feure, Febre, Faivre, Lefebvre, Lefevre, Lefebure, Lefeuvre, Lefeubre,** and **Faber.** There are numerous cognates and diminutive forms as well.

Feingold: German Jewish names originated in the early part of the nineteenth century when European Jews were compelled to take surnames. Many chose purely ornamental names, of which Feingold is an example that means 'fine gold.'

Ferguson is a Scottish patronymic name, derived from the Scottish and Irish surname **Fergus,** from the Gaelic given name *Fearghus.* The Gaelic elements *fear* = man + *gus* = vigor, force are the elements of Fearghus. Variations are **Ferris, Farris, Fergie** (diminutive), **Ferguson, Fergyson** (patronymics). Many of the Irish versions are preceded by the O' -- which meant *descendant of Fearghus.*

Fielding is a variation of the English place name **Field,** for the man who lived on land that had been cleared of trees, and derived from Old English *feld* = pasture, open country. **Fielden, Feilden, Velden, Fielder, Fielding, Atfield, Attfield,** and **Delafield** are variations.

Finn isn't always Irish, of course, but when it is -- it's derived as an Anglicized version of the Gaelic nickname *Fionn,* meaning 'white,' which could have denoted prematurely white hair, or fair complexion, etc. When Finn is of English origin it is derived from the Old Norse given name *Finnr* with the same meaning. Occasionally, the name is of Ashkenazic Jewish origin, but its exact meaning in that context isn't clear. Variations are **Finne, Fynn, Phinn, McGinn, Finsen** (Danish), **McKynnan, Kinnan, O'Finn, O'Fionn,** and many others.

Findlay is a variation of the Scottish patronymic name **Finlay,** derived from the given name *Fionnlagh,* which is comprised of Gaelic elements *fionn* = white, fair + *laoch* = warrior, hero. Other variations are **Findley, Finley, Findlow, Finlow.** Patronymic variations are **Finlayson, Finlaison, Finlason.**

Fiske is a variation of **Fisk,** which is an English (primarily East Anglia) occupational name for the fishseller. Fisk is listed in the Domesday Book in Norfolk and to this day is largely found in that area.

Fix is a German patronymic cognate of the Italian name **Vito,** which is from a medieval given name derived from Latin *Vitus > vita* = life. It was a popular name during the Middle Ages due to an Italian martyr whose cult following spread into Germany and western Europe. Variations of Vito are **Vitti, Viti, Vido, Vio, Bitto, Biti, Bitti.** Other German cognates are **Veitle, Vaitl** and German patronymic cognates are **Fiex, Vix.**

Flaherty is an Irish patronymic name, which is Anglicized from the Gaelic name *O' Flaithbheartaigh,* which meant "descendant of *Flaithbheaertach* " -- a nickname that meant "generous." It is drawn from the Gaelic elements *flaith* = prince, ruler + *beartach* = acting, behaving. Variations are **O'Flagherty, O'Flaherty, Flagherty, Flaverty,** and **Flarity.**

Flanery is a variation of the Irish patronymic name **Flannery,** which is an Anglicized form of the Gaelic name *Ó Flannghaile,* which means "descendant of *Flannghal* " whose name was taken from the word *flann* = reddish, ruddy + *gal* = valour. Other variations are **Flannally, O'Flannelly, O'Flannylla.**

Flax is an English and Jewish (Ashkenazic) name for the man who sold, grew, or otherwise treated flax that was used for weaving linen in early times, and is derived from the term that carried through from Old English. It's generally an occupational name. Variations include **Flaxman** and the English forms **Flexman, Flexer.** Jewish variations include **Flaks, Flacks, Flachser, Flachs, Flaxer, Flakser, Flaksman, Fleksman.** The German form is **Flassmann, Flass.** The Dutch version is **Vlasman.**

Fletcher is the English occupational name for the maker of arrows, commonly called the arrowsmith, or "fletcher" from the Old French word *fleche* = arrow. **Flechier, Flecher, Fleche** are French cognate forms.

Folk, Folkes, Foulkes, Fulkes, Foukx, Foakes, Fowkes, Fewkes, Volkes, Volks, Vokes, Folke, Fulke, Fulk, Fuke, and **Voak.** These are patronymic names from given names with the first element *folk / volk.*

Folkard is an English patronymic name from Middle English given name *Folchard,* a Norman name of Germanic origin that is composed of *folk* = people + *hard* = brave, strong.

Foot is an English name generally found in the Devon area, while **Foote** had its origins in the Somerset area, and is derived from a nickname given to the man with some peculiarity about his foot, and derived from the Middle English *fot* = foot. It was used in the context of defining one man from another, as in:

"Robert - William's son, you mean?" he asked.

"No," came the terse reply. "Robert, with the – you know -- the *foot.*"

"Ah! Robert *foot,* then."

"Aye, Robert Foote."

Forsgren is a variation of the Swedish ornamental name **Fors,** which means 'waterfall.' The Swedes were among the last to adopt surnames, and did so somewhat arbitrarily, picking nature-related suffixes and prefixes to acquire pleasant-sounding combinations that were approved by the government. Other ornamental names with the waterfall element are **Forsgren** (waterfall branch); **Forsberg** (waterfall hill); **Forslund** (waterfall grove); **Forsstrom** (waterfall river). **Forssen, Forss, Forssell, Forselius, Forsling, Forsman** are variations of Fors.

Fort: English/French Place/Descriptive name...Fort is found in several countries, all deriving from an English/French term meaning strong/brave that was derived from the Latin word *fortis.* Some with the name were descendants of a strong/brave person -- others were those who lived at or near the fort, which was the term eventually used to describe a strong or fortified location.

Fortner is a German version (cognate) of the English surname **Ford,** which is a place name for the man who lived near a ford -- a river or stream crossing point. Other German cognates are **Furt, Forth, Furtner, Further, Furterer, Furterer, Forther, Fortner, Forthmann;** Low German cognates are **Fuhr, Fuhrman, Fohrmann, Tomfohr, Tomforde, Tomfort.**

Foster/Forester: In the English Middle Ages, the forests and woods were almost always owned or controlled by the lord of the manor -- but people had no reservations about sneaking in and taking firewood, game, or whatever else they might require. To keep the poaching to a minimum, the lord retained a man to watch the forest -- often called a Forester, and sometimes called a Foster. The name stuck as an English Occupation surname when they became adopted.

Fowler is an English occupational name for the keeper or catcher of birds, a regular job during the Middle Ages. It is derived from Middle English *fogelere* > OE *fugol* = bird. **Fugler, Vowler** are variations. Cognates include **Vogeler, Vogler**

(German); **Vageler** (Low German); **Vogelaar** (Dutch); **Vogler, Fogler** (Ashkenasic Jewish).

Fox: Although in some cases Fox refers to the nature of its originator -- as in sly as a fox, most animal names were derived from the pictures that decorated the signs at the medieval roadside inns. Literacy was an issue, most could distinguish the pictures, and the family at the sign of the Fox often took that as a surname.

Franco is an Italian cognate of the English (from Normans) nickname **Frank,** an ethnic term for the Germanic people known as the Franks who inhabited the lands near the Rhine river during Roman times. **Franchi** is another Italian version. An English variation is **Franck; Franke, Francke,** and **Franck** are German variants, while **Franken** is the Jewish version.

France and **Frank** generally described the man whose place of origin was France, although occasionally they are variations of the name **Francis,** a popular Middle Ages given name, which is **Franz** and **Francke** in Germany, **Franzen** in Sweden, **Franczyk** and **Franczak** in Polish, **Franco** in Spain; **Francisco, Cicco, Ciccolo, Ciccone** in Italy.

Franta is likely a cognate form of **Francis** (which evolved in many forms as surnames) a very popular medieval given name from the Latin *Franciscus,* and introduced into England as *Francois* (from Old French). It originally meant 'Frenchman' but later lost that connotation in the popularity of the name. **Francies, Frances, Franses** are English variations. Cognate forms include **Francois, Francais,** (French); **Frances** (Provencal); **Francesco, Franceschi, Francisco, Franseco, Cesco, Ceschi, Cissco** (Italian); **Francisco, Franca** (Spain); **Frantz, Franz** (German); **Franc** (Polish); **Ferenc, Franc** (Czech); **Ferencz, Ferenc, Ferenczi, Ferenczy** (Hungarian); **Frantz, Franz, Franc** (Polish Jewish); **Ferencz, Ferentz, Ferenz** (Hungarian Jewish). Diminutive forms are numerous in all languages.

Elsdon Smith, in his book *AMERICAN SURNAMES,* says **Frazier** is the name given to the man from Friesland, and he maintains a separate listing for **Fraser.** *Hanks and Hodges* list Fraser as a Scottish place name of uncertain origin, recorded as early as the 12th century as *de Fresel, de Frisell,* and *De Freseliere* -- appearing to be Norman, but without a known city by that reference. They may be a corruption of a Gaelic name, such a **Friseal,** which is sometimes Anglicized as **Frizzell. Frazer** is a Northern Irish variation and **Frazier** is more commonly found in the US.

Frederick is an English patronymic name from a given name of Germanic origin, composed of the elements *frid/fred* = peace + *ric* = power. The Normans brought the name into England when William the Conqueror paid his visit to the Isles. The 9th Century bishop of Utrecht was canonized -- which always gave a name a surge of popularity. There are numerous cognates in various languages, as well as diminutive, patronymic, pejorative, and variant forms.

Free is the term used to identify a man that was free-born, as opposed to those born as serfs during the feudal system of the middle ages. It is derived from Old English *freo* = free. **Freeman, Freebody** are variations. Cognate forms include **Frei, Freier, Freyer, Frey, Freimann, Freymann (German);** Frig, Frigge, Frige, Frie, Friehe, Freye, Friemann (Low German); **Frey, Frei, Freyman, Freiman** (Swedish).

French is the English ethnic name for the man who came from France, from the Middle English word *frensche* = France, although occasionally it was simply a nickname for the man who adopted French airs. Those of Irish descent may be descended from Theophilus de Frensche, who was a Norman baron who came to the isles with William the Conqueror, and who produced Sir John French as a descendant (he was Commander-In-Chief of the British Expeditionary Force in WW1).

Friedman is generally a Jewish (Ashkenazic) ornamental name, derived from Yiddish *frid* = peace, corresponding to German *friede.* Variations are **Frid, Freed, Friedemann, Friedman, Friedeman, Fridman, Fridmann, Friedler, Friediger, Friedlich, Fridnik.**

Frieri may be derived from the Old French and Middle English *frere* = friar, monk > Latin *frater* = brother. It was adopted into various nicknames for the pious person, or occasionally, a man employed at the monastery. **Freer** is the most often found version, with variations **Freear, Frere, Frier, Fryer, Friar, Fryar;** cognates include **Freire, Fraile** (Spain); **Freire** (Portugal). Patronymic versions include **Frearson, Frierson.**

Fritz/Fritsch/Fritzch: German Patronymic Name...The Germans were fond of using shortened or pet versions of names when acquiring surnames. Fritz is a patronymic surname taken from a pet form of **Friedrich,** which means "peace, rule." Fritsch and Fritzch are versions of the given name held by a long ago ancestor.

Froman: from the Old French *fromant* = corn, a French occupational name for the corn merchant.

The name **Fry** is an English nickname derived from the name **Free,** which described the man who was not a serf, but a free-man. It occasionally was derived as a nickname for a small person, from the Middle English word *fry* = child, offspring. **Frye** is a variation of the name.

Fulton: /English/Scottish Place name, In Scotland, Fulton was the 'fowl enclosure'

Fuller: English Occupational name for the dresser of cloth. The fuller scoured and thickened cloth by trampling it in water.

Fullerton: English Place name...for the 'village of the birdcatchers' in Hampshire. From Old English *fuglere* = bird-catcher (Fowler).

G

Gabeline is likely a diminutive form or other variation of the German occupational name **Gabler,** derived from German *gabel* = fork, and describe the man who made any of the forked agricultural tools (eating forks weren't around then in Germany...), or as a place name to describe the man who lived near the fork in the road or river. There is also a German location called Gabel, and **Gabler** and **Gabeline** could describe the man who emigrated from there. **Gabel** is a listed variant form of the more commonly found Gabler.

Gaches/Gache/Gachlin/Gachenot/Gachon: French Place / Occupational / Nickname. When the name originated in Provencal, it referred to the person living by the lookout spot. In more northern areas of France, the name was the occupational title for a wood sawyer. Less frequently, the name was a nickname given to a wasteful person, derived from Old French *gaschier* to spoil.

Gage is an English and French occupational name for the man who worked as an assayer, checking weights and measures, from Middle English *guage* = measure. Occasionally, it is a nickname for a moneylender or usurer, from Old French *gage* = pledge, surety. English variations are **Gauge, Gaiger.** Another French version is **Dugage.** Diminutive French forms include **Gaget, Gageot, Gagelin, Gagey.**

Gaertner is an Americanized version of **Gartner** (with an umlaut over the -a-) which is a German cognate of the English occupational name **Gardener.** The English version is drawn from Middle English, and Old Northern French *gardin* = garden and generally referenced the cultivator of edible produce in an orchard or kitchen garden rather than flowers or ornamental gardens. English variations are **Gardiner, Gardinor, Garner, Gairdner, Garden, Gardyne, Jardine, Jerdein, Jerdan, Jerdon;** French cognates are **Gardinier, Jardinier, Gardin,**

Gard, Dugardin, Jardin, Dujardin, Desjardin; Italian versions are **Giardinaro, Giardinieri, Giardino, Giardini, Giardinu**; a Portuguese cognate is **Jardim.** Other German cognates are G **artner, Garner, Gartenmann;** Low German cognates are **Gardner, Gartner,** and **Gartner.**

Gallant is a variation of the French nickname **Galland,** which described the high-spirited or cheerful person, and was derived from Old French *galer* = good humor, enjoy oneself. Gallant, as in 'observant of women's needs' came later, and partly as a result of this same origin. Variations are **Gallant, Galan, Galand, Galant.** Cognative forms are **Gallant** (English); **Galante** (Italian); **Galan** (Spain); **Galant, Galanciak** (Polish). Diminutive forms include **Gallandon, Galandin.**

Galloway is a Scottish place name derived from the location in SW Scotland which got its name from Gaelic *gall* = foreigner + *Gaidhel* = Gaelic. Before the area was a province of Anglian Northumbria the Gaelic residents there were called "the foreign Gaels" and they tended to side with the Norsemen rather than their fellow Gaels when push came to shove. The Irish name **Galway** is a derivative of Galloway.

Gamble is an English patronymic name derived from the Old Norse given name *Gamall* = old. It originally was a Norse nickname or byname, but was found in Northern England as a medieval given name. **Gambell, Gammell, Gammil, Gemmell, Gemmill** are variations. **Gambling, Gamlin, Gamling, Gamlen, Gamlane** are diminutive forms. **Gambles** is the patronymic variation most commonly found.

Garcia: Spanish Patronymic Name from the given name *Garcia* which means "spear, firm."

Garren may be a variation of **Garand,** the French nickname for the man who stood behind someone's behavior, or as a guarantor for someone's financial obligation, from Old French *garer* = to warrant, guarantee. **Garant, Garandel, Garanton** are variations.

Garrison: English Place/Occupational name, derived from Middle English *garite* = watchtower. The garrison were troops stationed at the fort or castle, and the name could also describe one who lived near the garrison's watchtower.

Garwood: English Place Name derived from the Old English *gara* (triangular land) and *wudu* (wood). The early Garwoods were those who lived by the triangular stand of trees.

Gascon is a variation of the French place name *Gascoigne,* which described the man from the province of Gascony (Old French Gascogne). The Basques formerly extended into this region but were displaced in the Middle Ages by the speakers of Gascon (related to French). Variations are **Gascogne, Gascoyne, Gascon, Gascone, Gasken, Gaskin, Gasking.** Cognates include **Gascogne, Gascoin, Gascon, Gasq** (French); **Guasch, Gasch** (Provencal); **Guasch, Gasco, Gasch** (Catalan); **Gascon** (Spain). **Gouasquet, Gasquet, Gasquie, Gasquiel, Gascuel** are diminutive French forms; **Gascard** is a perjorative version, and **Gaskens** is a patronymic English form.

Gaston is a French patronymic name from the Old French given name derived from *gasti* = stranger, guest. It is also found among the English as a result of the followers of William the Conqueror. **Gastou** is a cognate found in Provencal.

Gaunt: English Place name derived from the town of Ghent in Flanders from which skilled workers migrated to England during the Middle Ages. It was also the nickname given the thin or gaunt man.

Gay: English and French nickname for the cheerful person.

Gee: If the man named Gee didn't come from the town Gee in Cheshire, then it was a nickname he was given by his less-than-tactful associates who pointed him out by his lameness or infirmity.

Gehringer is a variation of the German patronymic name **Gehring** which is a descriptive form of the German name **Gehr** or **Geer,** from a Germanic compound name with the first element meaning "spear." Sort of confusing...but here is how it came about. When there were only given names, there were several Germanic given names such as *Gerhard* and *Gerald* -- the first part of the name taken from *geri,gari* = spear. That name was shortened by some to include only the first element, which wound up in some cases as the name Gehr, Geer, or other variations. The son of Gehr in German was sometimes called Gehring. The suffix -er is often used as an additional identifier, such as "one who" or "one from" ie. Berliner is the man from Berlin, or Schreiber as the man who scribes (writes). Gehringer may have been the man from Gehring's settlement, or simply a variation of the name Gehring.

Geise is a form of the name Gilbert, an English, French (Norman), and Low German given name from *Gislebert,* which was a Norman given name derived from the Germanic elements *gisil* = hostage, noble youth + *berht* = bright, famous. St. Gilbert of Sempringham (1085-1189) was responsible for making it a popular name during the Middle Ages. **Geiselbrecht** is the German cognate form and **Geise** is a diminutive version. Other cognates, diminutives, and patronymic forms also exist.

Gentry is a variation of the English nickname **Gentle,** although sometimes used in an ironic fashion, generally described the 'gentleman' from Old French and Middle English *gentil* = well-born, noble, courteous. Variations are **Gentile, Jentle, Gent, Jent** and **Gentry.**

The name *Geoffroi* from Old French, meant "God's peace" and in England became **Geoffrey,** the basis of numerous names such as **Jefferson, Jefferies, Jeffers, Jefery, Jeffrey and Jeffries.** People also had pet forms of the name which often stuck and became surnames in themselves. Such is the case with **Giffin,** a pet form derived from Geoffrey. During the Middle Ages, the hard and soft sounds of letter G changed in usage with many names and words, producing variations in pronouncing written forms. In addition to **Giffin, Giff,** and **Giffey** are also pet forms of Geoffrey that became surnames in England and the Isles.

Gerald was a patronymic name introduced with the followers of William the Conqueror, and comprised of the elements, *geri* = spear + *wald* = rule. Occasionally, Gerald is a variation of the surname **Garrett,** derived from another Norman given name *Gerard.*

Gerner is a variation of the English place name **Garner,** which described the man who lived near a barn or a grainery, or occasionally is derived as an occupational name for the man in charge of that place - from Anglo-Norman-French *gerner* = granery. **Garnier, Garnar** are other variations.

Getz and **Goetz** are both pet forms of the German name *Godizo,* which derives from the Germanic element for God as a name of praise.

Giesbrecht is a Low German (German lowlands) cognate of the English surname **Gilbert,** which was **Gislebert** in Germany. It is derived from the Germanic elements *gisil* = hostage, noble youth + *berht* = bright, famous -- and was an extremely popular name during the Middle Ages. Other Low German versions are **Geiselbrecht, Gelbrecht, Gilbrecht, Gilbracht.** Geoffrey Gilbert who died in 1349 was a representative in English Parliament in 1326, and it likely Giesbrecht as a cognate would have been in existance around that same time.

Gibson is a patronymic form of the Scottish and English name **Gibb,** which was taken from the pet name *Gip,* derived from *Gilbert.* **Gipp** is a variant. **Giblett** and **Gibling** are diminutive forms, and **Gibbs, Gibbes, Gipps, Gypps, Gibson, Gibbeson, Gipson,** and **Gypson** are patronymic forms.

Gifford is generally a variation of **Giffard,** which primarily was a cognate of *Gebhardt,* a Germanic given name derived of the elements *geb* = gift + *hard* = brave, hardy. St. Gebhardt was bishop of Constance during the 10th century and contributed to the popularity of the name throught the Middle Ages. Occasionally, Giffard comes as a nickname from Old French *giffard* = chubby-cheeked; and finally, Gifford is sometimes a place name from the place in Suffolk -- now called Giffords Hall, which was known in Old England as *Gyddingford.*

Giles is an English patronymic name from the medieval given name Giles > Latin *AEgidius* > Greek *aigidion* = kid, young goat. **Gyles, Jiles, Jellis, Jelliss** are variations. Cognates include **Gile, Gille, Gili, Gilli, Gilly, Gilles, Gilis, Gelis, Gire, Giri, Gely, Gelly** (French); **Gidy, Gidi** (Provencal); **Gilli, Gillo, Gillio, Gili, Zilli, Zillio** (Italian); **Gil** (Spain, Portugal); **Agidi, Egidy, Egyde, Giele, Gillig, Gilly, Gilg, Illige, Ilg** (German); **Giele, Gillis** (Flemish); **Jily** (Czech).

Gill is an English patronymic name from a shortened form of the given names Giles, Julian or William -- modern pronunciation of these names notwithstanding. When of North English origin, it is derived as a place name for the man who live by a ravine or deep glen, from the Middle English term *gil* = used in a transferred sense from the thin-slit gill of a fish. When of Scottish or Irish origin, it is derived from an Anglicized version of the *Gaelic Mac Gille* (the Scottish version) or *Mac Giolla* (Irish), as an occupational name for the servant, or a shortened form of any of the several names which were attached to the names of saints to mean "devotee of (insert Saint's name here)," or it is derived from *Mac An Ghoill,* where *ghoill* was a Highland reference to the English-speaking lowlander.

Galick, Galicki, Galecki, Gawel, Gala, Gal are all variations of the Polish cognate form of the French and German patronymic name **Gall,** (Gall is also found as a Celtic name, of origin other than described here...) derived from the Latin name

Gallus = cock, a common European given name during Medieval times. It was popular due to the 7th Century monk named St. Gall who established a Christian settlement which later housed a monastery. The second syllable came about by association with the Latin name *Paulus,* which became *Pavel* in Czech and *Pawel* in Poland -- the name Gall was interpreted as *Gallus* and transposed as *Havel* (Czech) and *Gawel* (Poland).

Gillies is a Scottish patronymic name from the Gaelic given name *Gilla Josa* (servant of Jesus). **Gillis** is a variation. Patronymic forms include **Gillison, McAleese, McAleece, McAlish, McLeish, McLees, McLese, McLise.**

Gilmore: Irish Occupational Name...In old Ireland, the words g *il, kil, maol,* and *mul* designated a follower, devotee, or servant" of someone. Those with the name Gilmore are descended from the "servant of Mary."

Gilreath is a variation of the Scottish and Irish patronymic name **McIlwraith,** Anglicized from the Gaelic *Mac Gille Riabhaich* (Scottish version) and *Mac Giolla Riabhaigh* (Irish) which means 'son of the brindled lad.'

Gittler is a variation of the German place name **Gitter,** which stems from the Germanic word *gitter* = grid, grating, and described the man who lived by the gate or barrier.

Glabb/Glab/Glabski: Polish Place name/Nickname, variation of Glab/Glabski, a low-lying spot or valley or a Polish Nickname for a fool (the literal meaning of *glab* is cabbagestalk). Better go with that first definition!

Glover is an English occupational name for the maker or seller of gloves, from Middle English *glovere* > Old English *glof* = glove.

Godfrey: is an English Patronymic name from the French given name *Godefrei,* comprised of the Germanic elements *god* + fred, *frid* = peace. Variations are **Godfray, Godfree,** and **Godfer.**

French cognatives include **Godefroi, Godefroy, Godefrey,** and others. German: **Govert, Goffer, Goffarth.** Flemish = **Govaard, Godevaard, Govard.**

Gold/Gould/Guild (Scottish): English Patronymic Name derived from the Old English masculine personal name from the precious metal.

Goldberg is generally a Jewish (Ashkenazic) ornamental name from modern German *gold* (Yiddish *gold*) + *berg* = hill. There are numerous forms of the "gold" ornamental names, which were taken for their pleasing sound, and had the elements "gold" + a suffix...including **Goldbach** (stream), **Goldband** (ribbon), **Goldbaum** (tree), **Goldberger** (person from Golden Hill), **Goldblat** (leaf), **Goldbruch** (quarry); **Goldfaden** (thread), **Goldfeder** (feather), **Goldfinger, Goldfajn** / **Goldfine** (fine as gold); **Goldfracht** (freight), **Goldgart** (garden), **Goldfried** (peace), **Goldgewicht** (weight), **Goldenhorn, Goldkind** (child), **Goldgrup** (mine), **Goldhar** (hair), **Goldkranc** (wreath), **Goldmacher** (maker), **Goldmund** (mouth), **Goldenrut** (red), **Goldschlaeger** (beater), **Goldstuck** (coin), **Goldstern** (star), **Goldenthal** (valley), **Goldwirth** (host) -- and countless others.

Gollaher, and the more frequently seen **Gallagher,** are Anglicized versions of **O'Gallchobhair,** which means descendant of *Gallchobhar,* derived from gall = Foreign, stranger + chobhar = help, support. Other variants include **Gallacher, Gallaher, Gallogher, Galliker, Gilliger, O'Gallagher,** and **O'Galleghure.**

Goode is a variation of the English nickname **Good,** from Middle English *gode* = good, and used to describe the "good man." Occasionally, it is taken from the Medieval given name *Goda,* a shortened form of several names with god as an element, such as Godwine or Godwyn. Other variations are **Goude, Gude, Gudd** and **Legood.** Cognates are **Gut, Guth, Gothe** (German); **Gode, Gude** (Low German); **Goed, De Goede**

(Flemish and Dutch). Patronymic forms are **Gooding, Goodinge,** and **Goodings.**

Gordon is a Scottish place name, from a so-named location in the former county Berwickshire (now part of Borders region) and named for Breton words that preceded Welsh *gor* = spacious + *din* = fort. Occasionally, it is an English place name from Gourdon in Saone-et-Loire, from the Roman given name Gordus, or among the Irish as an Anglicized form of the Gaelic *Mag Mhuirneachain* (son of beloved). When of French origin, it is a nickname for the heavy man, from Old French *gort* = fat. Those of Jewish heritage with the name likely derived it as a place name from the Belorussian city of Grodno. **Gourdon, Gurdon** are variations of all but the Jewish form. Two variations of the Irish name are **McGournaghan, McGournasan.** French variants are **Gordet, Gordin.** Jewish versions include **Gordin, Gordonoff, Gordonowitz.**
Gore is a French nickname for an individual (don't tell former Vice-President Al though!) that has versions **Lagore, Gouret, Gorron, Gorin, Goury, Gorel, Goureau, Gorichon** and **Gorillot,** among others.

Gorman is an English patronymic name from the Middle English given name *Gormund,* from Old English *Garmund,* composed of the elements *gar* = spear + *mund* = protection. When of Irish heritage, Gorman is an Anglicized form of the Gaelic *Mac Gormain,* and *O'Gormain,* which mean 'son of' and 'descendant of Gorman" whose name was derived from Gaelic *gorm* = blue. **Garmen, Garment** are variations of the English version, and **MacGorman** and **O'Gorman** are variants of the Irish.

Goss: Polygenetic (several sources)... It originated near the same time in England, France, Hungary, and Germany. As an English place name, it described one who lived near a moor or wood...a descendant of Goss -- a pet form of *Gocelin* "the just" was called by the name, as was the descendant of the Goth...The dweller at the sign of the goose was sometimes called Goss, as was the dweller at the thorns. There was a former Austrian town called Goss, and some residents took that as a surname. And if that isn't enough, Goss is also a shortened form of the Germanic element *god* - which means good. You can pick your favorite!

Goswick is an English place name comprised of the Old English elements *gos* = goose + *wic* = outlying settlement dependent on a larger village. The term *wick* was especially used to describe an outlying farm, dairy, or salt works. Goswick would be the outlying settlement known for geese. *Wick* was a common place name suffix, and the man who emigrated from one place to another was often known or identified by his former locale.

Gough: English Occupational Name...of Celtic origin for the man who worked as a smith, from the Gaelic *gobha* or *goff*. It was common in E. Anglia and was introduced by the followers of William the Conqueror. It is also sometimes derived from the Welsh nickname for a red-haired man... *coch* = red.

Goward is a pejorative form of the English name **Gough,** which is of Celtic origin. The pejorative form of a name is a form that is altered from the original in a less flattering or demeaning connotation. Gough is the occupational name for a smith, from Gaelic *gobha,* and Cornish/Breton **Goff.** The name is common in East Anglia, where the Goward variant is chiefly found. It was likely introduced there by followers of William the Conqueror.

Grandey is likely a variation of the English and Scottish surname **Grant,** which is also commonly found as **Grand,** derived from Anglo-Norman-French *graund* = tall, large. It was used as a nickname for the person of remarkable size, or to distingish between two people with the same name (as in, the larger of the two). Variations are **Le Grand, Grand;** cognates are **Grand, Legrand** (French); **Grandi, Grande, Grando, Lo Grande** (Italian); **Grande** (Spanish). Diminutive forms include **Grandel, Grandeau, Grandet, Grandon, Grandot** (French); Grandinetti, Grandotto (Italian).

Graves is a patronymic form of the English occupational name **Grave,** derived from Middle English *greyve* = steward. Occasionally it is a variation of the place name **Grove,** or if of French origin, the description for the man who lived on gravelly soil, from Old French *grave* = gravel (of Celtic origin). **Graveston, Graveson, Grayston, Grayson,** and **Grayshon** are other patronymic versions.
Gray is an English nickname for the man with gray hair, or a gray beard, from Old English *græg* = grey. Among the Scottish and Irish it is derived as a translation for several Gaelic names that come from *riabhach* = brindled, gray. It is occasionally found as a place name, for the English or Scotsman who originated in Graye in Calvados, from Latin *gratus* = welcome. **Grey, Legrey** are variations. Numerous cognates exist as well.

Greave is a place name that is often derived from the place in Lancashire by that name, and was used to describe the man who moved from that place. Greave is derived from Old English groefe = thicket, woodbrush. **Greve, Greaves, Greves, Greeves** are variations of Greave.

Green, when derived from an Irish context, is a translation of several Gaelic surnames originating from *uaithne* = green, and *glas* = grey, green, blue: *O hUaithnigh* was the surname that became **Hooney,** and *glas* became **Glass.** When an English surname, it is derived from the color as a Nickname for the man who liked to wear green, who played the "Green Man" in the May Day celebration, or who lived near the village green.

Griffeth is a spelling variation of the Welsh patronymic name *Gruffydd,* which came from Old Welsh *griff* + udd = chief, lord. The exact meaning of griff in Old Welsh isn't completely understood. **Griffin** is sometimes a variation of the name Griffeth.

Griffin: A mythical beast, half-lion and half-eagle -- that decorated signs at some of the roadside inns during the Middle

Ages. Most people did not read or write at the time, but all could recognize the pictures. The man who lived at the sign of the griffin was sometime called by that name.

Griggs is a variant of the English Patronymic surname **Gregory,** from the same given name that was popular throughout the Christian countries during the Middle Ages. It derives from the Greek *Gregorios,* a variant meaning 'to be awake or watchful' but was later associated with a term that meant 'good shepherd.' Sixteen of the popes were named Gregory, starting with Gregory the Great in 540 AD.

Grills is a patronymic form of the English nickname **Grill,** which described a cruel or mean person, from Middle English *grille* = angry, from Old English *gryllan* = to rage. Conversely, and somewhat ironically, when of German ancestry it is a nickname for the cheerful person, from German *Grille* = cricket, in an implied transfer of the supposed cheerful disposition of the chirping cricket. It is also sometimes a place name for the man who emigrated from the German settlement of that same name.

Grossbaier is a Jewish (Ashkenazik) compound name, one of numerous versions adopted when ordered by the government, and selected for their ornamental quality and pleasing sound. **Gross** is a German term for large, and as a surname Gross is a nickname for the large or heavy man, from Germanic *gross* = large, corpulent. The English vocabulary word didn't come around until the 1500's, to mean 'excessively fat.' **Grosse, Groos, Grossert, Grosser, Grossmann** are variations. The compound names include Gross = large + (noun) such as **Grossbaier** (baier = Bayer = man from Bavaria); **Grossbaum** (tree), **Grossboim** (another tree version); **Grossberg** (hill); **Grossfeld** (field); **Grossgluck** (good fortune); **Grosskopf** (head); **Grosshaus** (house); **Grossvogel** (bird); **Grosswasser** (water).

Guerin and **Geurin:** (spellings weren't standardized until the 1800's) are both versions of the surname **Waring,** being the

Irish form of the French given name **Geran.** That was taken from the Norman name *Warin* which meant 'guard.' Kind of a long way 'round to achieve an Irish Patronymic name.

Guignion is a variation of the French surname **Guignard,** a nickname given to the man with a squint, from Old French *guignier* = to wink, squint, look askance, plus the suffix *-ard.* Occasionally the name is drawn from a Germanic personal name composed of the elements *Win* = friend + *hard* = brave, hardy. Variations are **Guignier, Guigneux,** and of the second version **Guinnard** and **Guinard** are variations. Diminutive forms are **Guignardeau, Guinet, Guignot,** and **Guignon.**

If **Guley** isn't Anglicized from something like the Russian **Gulyaev** (from *gulyat* = to walk) then it is likely a variation of **Gully,** the English nickname for the giant man, or the large man, from Middle English *golias* = giant. You remember David and Goliath -- same name, different spelling. **Gully** as a place where water runs did not come about as a vocabulary word until the 17th century, long after Mr. and Mrs. Gully had passed the name down several generations from medieval times.

Kinkel is a variation of the German occupational name **Gunkel,** which described the maker or the spinner of spindles. It is derived from the German word *Kunkel* = spindle, distaff, from Middle High German *kunkel* < LL *conicula,* a diminutive form of *conus* = cone, peg. Other variations are **Kunkel, Künkel, Künkler.**

Gustafson is a variation of Gustavsson, a Swedish patronymic name that comes from an Old Norse given name Gustaf or Gustav, which is composed of the elements *Gaut* (*Geatas* in Old English) + *staf* = staff. *Gaut* (or *Geatus*) is the tribe of Scandinavians to which Beowulf belonged, and the term used by the English to reference that race. The son of the man named Gustaf was called **Gustavsson, Gustafsson, Gustafson.** The Norwegians and Danes generally used and single -s and an -en rather than the -sson of the Swedes, ie. **Gustafsen.**

H

Haase is a German Lowlands version of the English name **Hare,** which was the nickname for the fast runner, or a person of nervous or timerous nature. Other cognate forms are **Hase** (German); **Haas, Haase** (Low German); **De Haese** (Flemish); **De Haas** (Dutch); **Haas** (Jewish ornamental). Hare is also found among the Irish as an Anglicized form of **O hAichir,** which meant " *descendant of Aichear,* " whose name meant fierce, sharp. Variations of the Irish name are **Hair, Haire, O'Haire, O'Hare, O'Hagher, O'Hahir, O'Hehir.**

Habershaw is a variation of the English occupational name **Habersham,** derived from Middle English from Old French *haubergeon* = mail jerkin, derived from *hauberc* = coat of mail. It was the name that described the maker of chain-mail coats. When they became obsolete, the name was altered in various ways to give the appearance of a place name (as in - *shaw,* which designated a copse or thicket). Other variations are **Habershon, Habberjam, Haversham, Havisham, Habbeshaw, Habishaw.**

Hackney is an English Place name, comprised of the elements *Haki* (Old Norse nickname for a man with a crooked nose or hunched figure, meaning similar to 'hook') + Eld English *eg* = island, literally, Haki's Island, or Hook's Island. The man from there might take the name Hackney.

Haffner/Hafner/Hefner/Heffner: German Occupational Name...Lathes and potter's wheels have been around since ancient antiquity; in Germany, one who fashioned pottery was the hafner.

Hagan: It's an Irish Patronymic name for the son of Hagan. Originally from the Gaelic form *O'Hagain,* it's one of the many that dropped the -O- identifier.

Hagood/Haygood is a compound English nickname derived from the Old English elements *heah* = tall (which was also a Medieval given name) + *gode* = good. It would have described the man by that name or nickname that was noted for his congeniality.

Hain is an English place name derived from Middle English *heghen,* from Old English *gehoeg* = enclosure. Hain and **Hayne** are found in several locations across England as common minor placenames. Occasionally, Hain is derived from Hain as a Middle English given name, derived from Germanic *hagano,* which in its original form meant "hawthorne." Sometimes, Hain is a nickname for someone wretched, from Middle English *haine* = wretch. When Hain is of German origin, it is derived from Middle High German *hagen* = hawthorne, hedge...or from the Germanic given name as described above. Variations are **Haine, Hayne, Hayn, Hagen. Haynes, Hanes** are patronymic versions.

Hake is a Low German occupational name -- the name given to the peddler or street trader, from the Middle Low German term *hoken* = to carry things (especially on one's back). The English word *hawker* is derived from the 16th century borrowing of that term. Other Low German variants of Hake are **Hocke, Haker, Haacker, Hocher, Hockner, Heckner.** As an English name, Hake is derived from the Old Norse nickname *Haki,* which translates as 'hook' and was name given the man with a a crooked back or hooked nose. **Hakes** is a patronymic form.

Hall: English/German/Danish/Norwegian/Swedish Place name, derived from various words for "large house" including OE *heall,* and Old High German *halla.*

Hallaran is a variation of **Halloran,** which is an Anglicized form of the Gaelic *O'hAllmhurain,* which means "descendant of Allmhuran" whose name was derived from the term *allmhurach* = foreigner, from *all* = beyond + *muir* = sea. Other variations are **O'Halowrane, O'Halloraine, O'Halloran, O'Hallaran,**

O'Halleran, O'Halleron, Holloran, and of course, in many instances, the O' was later dropped.

Halstead is derived as a place name for the man who originally lived in one of the several so-named locations (Essex, Kent, Leicestershire, etc.) which are comprised of Old English elements *(ge)heald* = hut, shelter + *stede* = site. Variations are **Halsted, Alstead.**

Halterman: The southern Germanic term for hillside or slope is *halde* and the German Place name for the man who lived on the *halde* was **Halder, Halter, Haldermann, Halterman(n), Haldner, Hald, Halde,** or **Halt.**

Hamilton: is an English Place name, derived from its elements *hamil* =treeless hill + *tun* =settlement, for a literal translation of 'treeless hill town.' Hamilton was earlier described as **Hameldon, Hambledon,** and **Hambleton.**

The Old High German term for 'flat land beside a stream' was *ham,* and **Hammer** was the name that described the man who lived in that area. Hammer also described the maker of hammers, from Old High German *hamar* = hammer of stone. **Hammerbacher** is likely a Swedish Ornamental compound name derived from the elements *hammer* = hammer made of stone + *back* = stream. It translates literally to "hammer stream" + the suffix -er. The Swedes were among the last in Europe to adopt heriditary surnames and were encourages to take names that sounded pleasing, but did not violate good taste when translated. **Hammarberg, Hammargren** and **Hammarlund** are other versions of Swedish Ornamental. The name also may be of Jewish (Ashkenazic) origin, along the lines of **Hammerschlag** (hammer blow), and **Hammerschmidt** (hammer smith).

Hampton is an English Place name from *hamrh* = water meadow or homestead + *tun* = town or settlement/enclosure.

The man who lived at the settlement near the water-meadow was called Hampton.

Handlen: is a variation of **Hanlon/Hanlin** which is one of the 'Fighting Irish' surnames. A number of Irish names reference warriors, and Hanlon and its variations means 'great hero.'

Handley is an English place name from any of the so-named locations as in Cheshire, Derbyshire, etc. which derived their names from Old English *heah* = high + *leah* = wood, clearing. Occasionally, when of Irish origin, it is an Anglicized form of the Gaelic *Ó hÁinle,* meaning descendant of Ainle, whose name meant Champion. **Henley, Hanly** are variations of the English version, and **O'Hanley, O'Hanly, O'Hanlee** are forms of the Irish.

Hanna/Hannah/Hannay: English Place name...All three names are derived from the English place in Lancashire called 'Hanna's Island' and as spellings of surnames were not standardized until the 20th century, several variations exist. People who came from Hanna's Island came to be known as Hanna/Hannah/Hannay.

Hansen is a Flemish and Dutch version of the German surname **Hans,** a medieval given name that was actually an aphetic form of *Johannes* (John). **Hansen, Henson,** and **Haesen** are patronymic forms of the name (meaning 'son of Hans') found among the Flemish and the Dutch. Hans was a popular name and variations and cognates are found in several languages and dialects.

Hardcastle: English place name near Hebden Bridge in Yorkshire. It is derived from Middle English *hard* + *castel* = castle.

Harding: English Patronymic name, from the name Heard (hard,brave)

Hardy is an English and French nickname for the brave or foolhardy man, from Old French *hardi* = bold, courageous. **Hardey, Hardie** (Scottish), and **Hardi** (French) are variations.

Harsh may be an Americanized version of **Harsch,** a German nickname for the stern or severe man, from German *harsch* = harsh, stern. It is also occasionally an occupational name for the soldier, from Middle High German *harsch* = body of troops.

Hatfield is an English place name from any of the so-named locations in Esses, Nottinghamshire, Herefordshire, Worcestershire, and others -- from Old English *hæð* = heathland, heather + *feld* = pasture, open country. **Hatfeild, Hatful, Hatfull, Hadfield** are variations.

Hay is an English and Scottish place name for the man who lived near an enclosure, from Middle English *haye* > Old English *gehæg* = enclosure, which was later confused with Old French *haye* = hedge, after the Normans invaded. Occasionally, it is a nickname for a tall man, from Middle English *hay* = tall, high (from Old English *heah* = high). **Haye, Hey, Heye** are variations. **Hayes** is a patronymic form.

The closest I can find to the Hungarian **Harlacher** is the German name **Horlacher** from the place *Horlach* in Bavaria or *Horlachen* in Wurttemberg, from Old High German *hor* = mud, marsh + *lahha* = lake. Germany constituted the strongest influence on early Hungary and Hungarian names are similar to German although the language is distinctly different.

Harriman is an English occupational name for a servant who was in the employ of someone who had the given name - Harry...as in Harry's man.

Hasler is a variation of the English place name **Hazel,** derived from Old English *hæsel* = hazel, which was the name of the man who lived near the hazel tree or grove. Other variations are **Hazell, Hasel, Haisell, Hessel, Heazel, Haseler, Haselar,**

Heasler. The Swedish version of the name is **Hassel, Hessel. Hasling, Hazlett** are collective forms found in England. The ornamental compound names used in Sweden with **Hassel** as a first element include **Hasselberg** (hazel hill), **Hasselgren, Hesselgren** (hazel branch), **Hesselblad, Hasselblad** (hazel leaf).

Haylow is derived from Old English elements and as a place name, described the location where a medieval ancestor made his home. The Old English terms *heah* = high + *hlaw* = hill were used as a descriptive means of identifying the man who had his home on the high hill in the local area.

Hazeltine is a variant of the English place name **Hazelden,** from any of the several places so-named from Old English *hoesel* = hazel + *denu* = valley. Variations are **Haizelden, Hayzelden, Haiselden, Hayselden, Hasleden, Haselden, Hesleden, Heseldin, Hazeldon, Hayzeldene, Hazeldeane, Haseldene, Hazzeldine, Hazledine, Haseldine, Hazeltine, Haseltine, Hesseltin,** and others.

Herald is a variation of the English patronymic name **Harrod,** from the Old English personal name *Hereweald,* derived from *Haraldr* or *Herold,* which the Normans introduced into English under William the Conqueror. The Norman names stem from an Old Norse origin from Germanic elements *heri, hari* = army + *wald* = rule, and was recorded as early as the first century. It was also occasionally derived as an occupational name for the herald, from Middle English *herauld.* **Harrold, Harroll, Harrald, Harralt, Harrell, Herrald, Herrold, Herauld** are all among the many variations. **Harold, Herold, Herholdt, Haerlet** are among the German cognates.

Harju is a Finnish ornamental name derived from Finnish *harju* = ridge, and is among the many nature words adopted in the 1800's by the Finnish people when surnames became mandatory.

Herman is from the Germanic given name composed of the elements Heri, *hari* = army + *man* = man. **Harman** is the French cognate of the name, and **Harmon** is the English cognate (of Norman origin). The name **Hermann** is of ancient origin, and the Latin historian Tacitus recorded the name of the leader of the Cherusci as the first bearer of the name, in the 1st century AD. Numerous variants, cognates and diminutive forms exist as well.

Harris: is an English Patronymic name that comes from a pet form of the given name Henry. Some Henrys became known as Harry, and Harris was the descendant of Harry.

Harstad: In Norway, people lived on farms rather than villages as they did in other parts of Europe, and some can be traced all the way back to the Iron Age. There are several designations for the farms, and -stad is one of the later ones. Harstad is a Norwegion place name.

Harts is a patronymic form of the English nickname **Hart,** which described the man who had some resemblance to the stag, according to his fanciful neighbors. What aspect of the male deer isn't clear -- or may have varied. When of Irish origin, Hart is an Anglicized version of the Gaelic name *O hAirt,* meaning 'descendant of Art' whose name meant bear, or hero. Variations of the nickname are **Heart, Hurt, Hort,** and of the Irish patronymic name: **Harte, O'Harte,** and **O'Hart.** When of Jewish heredity, Hart is a variation of several similar-sounding surnames.

Hartley: The ending - *ley* on English surnames is derived from the Old English word *leah,* which described a 'clearing in the woods.' **Hart** is an old term for stag or deer, derived from OE *heorot,* and Hartley would be the man who lived near the clearing in the woods, where the deer were found.

Hasse is a variation of the German patronymic name Hass, and comes about this way. The old German given name Hadubert was composed of the Germanic elements hadu = battle + berht = bright, famous. Pet forms of names are generally diminutive variations, such as Bobbie is to Bob, Freddy is to Fred. Hasso was a pet form of Hadubert (don't ask me why it formed that way!). From Hasso, as a given name (in a pet form) the surname Hass evolved. The name did occasionally arise from less elegant origins, although nothing so distasteful as many surnames. Hass is the German word for hatred, and was occasionally used to describe the medieval man whose disposition was especially bitter or sullen. When the name is of Jewish (Ashkenazic) origin, it is one of the assumed or ornamental names taken when the government imposed a surname requirement, and may be derived from the same "nickname" origination.

Hatfield: English Place Name for the field that was covered with heather.

Hawkins is a patronymic form of the English surname **Hawkin,** from the given name Hawkin, which was a diminutive form of **Hawk. Hawking** and **Hawken** are variations.

My Mother's maiden name is **Harray.** Her family comes from the Parish of Harray in the Orkney Islands, which is the thirteenth parish of the Nordic parish system of twelve parishes around the outside and one in the middle.

Hawthorne is a variation of the English Place name **Hawthorn,** which described the man who lived by the bush or a hedge of hawthorn, from the Old English word *haguporn,* which was the name for the thorn used to make hedges and enclosures. The -e at the end was generally found in Northern Ireland. Cognates, or names from words in other languages that mean the same thing, are: **Hagedorn, Haydorn, Heydorn, Heidorn** (German); **Van Hagengoren** (Flemish), and **Hagedoorn** (Dutch).

Haydock is an English place name from the town so-named near Liverpool which derived its name from either the Welsh *headdog* = barley farm, or Old English *hoep* = heath + *hoc* = hook.

Hayne and **Hayn** are variations of the name **Hain,** an English place name for the man from any of the various places named from Old English *heghen* or *gehœg* = enclosure. Hayne is a common placename in Devon.

Hayward is an English occupational name that described the man who protected the enclosed forest or other land from damage by vandals, poachers, or animals. It comes from Old English *hay* = enclosure + *ward* = guardian. **Heyward, Haward** are variations.

Hazelett is a diminutive form of the English Place name **Hazel,** which described the man who lived near the hazel tree or grove, from the Old English word *hoesel.* Variations are **Hazell, Hasel, Haisell, Hessels, Heazel.** The Swedish cognate is **Hassel** or **Hessel,** while Swedish ornamental compound versions are **Hasselberg, Hesselberg, Hasselblad, Hesselblad, Hasselgrn,** and **Hasselqvist.**

Hazlett is an English (although now primarily Northern Ireland) place name for the man who lived near the hazel copse, from Old English *haeslett,* a derivative of *hoesel* = hazel. Variations are **Hazlitt, Haslett, Haslitt, Hezlett, Heaslett.**

Heard is an English Occupational name for the tender of animals, normally a shepherd or cow herder, derived from Middle English *hearde* and Old English *hierde* = herd, flock. Variants are **Heardman, Herd** (Scottish primarily), **Herdman, Hardman, Hird, Hurd, Hurdman, Hearder;** cognates are **Hirth, Hirter, Herter, Herder, Horter** (German) and diminutive forms include **Hirtel** and **Hirtle.**

Hebert: is an English Patronymic name from the given name *Hebert,* which means "combat, bright."

Heck/Hack/Hatch/Hatcher: English Place name...Surnames were often derived from the places where people lived at the time names were being adopted: Heck, Hack, Hatch, Hatcher were names that were used by those who lived at the gate or entrance to a park or forest, usually surrounded by a hedge.

Hedmark: Swedish Acquired Name...the Swedes were among the last to adopt formal surnames and had a tough set of criteria for making up family names. (They didn't want anything risque or socially offensive.) Many were combined from nature words that they linked to form a pleasant sounding family name. *Hed* means 'meadow' and *mark* means 'field' -- so Hedmark would be literally translated as meadow-field.

Hedemark: The prefix *Hede* is from Old Norse *heior* = heath, used in context as **Hedegard:** *hede* = heath + *gard* = enclosure, with Hedegard a Danish place name.

Hefner is a variation of the German and Jewish occupational name **Hafner,** from German dialectic *fafen* = pot, dish -- the name described the potter in South Germany and Austria. **Haffner, Heffner,** and Häfner are variations. **Hipfner** is more likely a variation of the German occupational name **Hopfner,** which described the grower of hops, or the seller of hops. It is derived from Middle High German *hopfe* = hops + *-er* = local suffix for agent nouns. Other variations are **Höpfer, Hoptner, Heptner, Heppner, Hepner, Hopfner, Hopf.**

Heilenman may be a variation of **Heilman,** the German nickname for the man who was considered to be exceedingly healthy or robust, or derived from Old High German *heilag* = holy.

Heldt is a variation of **Held,** the German, Dutch, and Jewish (Ashkenazic) nickname which is translated as "hero" from German *held* = hero. As a Jewish name, it is normally an ornamental surname. Variations are **Held, Heldmann, Heldman.** Other ornamental Jewish names with the element are **Heldenburg** (hero's hill), **Heldstein** (hero's stone), **Geldstein** (Russian influence).

Helfield: The lord's manor or hall was one of the easily recognizable features in the early countryside. The man who had a home near the hall was called **Heller** and the man who lived near the field by the hall was called Helfield. It's an English Place Name.

Hell (e): is a variant of **Hill,** an English Place name. The man who lived by the Hill (and there were many) sometimes came to be known as Hill, and less frequently, as Hell or Helle. When the name is of German origin, it is a place name for the man from **Heller,** from the German *heller* = light.

Helmrich is one of the many variations of **Helm,** a medieval German given name which was a shortened form of the many compound names containing *helm* = helmet. Others are **Helmel, Helmle, Helmecke, Helmchen, Helmker.**

Henley/Hensley: English Place name...Originating in Suffolk and Warwickshire, from Old English *heah* meaning high + OE *leah* meaning wood/clearing. A Henley or Hensley would be one who lived near the high clearing in the woods.

Henson is an English patronymic name derived from the Middle English given name *Henne,* which was a shortened form of Henry. **Henn** is the surname commonly associated with the name, with Henson as a patronymic form. **Henkin** is a diminutive form.

The English, French, and German patronymic name **Herbert** is composed of the elements *heri, hari* = army + *berht* = bright, famous. The name was brought to England with the invading Normans, who apparently carried a big bag of names with them. Kidding there. Variations are **Herbit, Hebbert, Hebbard, Hebard, Harbert, Harberd, Harbard, Harbird, Harbord** (all English); the French variations are **Hebert Herbet, Harbert;** the German variants are **Herbrecht, Herbricht.** Other diminutive forms found among the French are **Hebertet,**

Hebertot, Herbreteau, Herbelet, Herbelin, Herbelot, Harbelot, Harbulot.

Herbst is a German nickname, which at the time, made reference to "harvest." The rationale for the nickname has been lost, but may have been in reference to the man who had obligations to be met at harvest time. The term *Herbst* in modern German has come to mean Autumn, but it was in the "harvest" sense that the surname was taken. **Herbstman, Erbst** are Jewish variations. **Harfst, Herfst, Host** are cognate forms.

Heredia is a Spanish place name that described the man who moved to his new town or settlement from any of the several so-named locales (there is one in the province of Alava) which got their name from the plural form of the Late Latin term *Heredium* = hereditary estate, which was an estate that was passed down from generation to generation rather than being returned to the overlord of the region.

Herrington is an English place name from the so-named location in County Durham, from Old English *Heringtun* = "settlement associated with Here" which is a shortened form of any of several names that had here (army) as their first element.

Herrod is an English nickname, chiefly from the Nottingham area, derived from the given name *Herod,* origating as the Greek name Herodes, from *heros* = hero. Herrod was the name of the king of Judea who ordered that all male children in Bethlehem be slaughtered at the time of Christ, and during Medieval plays the part was depicted as furious tyrant. Generally, the man who held the role became known by the name of his character, although it was occasionally given as a nickname to a hot-tempered man.

Herron is polygenetic, in that it is derived from several sources. As an English nickname, it described the man who was tall and thin, like the heron, from Middle English *heiroun.* As an Irish patronymic name, it is Anglicized from the Gaelic *O hEarain,* meaning 'descendant of Earan' whose name meant 'fear, distrust.' It is also derived as an Anglicized version of the Gaelic *O hUidhrin* (descendant of *Uidhrin* = dun colored, swarthy) Finally, it is also derived as an Irish Anglicized version of the Gaelic *Mac Guilla Chiarain,* which means "son of the servant of St. Ciaran.' Nickname variations include **Herroun Herron, Haironn, Leherne. Heron, Hairon, Leheron, Aigron** are cognate forms.

Hester is a variation of the Low German place name **Heister,** which described the man who lived by a conspicuous beech tree, derived from Middle Low German *héster. Heester, Heesterman* are Dutch forms; **Hetre, Lehetre** are found in France. **Hester** is also the English cognate form of **Heister. Hetreau** is a diminutive French form.

Hewitt is an English Patronymic name from the given name *Huet,* which was a diminutive form of Hugh; occasionally it comes as a description of the man who lived in a newly-made clearing in the woods, from Middle English *hewett,* a derivative that meant 'to chop' or 'to cut.' Variants include **Hewit, Hewett, Hewat, Howett, Howatt, Huett,** and **Huitt.** Patronymic versions are **Hewitson, Hewetson, Hewison, Howetson, Howatson, Huitson,** and **Huetson.**

Heydrich: and its many variations are German Patronymic names from the given name Heidenreich, which is derived from Old German *headen* =heathen + *reich* =rule, and was a popular name during the Crusades when it proudly declared "power over heathens!" The other forms of the name include **Hedrick, Headrick, Heydrick,** and **Hydrich.**

Hibbard/Hibbert/Hilbert/Ilbert: English patronymic name from the Norman given name *Hilbert* or *Hildebert,* which was derived from *hild* = battle + *berht* = famous.

Hickey is an Anglicized Irish version of the Gaelic name *O'hIcidhe,* which meant "descendant of *Icidhe"* which was a nickname of sorts for a doctor or healer. It's also found as **O'Hickey, O'Hickee, Hickie, Hicky.**

Higgs is a variation of the English surname **Hick,** from the medieval given name *Hicke,* which was a pet form of the name Richard. The Norman pronunciation of the R gave the English trouble, so they wound up placing an H as substitution in the cases of several Norman-based given names (Hobb for Rob, etc.) **Hitch, Ick, Icke** are variations. Diminutive forms include **Hicking, Hickin, Hicken, Hicklin, Higgett, Higgitt, Higgon, Hitching, Hitchin, Hitcheon, Hitchcock, Hedgecock, Hitchcott, Hedgecote, Hitchcoe, Hickock, Hiscock, Hiscoke, Hiscott, Hiscutt, Hiskitt. Hickes, Hicks, Higgs, Hutches, Ickes, Hickeson, Hixon, Hitchisson** are patronymic forms.

Highland: English/Scottish Place name that quickly described where its owner lived -- on the high land. It was an easy way to distinguish between John in the valley from John on the hill.

Hill is an extremely common English place name that described the man who kept his home on or near a prominent hill, from Old English *hyll* = hill. The -y was pronounced in various ways in medieval England and the surname Hell developed from the same context with a different pronunciation. Sometimes the name was a shortened form of Hillary, or Hildabrand. **Hell, Hull, Hille, Hillam, Hills, Hiller, Heller, Hillman** are variations.

Hilliard: is one of the rare English Matronymic names -- that is, it comes from the name of the mother instead of the father. Hilliard is derived from the Norman female given name *Hildiarde/Hildegard,* comprised of Germanic elements *hild* = battle, strife + *gard* = fortress, strength. Variations include **Hilleard, Hillyard,** and **Hildyard.**

Hillon may be derived from **Hillion,** a diminutive form of the English patronymic name **Hilary,** which was a Medieval given name from Latin *Hilarius* > hilaris, cheerful, glad. Hilary was a popular name among early Christians and was borne by several saints. **Hillary, Hillery, Ellery, Elleray, Elray.** There are cognates in several languages.

Hines is a variation of **Hynes,** which is an Anglicized form of *O hEidhin,* which meant "descendant of of Eidhin" whose name was a derivative of *eidhean* = ivy. Occasionally Hines is a patronymic form of Hine, an English name for the servant lad in the household. **O'Heyne, Heynes** are variations of the Irish form.

Hinshaw: English Place name that is a variation of **Henshaw,** which was a 'woods where wild birds are' found, such as moor hens and partridges.

Hix is a shortened form of **Hixon,** which was a patronymic form of the English surname **Hick,** which in itself was a form of the given name *Hicke,* which was a pet form of the name Richard. Long story there! The change from -R- to -H- was due to the English inability to cope with the French-Norman -R- and created many variants in surnames. **Hitch, Ick, Icke** are variations of Hick. Many diminutive and patronymic forms also exist.

The Swedes were among the last to adopt surnames in Europe and did so at the urging of their government, which compiles lists of acceptable prefixes and suffixes that could be used in forming ornamental compound names. **Hogberg** is composed of the elements *hög* = high + *berg* = hill. The names do not have a specific meaning, but were simply chosen for their pleasing sound. **Höglund** (high grove) and **Högström** (high river) are other examples.

Hobb was a pet form of the name Robert (where there is a mention of Hobb). The Norman invasion in 1066 brought many names to England, but the locals had trouble pronouncing the Norman version of a preceding "R" so they used "H" in many cases, which was easier for them to say. That why Dick became a nickname for Rick (Richard), and Hobb was substituted for Rob (Robert). **Hob, Hopp, Hobbin, Hoblin, Hobling, Hoblyn** are variations. Patronymic forms include **Hobbes, Hobbs, Hobbiss, Hobbis, Hobson, Hopson, Hobbins.**

Hogg is an English and Scottish occupational name for the swineherd, from Middle English *hog* = pig. Occasionally, when of Scottish or Irish origin, it is a translation of the Gaelic *Mac an Bhanbh,* which means "son of the hog," but the meaning of that may be lost to obscurity.

Holder is a German place name that described the man who lived by an elder tree, from Old German *holuntar* = elder tree. When of English origin it is an occupational name for the man who kept animals, from Middle English *holden* = to guard. **Holderer, Holdermann, Holderbaum, Houlder** are variations; **Hölderlein, Hölderlin, Hölderle** are diminutive forms.

Holdsworth is a variation of the English place name Hallworth, from two places in West Yorkshire by that name, originally called 'Halda's enclosure.' Halda was an English nickname that meant 'bent.' The name **Hallworth** is comprised of *Halda* + OE *word* = enclosure. Variations are **Hallsworth, Holdsworth, Houldsworth, Holesworth.**

Holst is a Dutch, German, and Danish name for the man who lived near a patch of woodland, from Middle Low German *holtsate* > holt = wood + *sate* = tenant.

Hopkins: English Patronymic name...At the time of the conquest, the Normans brought the name Robert to England, and it had several pet forms that became the basis for surnames. *Rob* (which we still use), *Hob,* and *Dob,* were all pet names for Robert. **Hobbs** and **Hobson** were drawn from Hob, and Hopkins was yet another variation.

Hodge/Hudge/Hodgin/Hodgen: English Patronymic name from the pet name Hodge, which was derived from the given name Roger. Roger came to England as *Rogier* courtesy of the conquering Normans.

Hodinott: is the original version of (H)Od(d)en(n)not(t), which is a Welsh Place name from Hodnet in Shropshire or any of the various places called Hoddnant in Wales. It is derived from *whawdd* = pleasant, peaceful + *nant* = valley, stream. Other variations include **Hodinott, Hodinett,** now chiefly in Ireland.

Hoefling/Hoffling/Haefling: Americanized spelling of German name **Höfling,** a diminutive form of the nickname **Höflich.** From German *höflich* = polite, well-mannered, refined > Middle High German *hovelich* (an adjective derived from *hof* = court).

Hoffman: German Nickname Name...hoef (*hof* with the two-dots over the o = umlaut) means court or small farmer and Hoffman is a nickname for a farmer who owned his land rather than rented.

Hogarth/Hoggarth: English and Scottish Place name from an unidentified place with the second element *garth* = enclosure.

Hogeweide/Hochweide: German Place Name...From German *hoge/hoch* = tall + *weide* = willow, or "tall willow." One living near the tall willow would be Hogeweide or Hochweide.

Holbrook: English place name that described the man living by the stream in the deep ravine.

Holden is an English place name that described the man from any of the so-named locations in Lancashire and W. Yorkshire, named from the Old English elements *hol* = hollow, depression + *denu* = valley. **Houlden, Howlden, Houldin, Holding** are variations.

Holladay is a variation of the Northern English and Scottish nickname **Halliday,** derived from Old English *haligdoeg* = holy day, religious festival. It is believed that the term was adopted as a surname to describe the person born at Christmas or Easter. Variations are **Haliday, Halladey, Hallady, Halleday, Holiday, Holliday, Holyday, Holladay.**

Holland is an English place name that described the medieval man from any of the eight villages scattered around England at the time, which got their names from Old English *hoh* = ridge + *land* = land. A county of the Holy Roman Empire was Holland in the Netherlands, and it has long been used synonymously in English and occurs occasionally in English, German, Jewish, Flemish, and Dutch names to describe the man from that area. Also, less frequently, Holland (when of known Irish origin) is an Anglicized form of the Gaelic surnames Houlihan, Mulholland, or Whelen. Variations are **Hollands, Howland, Hoyland.** Of the Netherlands version, variations exits in the form of **Hollander, Hollaender, Holand, Holander, Goland, Golender.** Cognates are **Hollande** and **Hollenzer.**

Hollingsworth is an English place name derived from so-named locations in Cheshire and Lancashire (actually called Hollingworth) derived from Old English *holegn* = holly + *worð* = enclosure. Hollingworth is the other version also commonly found.

Holman is an English, Flemish, and Dutch place name for the man who lived in a hollow, from Old English *holh* = hollow, hole + *mann* = man. Occasionally, as a surname of English origin, it is derived from Middle English *holm* = holly + *man,* as a name that described the man who lived near a prominent holly tree, or holly grove. **Hollman, Holeman, Homan** are English variations, and **Holleman** is found among the Dutch and Flemish.

Holmes is a patronymic variation of the English and Scottish surname **Holme,** derived from the Middle English word *holm,* from Old English *holegn,* which derived eventually into the word 'holly' and described the tree. Holme was the man who lived near the holly tree. Occasionally, it is derived from Northern Middle English *holm* from Old Norse *holmr* = raised land in a fen or partially surrounded by streams, and used to describe the man who lived on a tiny island of raised land. Other variations are **Hulmes, Home, Hulme, Hume.**

There are names that have equivalent forms in different languages. The name **Holt** in England described 'the man who lived by the woods.' The same description in Germany was known as **Hoelzler** (actually written **Holzler,** with an umlaut over the -O-). A diminutive form of that name is **Holzl,** and Americanized as **Hoelzl.**

Holton is an English place name that described the man who emigrated from any of the several locations by that name, which were named from the Old English elements *hoh* = spur of the hill + *tun* = settlement, enclosure. Holton locations in Oxfordshire and Somerset were named from OE *halh* = nook, recess + *tun* = settlement, enclosure.

Hopp is generally a variation of the English patronymic name **Hobb,** which was a medieval given name spelled alternately *Hobbe,* and *Hobb,* which was a pet form of the given name Robert. Hob is another variant, while diminutive forms are **Hobbin, Hobling, Hoblyn,** and **Hobbes, Hobbs, Hobbis,** and **Hobbiss** are patronymic variations. As a name of German origin, Hobb is likely a spelling variation of the Low German name **Hoppe,** which is a cognate for the German occupational name **Hopfner,** the grower of hops, or dealer in hops, and occasionally used as a nickname for a brewer due to the hops used in the making of beer. The name is derived from the German *hopfen* = hops + *er* = suffix applied to nouns. Variations are **Hopfer, Hoptner, Heptner, Heppner, Hopfner,** and **Hopf** (Bavaria). **Hoppner** is another Low German cognate, while **Hopman** and **Van Hoppe** are the Dutch versions.

Horne is an English occupational name for the man who made small items from horn material, a common practice during medieval times. It is also derived from the occupation of horn-blowing, which was both a form of entertainment, and signalling. **Horne** is a variation. Occasionally, Horn was an unflattering nickname for the man who had some quality that reminded his neighbors of a horn, or horned animal. Also, it was occasionally derived as a place name for the man who lived near the horn-shaped hill or outcropping. **Horner, Horner, Hornor** are English variations. **Horner, Hörner, Hornemann, Hormann** are German cognates. **Van den Hoorn** is a Dutch cognate of the place name.

Hornsby is an English place name from place by that name in Cumbria, from the Old Norse name *Ormr* = serpent + *byr* = farm, settlement.

Horry is a Norman-form variation of the English surname **Wooldridge,** a patronymic name derived from the Middle English given name *Wolfrich, Wolrich* -- which came from Old English *Wulfric,* from Old English *wulf* = wolf + *ric* = power. Other Norman versions are **Horrey, Hurrie, Hurry, Hurrey, Orrey, Orry, Urie, Urey, Urry, Ury.** Other English versions are **Wolveridge, Woolveridge, Woolridge, Woolrich, Wolrich, Woolright.**

Houle is a variation of the English place name **Hole,** which described the man who lived in a low area or depression (geographic, not mental!) and derived from Old English *holh* = hollow, depression. **Hollow, Holer, Holah, Holman** are variations. **Hohler, Hohl** are German cognates. **Holla** is the Frisian version. **Höl** is found among the Flemish and Dutch.

Houlihan is an Irish patronymic name Anglicized from the Gaelic *O' hUallachain,* meaning "descendant of *Uallachan* " a given name derived from another form that meant "proud, arrogant."

Houston/Huston/Houstoun/Heuston: Scottish Place Name...From a place near Glascow, from the medieval given name Hugh + the Medieval English word *tun* = enclosure, settlement. Hugo de Paduinan held the location circa 1160. Hugh's town was Anglicized to Houston, the most common form.

Houtz is likely a Dutch or Low German cognate form of the name **Holt,** a place name that described the man who lived by a wood or copse. **Hout, Van Houten, Houtman** are other Dutch cognate forms.

Howard is an English patronymic name from the Norman given name *Huard, Heward,* which came from the elements *hug* = heart, mind + *hard* = hardy, brave. It is also derived from an Old Norse name *Haward,* from Norse elements *ha* = high + *varðr* = guardian. **Heward, Hewart, Huart** are variations of the Norman form, **Haward** is a variation of the Norse. English/Norman patronymic versions include **Hewartson, Hewertson, Huartson, Huertson.**

Howell is a Welsh patronymic name, from the given name *Hywel,* which meant 'Eminent' -- a popular name since the Middle Ages due to the Welsh king by that name. Occasionally it derives as an English Place name from a place in Lincolnshire from the Old English name *Huna* > *hun* = bear cub + *well* = spring, stream. **Howl** and **Howel** are variations; patronymic forms include **Howels, Howells, Powell, Bowell.**

Howey is a Northern English and Scottish patronymic name, derived from a dimunitive form of the given name Hugh. Occasionally, when of Irish origin, it is an Anglicized version of the Gaelic *O'hEochaidh,* which meant 'descendant of Eochaidh,' whose name meant "Horseman." **Howie** is another variation of the Scottish name, while **Hoy, Huey, Hoy, Houghy, O'Hohy, O'Huhy** are variations of the Irish. **Howieson, Howison** are patronymic forms.

Hoxie/Hochzeit: German Acquired Name...Hoxie is that it is derived from the German Acquired name Hochzeit (many names were altered to make them easier to spell) whose elements are *hoch+zit* which meant "high time" in Middle High German. It was associated with weddings and could have been taken by a man who was being married and had not yet become known by a specific surname.

Hoyal is another variation of the English place name **Hole,** in the same fashion as **Hoyle** which reflects a regional (Yorkshire and Lancashire, primarily) pronunciation of the word. Hole was the name that described the man who lived in a hollow or depression. Other variations are **Hoile, Hoyles, Hoiles.**

Hudec is a Czech occupational name for a fiddler, derived from the Czech word *hudec,* from *housti* = to play the fiddle. **Hudecek, Houdek,** and **Hudek** are diminutive forms of the name.

Hudson is a patronymic version of the English patronymic name **Hudd,** derived from the popular given name *Hudde,* which was a pet form of the name Richard (like Hobb and Dobb), and also from *Huda,* an Old English given name. **Hutt** is a variation. **Huddy, Huddle** are diminutive forms. **Hudson, Hutson** are patronymic variations.

Huff: English Place Name...from the Old English *hoh* = heel, and referred to one who lived at the spur of a hill.

Hugh is an English patronymic name, from the Old French given name *Hue* or *Hughe,* which was brought to England by the invading Normans. There are any number of given names with the Germanic element *-hug* = heart; Hugh is a shortened form, and was a popular name in England, partly due to St. Hugh of Lincoln (d. 1200). Variations are **Hugo, Hewe, Hew.** Cognates include **Hugo, Hugues, Hue, Hugon, Gon,** (French); **Huc, Uc** (Provencal); **Ugo, Ughi** (Italian); **Hugk, Hug, Huge** (German), **Haugg, Hauch** (Franconia); **Huyghe** (Flemish). **Hughes** is a patronymic version, as are **Hughs, Huws, Hewes,**

Hews, Hughson, Hewson, Howson, Hooson, FitzHugh, D'Ugo, Hauger, Huygens.

Hulse is a Low German cognate of the German place name **Hilse,** which described the man who lived by a holly tree, and was derived from Middle High German *huls* = holly. Huls, **Hulse, Hulss, Hulst, Hulster, Hulsemann, Ophuls** are other Low German cognate forms. **Van der Hilst, Van Hilst, Van Hulst, Van der Hulst, Verhulst, Hilster, Hulsenboom, Hulsman** (Flemish Dutch); **Lehoux, Duhoux** (French).

Sometimes all the clues have to be added together to come up with an origin. If your family knows that your ancestors came from Germany, then **Humble** is likely an Americanized version of the German patronymic name **Humboldt,** from the elements *hun* = beare cub + *bald* = bold, brave. This was a fairly rare name and isn't found in other languages, but also appears as **Humbolt.**
Humble with the English spelling is generally an English Nickname for the meek or lowly person, from Middle English and Old French *humble/umble,* from Latin *humilis* = lowly.

Humby - the suffix *-by* is from Old English *by* > *buan* = to stay, dwell, live and designates a place name derived from a settlement. In this case, it may be Humm's settlement, with Humm a given name from Anglo-Norman-French which meant "man."

Humiston is an English place name, as determined by the suffix *-ton,* derived from Old English *tun* = settlement, enclosure. **Humis** is likely a condensed form of a medieval given name, or a now-unrecognized given name.

Hunnicutt is an English place name -- distiguished by the suffix *-cutt,* which is derived from Old English *cot* = shelter, cottage. Such names are generally prefixed by the owner of the shelter, and in the case of Hunnicutt, it is likely *Hunnibal's* cottage in a contracted form. *Hunnibal* was a medieval given name that was adopted later as a surname with several spelling variations.

Hunter/Hunt: Scottish/English Occupational name, variation of Hunt, Old English *hunta* = to hunt.

Hutchin is an English and Scot patronymic name from the medieval given name *Huchin,* which is a diminutive form of **Hugh. Hutcheon** is a variation found mainly in Scotland -- other variations are **Hutchen, Houchen, Howchin. Hutchins, Hutchings** are primarily found in Devon and Somerset as patronymic forms; Scottish patronymic forms include **Hutchison, Hutcherson, Hutcheson. Hutchinson** is found all over, but is most common in Northern Ireland and Northern England.

Hutin/Hooten/Hustin: French Nickname for a quarrelsome person.

I

Ide is an English and Low German patronymic name from the German given name **Ida,** from the element *id* = to work or perform, and was a name used by both men and women. It was a popular name among the Normans and was brought to England with William the Conqueror. It fell into disfavor as a given name about the mid-14th century. Variations are **Hyde** and **Ihde; Itt** is a Low German cognate, and **Ikin** is a diminutive form found in England.

Ingersoll/Ingersall/Inkersall/Inkersole/Ingsole: English Place Name from Derbyshire which was written in the 13th Century as Hinkershill and was derived from Old Norse name *Ingvair* + the Old English term *hyll* = hill; literally Ingvair's Hill.

Inman is an English occupational name for the keeper of the public house, or inn, from Middle English *innmann,* from Old English *inn* = abode, lodging + *mann* = man. This is distinctly different from the tavern, where beverages were sold, but no lodging was offered.

Yisek is a variation of the Jewish, English, and French name Isaac, derived from the given name *Yitschak,* derived from Hebrew *tsachak* = to laugh. **Isaac** has always been a popular name among Jews but was widely used by Christians as well during medieval times, and as a result, gentile families bear the last name as well. Variations are **Isac, Isaak, Issac, Issak, Izac, Izak, Itshak, Itzshak, Yitzhak, Yitzhok, Jzak, Eisik, Eisig, Aizik, Aizic, Aysik, Ajsik, Ishaki, Izchaki, Izhaki, Izhaky, Yitschaky, Yitshaki, Yitzchaki, Yizhaki, Yithaky, Jizhaki, Itzchaki.** Numerous patronymic forms exist as well.

J

Jack is a Scottish and English patronymic name, from the Old French given name **Jacques,** which was the French form of the Latin *Jacobus.* It is also a Scottish and English pet form of John, borrowed from Low German and Dutch pet forms *Jankin* and *Jackin,* which come from Jan (the German version of John). Occasionally Jack is derived as an Anglicization of similar-sounding Jewish names. Variants of the English form are **Jake** and **Jagg, Jacques, Jaquith.** Cognates include **Iago** (Wales); **Jagoe, Jago, Jeggo** (Cornish); **Jacques, Jacque** (French); **Jacq** (Provencal); **Giachi, Giacchi, Iacchi, Zacchi, Zacco** (Italian). **Jacks, Jags, Jakes,** and **Jackson** are all patronymic forms of Jack.

Jackson: is an English Patronymic name from the Old French given name Jacque, which was the French form of Jacob (*Yaakov* in Hebrew, meaning heel -- it's a long story...)

Jacobs is a patronymic form of **Jacob,** an English, Jewish, and Portuguese surname from Latin *Jacobus* < Hebrew *Yaakov.* **Jacob, James,** and **Jack** are all derived from this source. Variations include **Jacobb, Jacobbe, Jeacop, Jecop** (English); **Jakov, Yakob, Yaakov, Yakov, Jacobi, Jacoby** (Jewish). Cognate forms include **Giacobbo, Giacobo, Giacubbo, Giacoppo, Iacobo, Iacopo, Iacovo, Iacofo, Copo, Coppo** (Italian); **Jakob** (German); **Kobus** (Flemish, Dutch); **Jakubski, Kobus, Kobiera, Kobierski, Kobieraycki, Kubas, Kubisz, Kupisz, Kubacki, Kubicki, Kubera** (Polish); **Jakoubec, Kubu, Kouba, Kuba, Koba, Kob, Kopa, Kopac, Kopal, Kubal, Kubala, Kubat, Kubec, Kubes, Kubin, Kubis, Kubista, Kupec** (Czech); **Jakab, Kabos** (Hungarian). Numerous diminutive forms are found, as are patronymic versions such as **Jacobs, Jacobson** (English); **Jakobsen, Jakobs** (Low German); **Jacobsen, Jakobsen** (Danish, Norwegian).

James is an English patronymic name derived from Hebrew Y *aakov > Latin Jacobus > Late Latin Jacmus* -- and believed originating in the Hebrew term *akev* = heel. A biblical story contains the mention of a heel in the birth of Jacob. In English, Jacob and James are distinctly separate names, but throughout the rest of the world, the two are considered the same name in cognate form. Cognates of James are **Jacqueme** (French); **Jayume, Jaulmes, Jaume, Jaumes** (Provencal); **Giacomo, Giamo, Giacomi, Iacomo, Iacomi, Como, Comi, Cumo** (Italian); **Jaime** (Spanish); **Juame** (Catalan). There are dozens of diminutive forms of James. Patronymic forms include **Jameson, Jamisom, Jamieson, Jemison, Jimpson, Jimson, Gemson, Gimson** (English); **McKeamish, McJames,** (Scot); **Di Giacomo** (Italian); **Jaimez** (Spanish).

Janson is a variation of the English Patronymic name **Jane,** derived from the Middle English given name **Jan,** a variant of John. The feminine name Jane was not around during the period of time when surnames originated. Other variations are **Jaine, Jayne, Jean, Jenne, Genn, Jaynes, Jeynes, Jannis, Janns, Jenness,** and **Jennison,** among others.

Janzen is one of the many cognates of the Patronymic surname -- John -- which was from the Hebrew name *Yochanan,* meaning 'Jehovah has favoured me with a son.' It was adopted into Latin as *Johannes* and throughout the early Christian era in Europe (and still today!) enjoyed great popularity as a given name. In Wales the name is called **Evan,** or **Ioan,** in Scotland it is **Ian** or **Iain,** the Irish version is **Sean,** the German is **Johann** and **Hans;** in Dutch and Flemish it becomes **Jan;** in French it is **Jean;** Italian is **Giovanni, Gianni, Vanni;** in Spain it is **Juan;** it Portugal John becomes **Joao;** the Greek form is **Ioanni;** Czechoslovakians have **Jan,** while Russians prefer **Ivan.** In Poland it becomes **Jansz** or **Iwan.** The variation Janzen is found in several languages as a patronymic form of Jan (John), including Low German, Dutch, and Danish. Other German patronymic forms are **Johansen, Jansen, Johanning, Jans, Jahns, Jantzen, Janz, Janning;** other Dutch forms are **Jans,**

Johansen, Janse, Jansen, Janssen; and other Danish versions are **Johannesen, Johansen, Johnsen, Jensen, Joensen, and Jantzen.**

Jarrett is a diminutive form of the French occupational name **Jarre,** which described the potter, from Old French *jarre* = earthenware vessel. **Jerrier** is a variation of Jarre. **Jarron** is another diminutive form.

Jarvis is an English patronymic name, from the given name *Gervase,* brought to England by the conquering Normans, and comprised of the Germanic elements *geri* = spear + *vase* = meaning unclear. Jarvis is also a place name, from *Jervaulx* in Northern Yorkshire, the site of a Cistercian monastery and named from the Anglo-Norman-French name of the river Ure + *vaulx* = valley. **Jervis** is a variation of the first case, and **Gervis, Gervase,** and **Jarvie** are variations of the second origin.

Jarzembek is a variation of the Polish place name **Jarzebowski,** derived from Polish *jarzab* = service tree + *-ow* = possessive suffix + *-ski* = suffix of local surnames. Other variations are **Jarzebski, Jarzabek.**

Jeanes/Jeanne/Jayne: Norman-French Place Name....Guido de Genez came to England with the Norman Conquest and was granted lands there. Genez is a placename in Normandy. Anglicized to Jeanes; also **de Genes, Jenis, Janes, Jans, J'Anes, Jeanne, Jeynes, Jayne, Jane, Janns.**

Jenks is an English Patronymic name derived the long way around from the given name Jenkin (normally suffixes are added rather than taken away), in this case, the Anglo-Norman suffix -in is removed. Jenkin was a Middle English given name that came as a diminutive form of John.

Jennings is an English patronymic name from the Middle English given name *Janyn,* a diminutive form of John (from

Hebrew -- Jehovah has favored me with a son). Variations are **Jannings, Jennins, Jennens.**

Jennison is a variation of the patronymic name **Jane** (not to be confused with the female given name Jane, which didn't appear until the 17th century). Jane evolved from *Jan,* a Middle English version of John, which was found primarily in the Devon and Cornwall areas of England. Jennison is a patronymic form designating the "son of Jan." Other forms are **Jain, Jaine, Jean, Jenne, Jenn, Genn, Janet, Jennett, jankin, Janes, jaynes, Jeynes, Jeanes, Jeans, Jeens, Jeneson, Jannis, Jans, Janson, Jenns, Jenness, Jenison, Jennison.**

Jeter is a French vocabulary word (pronounced jshuh-tay -- that's as close as I can get without a soft-J pronunciation symbol) that has several contexts with which it is used, but as a place reference, a *jeter* is a common expression for an "empty river" and may have developed in that context.

Juliard/Julliard/Julianus/Julius: French Patronymic Name....Juliard is a French version of Julian/Julianus/Julius which derived from the Latin *Julius* meaning youthful looking -- literally as "downy-bearded."

John is one of the most popular of the medieval names, and took several forms even in medieval times. John derived from Hebrew **Yochanan** (God has favoured me with a son). **Jahncke** (Jähncke) is a diminutive form of the German (of Slavic origin) cognate of John, including **Jann, Jahn** (Low German). Other diminutive forms include **Johnikin, Johnigan, Jonikin, Jonigan** (English/Irish); **Jeannet, Jeanet, Joannet, Jouandet, Jeandet, Jantet, Jentet, Jouanneton, Jeannin, Jouannin, Jouanny, Jany, Janny, Jeandin, Jentin, Jeannenet, Jeannot, Jouanot, Jeandon, Janton, Jenton, Jeannel, Jeandel, Jantel, Jeanneau, Jeandeau, Jenteau, Jeannequin, Jannequin, Johanchon,** (French); **Giovannelli, Gianelli, Giovannilli, Gianiello, Gianilli, Cianelli, Iannelli, Ianello, Ianniello, Iannilli, Zannelli, Zuanelli, Zuenilli, Vannelli, Nanelli,**

Giovannetti, Ninotti, Zanetello, Zanettini, Nannini, Notti, Noto (Italian); **Jähnel, Jähne, Jäne, Jähndel, Jähnel** (German); **Juanico** (Spain); **Johnke, Jönke, Jenne, Jennemann** (Low German); **Jansema** (Frisian); **Jähncke, Jäncke, Jänke, Jahnisch, Janisch, Jansch, Jannuscheck, Janoschek, Jenicke, Jentzsch, Jentsch, Genicke, Genike, Gentzsch, Gentsch, Wahnncke, Wanka, Wanjek, Wandtke, Nuschke, Nuscha** (German of Slav origin).

Johnson: English Patronymic Name:One of the earliest first names was John (gift of God), which in the 17th century replaced William as the most popular name for a male. As a patronymic name, Johnson from England and Scandinavia became the most widely found name in America, and its Welsh version Jones the fifth-most prolific.

If **Joines** is not derived as a variation of the English occupational name **Joiner** (the man who created wooden furniture) it is a patronymic version of the French surname **Jouvin,** from the Latin given name *Iovinus* = Jupiter, the principal god of pagan Rome. An early saint in France (obscure now) bore the name, which allowed Jouvin to survive as a given name into the Middle Ages. **Jovin, Join, Jouin, Jevain** are variations. Diminutive forms include **Jovignet, Jovelin, Jovelet, Joindeau, Joinet, Jouon, Jout, Jouet.**

Jones: English Patronymic Name:One of the earliest first names was John (gift of God), which in the 17th century replaced William as the most popular name for a male. As a patronymic name, Johnson from England and Scandinavia became the most widely found name in America, and its Welsh version Jones the fifth-most prolific.

Josselyn is a variation of **Jocelyn,** taken from an Old French name by circuitous route, by way of *Goscelin, Gosselin, Joscelin,* which was brought to England before the Conquest but was spread by the Normans' widespread usage of the given name. Most versions have Germanic origins from *Gauzelin,* a variation of several names with Gaut (a tribal reference) as part of the name. It was eventually adopted as a diminutive form of the Old French given name *Josse.* Variations are **Joscelyne, Joscelyn, Joselin, Joslen, Josling, Joseland.**

Jovan: Slavic Patronymic name...Likely Anglicized version of **Jovanovic,** a Slavic version of the given name John, which came from the Hebrew Yochanan, which meant `Jehovah has favored me with a son.'

Joy comes from Middle English, by way of Old French *joie,joye* = joy, which described the cheerful person. Variations are **Joye, Joie, Joyet.**

Jurista / **Yurista** are likely variations of a Slav cognate of the surname **George,** a popular name during the Middle Ages, derived from Germanic *georgos* = farmer, a compound form of *ge* = earth + *ergein* = to work, till. Germanic cognates of Slavic origin include **Jerschke, Jurick, Juschke, Juschka, Gorcke, Goricke;** Czech forms are **Jirik, Jiricek, Jiricka, Jiracek, Jirasek, Jurasek, Jiranek;** Polish forms are **Jurek Juczyk;** Ukrainian is **Yurchenko;** Patronymic forms include **Juris, Jurries, Jorger** (German); **Yurov, Yurevich** (Beloruss) and others.

Justice: English Patronymic name that is derived from the given name Justus which means 'the just,' and in some cases was applied to the man who performed the duties of the judge. If nowhere else -- you can find Justice on these pages!

K

Kampert is likely a variation of **Kamper,** a Low German cognate of the French place name **Champ,** which described the man who lived near an area of open country or a field and was derived from the vocabulary word *champ* = field > Latin *campus* = plain, open expanse.

Kanner is a variation of the German and Jewish (Ashkenazic) occupational name **Kannengiesser,** which described the man who made vessals from metal, generally speaking, the man who worked in pewter. Variations include **Kannegiesser, Kanngiesser, Kannegieter, Kannegeter.**

Kantor: German Occupational Name...Kantor is the one who sang liturgical music in the synagogue.

Karle is a variation of **Charles,** a French, Welsh and English surname, from the Germanic given name *Carl* = man. **Karl,** the German cognate form, was not in use as a given name during the Middle Ages, and is rare or unknown as a German surname since it was restricted to nobility. English variations of Charles are **Karl, Karle, Carle.** French forms are **Charle, Charlon, Carle, Chasles, Chasle.** Cognate forms are **Carlo, Caroli, Carlesi, Carlisi, Carlesso** (Italian); **Carlos** (Spain); **Carles** (Catalan); **Kerl, Kehrl, Keerl** (Low German); **Karl** (Jewish Ashkenazic); **Karel, Kares** (Czech); **Karoly, Karolyi** (Hungarian). Patronymic forms include **Charleston** (t-added); **McCarlish** (Scottish); **De Carlo, De Carli, Di Carlo, De Carolis** (Italian); **Carlens** (Flemish/Dutch); **Karlsen, Carlsen** (Norwegian); **Karlsson, Carlsson** (Swedish); **Karlowicz, Karolak, Karolczak** (Polish).

Kasparek is a Polish diminutive form (if you remove the diacritical marks from the Czech version, it is also the Czech form) of the German and Polish patronymic name **Kaspar,** from the given name which originally meant "treasurer" in

Persian. It is supposed to have been one of the three Magi's names and gained popularity in Europe after the 12th century. Variations include **Kasper, Kesper, Casper** (German); **Kasparski, Kasperski, Kasper, Kaszper, Sperski** (Polish). Cognate forms include **Jaspar, Jasper, Jesper** (Low German); **Jesper** (Flemish); **Jasper** (English); **Kaspar, Kasper** (Czech); **Gaspar** (Hungarian); **Casperii, Gasperi, Gaspero, Gasparri, Gasparro, Gaspardo, Gaspardi, Gasbarri, Parri** (Italian).

Keach: is an English nickname given the man who was a little chubby. From the Middle English keech = fat, with variants Keech, Keetch, Keatch, and Keitch.

Keen, the English nickname for the brave man, from Middle English *kene* > Old English *cene* = fierce, brave. **Keene** is a variation, and **Kenning** is a patronymic form.

Keesee is a variation of **Keese,** which is a Low German cognate of the occupational name known as **Cheeseman** in English-speaking countries, which described the maker or seller of cheese. The English word is derived from Old English *cyse* = cheese + *mann* = man. **Cheesman, Cheseman, Chesman, Cheasman, Chiesman, Chisman, Chessman, Chismon, Cheese, Chiese, Cheesewright, Cheeseright, Cheswright, Cheeswright, Cherrett, Cherritt** are variations of the English form. Other cognate forms are **Käsmann, Käser, Keser, Käs, Käse** (German); **Kaasman, Kaas, Keesman** (Low German); **Caesman** (Flemish); **Kaes, Kaas, Kaaskooper** (Dutch); **Keizman, Keyzman** (Jewish); **Chasier, Casier, Chazier, Chesier, Chezier, Chazerand** (French); **Casari, Casaro, Caseri, Caser, Casieri, Casiero, Case** (Italian); **Queyeiro, Queyos** (Portuguese).

Kellett is an English place name from so-name locations in Lancashire and Cumbria which derived their names from Old Norse *kelda* = spring + *hlid* = slope, hillside. **Kellet** and **Kellitt** are variations.

Kelso: Scottish Place name that was used to describe the man who lived near the 'chalky height' -- a place they would have recognized during the Middle Ages when surnames were adoped there.

Kempf is a German cognate (same meaning, different language) of the English surname **Kemp,** the Occupational name for the man who was a champion at jousting or wrestling. It is derived from the Middle English word *kempe,* which came from Old English *cempa* = warrior, champion, which itself came from Latin *campus* = field, plain of battle. **Kempe** is a variation of the English name, while other cognates include **Kampf, Kömpf** from Germany; **Kempner, Kempe** from German Low Regions; **Kemper** from Holland. Patronymic versions include **Kempson, Kempers,** and **Kemppainen** (Finnish).

Kemplay is likely a variation of **Kempfle,** a diminutive form of **Kempf,** the German surname for the wrestling or jousting champion.

Kern/Kerns/Curn: Many German names are taken from the short, or pet form of a given name. Kern (of which Curn may be a derivative) is taken from *Gernwin* (spear, friend) when it isn't the man who emigrated from Kern, the German town. It's a German Patronymic name when not from the town, and a German Place name in that case.

Kerwin, Kirwan and others are commonly accepted as Irish surnames that described the swarthy man, or black-haired man. Spellings are varied because none of these names were Anglo to begin with, but were actually the Gaelic name *O Ciardhubhain,* which means "descendant of *Ciardhubhan*" whose name was composed of the elements *ciar* = dark + *dubh* = black + the diminutive suffix *-an.* When the name was Anglicized, it took a number of versions: while Kirwan is the most commonly found, these also derived from *O Ciardhubhain* -- **Kirwen, Kirwin, Kirivan, Kierevan, Kiervan, O'Kirwan, O'Kerevan, O'Kerrywane.** Since most of the population was illiterate, spellings were often the whim of whoever recorded the name at a particular point in time, and whether that spelling managed to survive until recorded on deeds or similarly abstracted materials.

Kerr is a Scottish and North English place name for the man who lived by the area of wet ground that was covered with brushy growth, from the Middle English (Northern) term *kerr,* from Old Norse *kjarr.* It is generally pronounced like the auto -- car -- which reflects the dialect and a Middle English misconception about the pronunciation of the -er spelling. Similarly, the name for the clerk was pronounced "clark" and the merchant was called the "marchant." Carr is a spelling variation based on the pronunciation. Scholars later re-educuated the public about the sound and some surname pronunciations were changed at the same time. Being in Scotland, and exposed to the Gaelic term *cearr* (wrong, left-handed), it became part of the local folklore that the Kerr family members were left-handed. **Keir, Ker** are variations. **Kjair, Kiaer** are Danish cognate forms. **Karrstrom** is a Swedish adopted ornamental name from Swedish elements meaning (marsh + river).

Kesterson: Some names are a combination of types: In Germany, the official in charge of the church sacristy was the **Kuester** (the English equivalent was Sexton) and **Kiester, Kester** and **Koester** are variations of that occupational name. The - *son* at the end is a Patronymic designation that denotes the descendant of the Church Kuester.

Ketchum could have been the speedy man, that no matter how quick his prey, he could always ketch'um...just fooling. It sounds plausible, but in reality, Ketchum is an English Place name for the man who resided at *Caecca's homestead* or settlement, derived from the elements *Caecca* + *ham* = homestead, settlement.

The name **Kettle** is derived from the Old Norse given name *Ketill,* which was a shortened version of several compound names that had that element included, derived from *ketill* = cauldron. Variations are **Kettel, Kettell, Ketill, Kitell, Kittle,**

Kell. Patronymic forms include **Kilsson, Kjeldsen, Ketelsen, Kettelson, Kells, Kettles, Kettless. Kelling** is a diminutive form of the variation Kell.

Keunemann is a Low German diminutive form of the German patronymic surname **Konrad,** derived from the elements *kuoni* = daring, brave + *rad* = counsel, an extremely popular name during the Middle Ages, and found as an hereditary name in several ruling families. Pronunciation is very close to **Kinnamon,** and other variants of Konrad exhibit an -I- sound. The German equivalent of the saying "every Tom, Dick, and Harry" was *Hinz und Kunz* which were shortened forms of the name Henry and Konrad. Other German diminutive forms are **Kiendl, Kienl, Kienzle, Kienle, Kienlein, Kienle, Kaindl, Kainz, Kuhn, Kuhndel, Kunzelmann, Konzelmann, Kullmann,** and **Kiehne,** among others.

Key: as you might expect, was the man who made keys, or occasionally -- the man in the largely ceremonial office of 'key-bearer.' **Kay** is another version of that English Occupational name.

Kidd: English Occupational/Nickname...Most surnames relating to animals had their origin in signs that were displayed at inns throughout the countryside. In early times, when travel from one location to another could not be completed in a day -- people took travellers into their homes -- many doing so as a business. Animals pictures were popular additions to the signs. Kidd came from the picture of the "little goat" at an English inn...in France, the counterpart was **Chevrolet.**

Kille is a variation of the Irish Patronymic name *Killeen,* which is an Anglicized version of the Gaelic *Cillin,* a dimunitive form of *Ceallach.* Phew! -- a long way of saying *descendant of Kelly.* John Kyllyk is the first known bearer of the name. He was a vintner in London whose will was proven in court in 1439

Kimball and **Kimble** are English place names from the place so-named in Buckinghamshire that is taken from Old English elements that mean 'royal hill' and the man who emigrated from that town sometimes became known by the name of his former location.

The Old English origin of **Kimbrough** was *cyne* = royal + *burh* = fortress, stronghold. Cyneburh was an Old English female given name derived from those elements. The daughter of King Penda of Mercia, who lived in the 7th Century) bore the name, and was an early convert to Christianity, over her father's oppposition. She founded an abbey, and was venerated as a saint, which led to all kinds of youngsters being named for her. **Kimber** is another form of the matronymic name.

Kincaid: Scottish Place Name...Kincaid was derived from a place near Lennoxtown in Campsie Glen, north of Glascow. It was referenced in 1238 as Kincaith which means 'top pass.'

King is an English nickname, derived from Old English *cyning,* originally meaning tribal leader, but it evolved to modern vocabulary as king. The name was already in use before the Norman conquest, and was a common nickname for the man who carried himself like royalty, or to the man who had played the part of the king in a medieval pageant (several surnames were derived from medieval pageants -- must have been quite the attraction -- and the players must have been celebrities of sorts, as a result). Rarely, the name was given to the man who worked for royalty as a footman or servant. Among Ashkenazic Jews, it is an Anglicized version of **Konig** (umlaut over the -O-). **Kinge** is a variation of the English nickname.

Kingdon: It's an English (Devon) place name from High Kingdon in Alverdiscott, Devon. The name elements are from Old English *cyning* = king + *dun* = hill for a literal translation of 'king's hill.'

Kinkel is a variation of the German occupational name **Gunkel,** which described the maker or the spinner of spindles. It is derived from the German word *Kunkel* = spindle, distaff, from Middle High German *kunkel* < LL *conicula,* a diminutive form of *conus* = cone, peg. Other variations are **Kunkel, Künkel, Künkler.**

Kinney: Variant of the Scottish Patronymic name **Kenney** derived from the Gaelic given name *Cionaodha,* of unknown origin, but likely composed of the elements *cion* = respect + *Aodh* = pagan god of fire. Occasionally Kenney is derived as an Irish Patronymic name through the Anglicizing of *O'Coinnigh* -- 'descendant of *Coinneach.* Variations are **McKinney, McKenney, McKenna, McKinna,** and **McKennan,** among others.

Kinsey is an English patronymic name derived from the Old English personal name composed of the elements *cyne* = royal + *sige* = victory. **Kincey, Kynsey, Kinzie** are among the variations.

Kirkland: Scottish Place name; the man who took it as a surname lived on land adjacent to the church property, often the parish cemetery. The Scottish church is referred to as the Kirk.

Cline is an Anglicized spelling of the German, Dutch, and Jewish nickname **Klein,** which described the small man, from German and Dutch *klein* = small (Yiddish *kleyn* = small). Cline is generally found among those of Jewish ancestry along with **Kleiner, Kleinerman, Kleinman, Klainer, Klain, Klainman, Kline, Kliner, Klyne, Clyne.** German variations include **Kleintert, Kleiner, Klaint, Kleinmann.** Dutch variations are **Kleine, Klene, Kleijn, Klijn, Kleyn, Klyn.**

Kleinkauf is a Jewish ornamental surname comprised of the Middle High German elements *kleine* = small + *kauff* = seller, dealer. Although this has the sound of an occupational name (and it may well be), most of the Klein+suffix names were strictly ornamental and adopted when ordered to do so by the government.

Klink: Dutch Place name for the man who lived near the rushing mountain stream.

Knapp: As an English place name, Knapp was the man who lived at the top of the hill.

Knapik is a diminutive form of the Polish and Czechoslovakian occupational name **Knap,** which -- in German -- is translated to the name **Knapp,** from Middle High German *knappe* = boy, lad...a term used for a servant or squire. **Knappe, Knabbe, Knabe** are German variations. **De Knaap** is the Flemish/Dutch form.

Knight: English Status Name from the Old English *cniht* which referred to a boy or serving lad. During the Middle Ages, Knight was used as a given name before the Norman conquest, after which it became a term for a tenant farmer who defended his lord on horseback. As only those men of some stature owned horses, it became a term for a man of prominence, and later, was converted to an honorary title.

Knopf: is a German and Jewish occupational name for the maker of buttons, or the man who lived by a rounded hillock. In the second case, it's a Place name.

Knutson is found in Sweden and Norway and a patronymic name meaning "son of Knut" or "son of Canute" -- given names that meant "hill" or "white-haired."

Koche is the German occupational name for the cook, taken from the German word *Koch* = cook. Variations are **Kocher, Kochmann.**

Kolberg is likely an ornamental name of either Jewish or Swedish extraction. The element *-berg* means "hill" and is used in a number of ornamental names (names adopted for their pleasing sound, without connotation to the bearer). *Kohl* is a

German word for cabbage, and the element *Kol* may be derived from this or a similar vocabulary word (usually words that were nature-oriented were selected, as in **Lundberg** (Swedish grove-hill).

Many surnames were Americanized when the recent arrivals wanted to blend in with their established neighbors, and **Coons, Cooncе,** and others are examples of spelling that was less reflective of their origin. **Konrad** is a German given name composed of the elements *kuoni* = daring, brave + *rad* = counsel. It was extremely popular during the Middle Ages, and as a result led to a number of surnames and variations. **Kunrad, Kuhnert, Kunert, Kundert, Kuhnhardt Kuhnt, Kundt, Kurth** are variations. Cognates include **Konert, Kohnert, Kohrt, Kordt, Kort** (Low German); **Koenraad** (Dutch), **Kunrad, Konrad** (Czech); **Kondrat** (Polish); **Corradi, Corrado, Cunradi, Cunrado** (Italian). Diminutive forms include **Kuhn, Kuhne, Kuhndel, Kiehnelt, Kaindl, Kainz, Kunz** (from which Coon and Coonce were derived, among others), **Kuntz, Kienzelmann, Kunze** (German); **Cohr, Keuneke, Keunemann, Keuntje, Kohneke, Konneke, Kunneke, Kohnemann,** and others (Low German); **Koene, Keune** (Dutch); **Kuna, Kunes, Kunc** (Czech); **Kondratenkko, Kondratyuk** (Ukrainian). There are other versions of this name as well.

Kostmeyer is a German compound name comprised of the elements *kost, kostner* = sacristy official + *meyer* = household head servant or officer. It may have designated the man who was the head of the household for the sacristy official, or depending on the family heritage, it may be one of the Jewish compound names taken as ornamental surnames when they became required.

Kragh is the Danish cognate for **Crow.** The nickname was used in numerous languages to describe a man that seemed to fit that monicker, for whatever reason. **Krah, Krahe, Kroh, Krohe, Kräh, Krähe, Krehe, Krach, Kray, Kra** are all German forms of the name. **Krey, Krei** are the ones used in the German lowlands. **Craey** is the Flemish version. **Kraaij, Kraay** are the Dutch forms. **Krag, Kragh** are found among the Danes. **Crowe** is the form found in Ireland, and **Craw** is an English variation. Crow comes from the Old English word *crawa.* When of known Irish origin, the name is sometimes a translation of any of the several Gaelic names that meant "raven" or "crow."

Kroeger: From the Middle Ages through colonial times - innkeepers and tavern owners were people of prominence in the community, and were the only place of refuge for travelers. More often than not, the host of the inn took that as a surname: **Host** and **Hostler** in England, in Germany it was **Krueger, Krug,** and **Wurtz.** The Dutch form was **Kroeger.**

Kruse/Krusekopf: German Nickname...Kruse is a Low(land)German version of the surname **Kraus,** which -- along with Kruskopf -- was given as a nickname for one with curly hair. Kraus means curly. **Cruise,** (as in Tom Cruise) on the other hand, is an English nickname from the Middle English *crouse* =bold, fierce.

Kusnerek is a Slavic diminutive variation of the German occupational name **Kurschner** (umlaut over the U) from the Middle High German word *kursen* = fur garment, which described the man who worked as a furrier. **Kurssner, Kierschner, Korschner** are variations. **Kusnierz** is a Polish cognate; **Kushnir** is found in the Ukraine, **Kurshner** is a Jewish form Anglicized from German, **Kirschner, Kirsner, Kerschner, Kersner** are other Jewish cognates.

Kyle: In early times, the man who lived by an important river was referred to by the name of the river. In England, the Kyle River was the "narrow" river. Kyle is an English Place name.

Kyser is a spelling variation of **Keiser,** which is a variation of **Kaiser,** the German nickname for the man who lived in a stately manner -- derived from German *Kaiser* = emperor, from the

Latin title *Ceasar.* It may also have been a nickname for the man who played an emperor in the village pageant (many of the well-played parts stuck as nicknames, which became surnames). Kaiser is also found as a Jewish ornamental name. German variations include **Keser, Keiser, Kayser, Keyser.** Jewish forms include **Kaiserman, Keiserman, Keiser, Keizer.** There are also cognate forms in several languages.

L

Lacey is an English and Irish place name of Norman origin, derived from **Lassy** in Calvados, which got its name from a Gaulish given name *Lascius* + *-acum* (a local suffix). Lacey is most common in Nottinghamshire, but is found all over. Variations are **Lacy, Lassey, De Lacey, De Lacy, Leacy** (the last occasionally found in Ireland).

LaCroux is a Provencal variation of the surname **Cross:** English Place name for the man who lived near the stone cross set up by the roadside or marketplace, from Old Norse *kross.* Cognitives include **De(la)Croix, Croix,** (French); **Croux, Lacroux, Lacrouts, De(la)croux** (Provencal); **Croce, DellaCroce, Croci** (Italian); **Cruz** (Spanish); **Kreutzer, Kreuziger** (German); **Vercruysse** (Flemish), **Krzyzaniak** (Polish), and **Van der Kruijs** (Dutch).

Laird: is a Scottish name taken from the term used to describe the caretaker of land under which the peasant farmers rented land and sought protection during the height of the feudal period. The laird offered protection to the serfs who fought for him when attacked by neighboring lairds. They tended to raid each other often, for livestock, and as a relief for boredom.

You'd think that **Lakey** had something to do with a "lake" but that word as we understand it today was an addition to the English language from the French after surnames had already been fairly widely adopted. The Old English word *lacu* meant "stream" and the man who lived by the stream was often described as lacu, or **Lake, Lack, Lakes, Lakeman.** Diminutive or pet forms of names are often achieved by the addition of a *-y* or *-ey,* much the way Bobby is a pet form of Bob.

Lambert: English/French/German Place name from Old German *land* =land + *berht* = famous...literally, famous-land.

Lambkin/Lumpkin/Lamkin: English Patronymic names derived from "Little Lamb" which was a pet form of the given name Lambert (land, bright).

Land is an English place name that described the man who lived in the country rather than in a town. The term had a more specialized sense in the Middle Ages, and was also applied to a forest glade from Middle English *lande* = heath. Occasionally, it described the man from Launde in Leicestershire, which was named from the same term. **Lawn** is a variation. Cognates include **Landt, Land** (German); **Landh, Landell, Landelius, Landen, Landin** (Swedish ornamental); **Landberg, Landegren, Landquist, Landstrom** (Swedish compound ornamental).

Lamond(e) is a variation of the Scottish and Northern Irish patronymic name **Lamont,** from the medieval given name *Lagman,* from Old Norse *Logmaðr,* with the elements *log* = law + *maðr* = mann/man. **Lammond, Lamond, Lawman** are variations. **McLamont, McLamon, McClemment, McClements, McClymond, McClymont** are patronymic forms.

Langdon: English Place Name...from settlements in Devon, Dorset, Essex, Kent, and Warwick in medieval times. It is derived from Old English *lang* + *dun,* which meant long hill.

Lange is a cognate of the English nickname for a tall person -- the name is **Long** among English speaking countries and Lange is found among the Dutch, Norwegians, and Germans. **Lang, Lange,** and **Langer** are the German versions, while **DeLanghe** is the Flemish, **De Lang** is Dutch and **Lang** and **Lange** are the Danish and Norwegian versions.

Langworthy: is an English Place name that is derived from two elements, - *lang* which meant 'long' and - *worth* which designated an enclosure or settlement. Langworthy was the man who hailed from the long settlement or enclosure.

Laporte: French version of the place name Port which described someone who lived near the gateway to the town, or by a harbour.

Lapsley: is an English Patronymic name from the Old English given name, *Hlappa* + *leah* =woods, for a literal meaning of 'Hlappa's woods' or more specifically, 'Hlappa's clearing in the woods."

Larson/Larkin/Lawson,/Lorenzo: The name Lawrence was derived from 'laurel' - symbol of victory, and was popularized by St. Lawrence, a papel deacon who was martyed in the Middle Ages. **McLaren** is the Scottish form of the name, **Larson, Larkin,** and **Lawson** are among the English variations and **Lorenz** is a German form. Spanish speaking languages are among those that would have **Lorenz** and **Lorenzo** as a variants of Lawrence, which is a Patronymic name -- from the name of the father with that given name.

Law: is an English and Scottish Patronymic name from a Middle English pet form of the given name Lawrence; occasionally it is an English Place name for the name who lived by the hill, derived from Northern Middle English *hlaw* = hill or burial mound. **Lawes** and **Lawson** are traditional Patronymic versions of Law. Richard Law emigrated to America in 1638 and was one of the founders of Stamford, Connecticut.

Lawton: English Place name from settlements common in Lancashire and Yorkshire, from Buglawton or Church Lawton in Cheshire, which derived their names from Old English *hlaw* = hill, burial mound + *tun* = enclosure, settlement. The literal meaning would be "hill settlement" and someone from that place might be identified as Lawton.

Layland is a variation of the English surname **Leyland,** a place name derived from Middle English *layland* > Old English *lægeland*

= fallow land, uncultivated. Most bearers of the name have origins in the location so-named in Lancashire.

Leach: is an English occupational name for the doctor, from the Old English word *loece* (the -o and -e are attached with a long-vowel mark above.) Originally, the animal was known by that term with reference to 'healer' rather than physicians being compared to a bloodsucker -- but times do change. Variations are **Leche, Leetch, Leitch.**

Lee/Lea: The surname Lea is derived from the Old English word *leah,* which meant 'clearing in the woods' and the ending -ley- is the second-most common among English surnames. Lee and Lea were also the names of many small towns that were in the valley or the 'clearing in the woods.

Lease is a variation of Lees, an English name that is derived from several sources, one of which is the same as **Lee** and **Lea.** In medieval times, the Old English word *leah* meant "wood" or "clearing" and the name Lee (or Lea) described the man who lived near a meadow, pasture, or patch of arable land. Leas/lees is the plural form of 'lee' which was the Middle English form of 'leah.' The man named Lees/Leas (and its variations) lived on or near the fields or pastures. Also, several settlements arose with the name Lee or Lees, and people who lived there were often described that way, when no other description was more appropriate. There is a Lees in Ashton-under-Lyne and a Leece in Barrow-in-Furness. Occasionally -- although somewhat rarely -- Lees is derived as an English Matronymic name. Names taken from the mother are pretty scarce, but in the case of Lees and Lease, some derived their name from the female given name *Lece,* a short form of *Lettice.* Finally, some with the name Lease or Lees are descended from Scots with the surname **Gillies,** where the first part of the name has been lost through aphesis, when a short beginning syllable is dropped through lazy pronunciation, as in squire, derived aphetically from esquire. Gillies is a Scottish Patronymic name from the Gaelic given name Gilla Iosa (servant of Jesus). Variations include **Leese,**

Leece, Leish, Leishman, Leeson, Leason, Lesson, and **Lisson.**

Leith is a Scottish place name for the port near Edinburgh, which gets its name from the river nearby. The river name is from Gaelic *lite* = wet, similar to Welsh *llaith* = damp, moist. Of course, the man who ran the mill on that river was a Miller Lite (yuk yuk < Latin yukkius).

Leitherland is a variation of **Litherland** -- an English place name from a so-named district consisting of Uplitherland and Downlitherland, and derived from Old Norse *hliðar* < hlið = slope + *land.* **Leatherland** is another variation.

Leo is an Italian version of the English Nickname **Lyon,** given to the brave or fierce warrior, from the Old French *lion,* from Latin *Leo/Leonis.* Also it is taken from the given name Leo = lion, borne by numerous early martyrs and popes. English versions are **Lion,** and **Leon,** French are **Lion, Leon;** Italian versions are **Leoni, Leone, Lione, Liuni,** and **Lio.** The Spanish version is **Leon,** Portugese is **Leao.** Patronymic forms are **Delion, De Leone, Di Lione, De Lionibus, De Leo, Di Leo,** and **Leoneschi.**

Leonard: Almost all given names that were around during Medieval times have continued through the ages as surnames. Leonard is one such name, the meaning of which is "lion, bold."

Lippard is a variation of **Leppard,** an English name derived from Middle English and Old French *lepard* = leopard, from Late Latin *leopardus* (*leo* = lion + *pardus* = panther). It was derived as a nickname for the stealthy and powerful man, and or as a place name indicating a home at the sign of the leopard. It is believed that the surname evolved from a single family in E. Sussex, England. Variations of the spelling are **Liopard, Lepperd, Lippard.** Cognate forms found in other countries (not blood-relations to the English versions) are **Leopardo,**

Leopardi (Italian); **Llopart** (Catalan); **Lebart, Lebert** (Germany).

Leavenworth is an English place name as determined by the suffix -worth, from *word* = enclosure. It would literally mean "Leaven's enclosure" although the actual name might have been Lefred, Leofroed, Lefric, Leofwaru, Leu, etc.

Leighton: an English place name for the man who emigrated from any of the so-named locations in Bedfordshire, Cambridgeshire, Cheshire, Lancashire, Shropshire, et.al., which were named from Old English *leac* = leek + *tun* = settlement, enclosure, and translated as "settlement at the place of the leeks." Although **Laughton, Layton, Leyton** were drawn from the same origin, those names are polygenetic and were drawn from other origins occasionally as well.
Leurman is a variant spelling of **Lauerman,** the German occupational name for the tanner, from Middle High German *lowoere* = a German reference to the substance extracted from tree bark used to tan leather + *mann* = man, occupational suffix.

Lewis is an English patronymic name from the given name **Lowis,** *Lodowicus,* and comprised of the elements *hlod* = fame + *wig* = war. The founder of the Frankish dynasty bore this name, and it was popular throughout France during the Middle Ages before being introduced into England by the conquoring Normans. When of Welsh extraction, it is an Anglicized form of **Llywelyn.** The Scots version is a local place name for the Hebridean island of Lewis, or as with the Irish, it is sometimes an Anglicized form of the Gaelic *MacLughaidh,* meaning "son of *Lugaidh.*" Lugh was the Celtic god - 'Brightness.' Among the Jewish heritage, Lewis is a patronmymic form of **Levi,** or an Anglicized version of a similar Jewish name.

Lichtsinn: is a variant of the surname **Licht,** which is a German Occupational name for a chandler. It is derived from the German *licht* =light. Variations include **Lichtner, Lichtmann,** and **Lichtzer,** among others.

Lilegdon: surnames with the suffix *-don* are generally derived from Old English *dun* = hill. Possible an English place name from OE *lilie* = lily + *dun* = hill, and would have described a location where the man who first bore the name lived.

Lindsey is a spelling variation of Lindsay, an English and Scottish Place name from Lindsey in Lincolnshire, first found in the form *Lindissi,* a derivative of the British name Lincoln. The Old English element *eg* =island was added since the area was virtually cut off from the surrounding fenland. **Lincey** and **Linsey** are other variations.

Little is an English nickname given to the small man, or the younger of two men who bore the same given name, from Middle English *littel* > Old English *lytel* = little. Variations are **Littell, Lyttle, Lytle, Littler.** Among the Danish and Norwegians the name is **Litle.**

Littlefield: English Place Name...Field comes from the Old English word *feld,* which meant pasture, or meadow that was flat and uncultivated. Littlefield is a place name given to one who lived near the small uncultivated meadow -- the 'little-field.'

Lytton is a spelling variation of the English place name **Litton,** which described the man whose original home was in one of the several so-named settlements in Medieval England, which were named from Old English *hlyde* = torrent + *tun* = enclosure, settlement, and believed to describe a settlement near a loud or roaring stream.

Livesey is an English place name from the so-named location in Lancashire, derived from Old Norse *hlif* = protection, shelter + Old English *eg* = island. **Livesay, Livsey,** and **Livesley** are variations.

Lloyd is a Welsh nickname for the man with grey hair, or the man who was always seen wearing grey clothing. It comes from the Welsh word *llwyd* = grey. Variations are **Loyd, Floyde, Floyd, Floyed. Bloyd, Blood,** and **Blud** are patronymic versions of the name formed from the Welsh patronymic prefix "Ap" which meant "son of." When "Ap Lloyd" (son of Lloyd) was said quickly, the p-l often became indistinguishable from b-l. When the Ap portion was dropped many mistakenly retained the B sound to produce names such as Bloyed, Bloyd.

Logan: Scottish Place name and colonial frontier family, including General Benjamin Logan who founded Logan's Station (Stanford, KY). The name originated in the Scottish Lowlands, and designated the man who lived near the 'little hollow.'

Logerstedt is likely a spelling variation or Americanized spelling of **Lagerstedt,** a Swedish compound ornamental name derived from words describing natural phenomena that were used when surnames were adopted there in the late 1800's and early 1900's. (They were late bloomers, surname-wise!) Lagerstedt is a combination of *lager* and *stedt,* meaning literally "laurel homestead." Other Lager names along the same line (the first element *lager* = laurel) **Lagerbach** (stream), **Lagerberg** (hill), **Lagerborg** (town), **Lagerkrantz** (wreath), **Lagerdahl** (valley), **Lagerfeldt** (field), **Lagerfors** (waterfall), **Lagergrehn** (branch), **Lagerquist** (twig), **Lagerlof** (leaf), **Lagerstrandt** (shore), and **Lagerstrom** (river).

Long: English Descriptive name. During early times when surnames were being adopted, the man they called Long was especially tall and lanky.

Loomes is a variation of the English place name **Lumb,** from any of the several so-named locations in Lancashire and W. Yorkshire, named from Old English *lumm* = pool > dialectic *lum* = well for water in a mine. **Lum, Loom, Limb, Loombe, Lombe, Loomes** are all variations.

Lopez is a patronymic form of the Spanish surname **Lope,** which was also a medieval given name, likely from Latin *lupus* =

wolf. **Llop** is the way the name is found in Catalan, and in Portugal the patronymic form is **Lopes.**

Lovell is an English diminutive variant of the name Low, when it meant a crafty or dangerous person, a Nickname derived from the Anglo-Norman French *lou* = wolf + - *el,* a diminutive suffix. **Lovel** and **Lowell** are variations.

The surname **Loving** comes from Louvain, a place in Belgium that came from a French word meaning 'lions."

Lowery is a variation of **Lowry,** the English and Scottish patronymic surname, which is a deminutive form of the name Lawrence (man from Laurentum). When of Irish heritage, Lowry is derived as an Anglicized form of the Gaelic *O Labhradha,* "descendant of *Labhradha,"* whose name meant 'spokesman.' Other variations are **Lowrey, Lowerie, Lorrie, Lorie, Loury, Lory, Lourie;** Irish variations include **O'Lowry, O'Lawry.** Patronymic forms are **Lowries, Lowrieson, Lorrison, Lorriman.**

Lukacsko is a cognate form of the English, French, Spanish, Portuguese, and Flemish/Dutch patronymic name **Lucas,** from Greek *Loucas* = man from Lucania (an area of Southern Italy). **Luke, Luck** are English versions. **Look, Lock** (Scotland); **Lugg** (Devon); **Luc** (French); **Lukas** (Flemish/Dutch).

Lund comes from the Old Norse term *lundr* = grove, and is an English, Swedish, and Danish Norwegian place name for a person who lived in a grove. It is also among the most popular of names adopted by the Swedes when they were compelled to take last names in the 19th century. It is also used in combination with other Swedish nature words, to form compound names such as Lundquist and Lundgren. Variations are **Lunt, Lunn** (English); **Lundh, Lundell, Lunden, Lundin, Lundman** (Swedish).

Lumby is an English place name that described the man from the so-named location between Leeds and Selby, the name derived from Old Norse *lundr* = grove, wood + *byr* = farm, settlement.

Lundquist: Swedish Acquired Name...Adopted when surnames became required; the Swedes acquiring surnames much later. Acquired names were chosen for a pleasing sound; Lundquist is literally "grove twig." Swedish immigrants to American often added Lund or qvist/quist to surnames because it gave the appearance of increased social status. Lundquist is simply a surname prefix with a suffix attached.

Lux: may be the shortened form of Luxton, a place in Devon, England. The ending -ton came from Old English *tun* = settlement and Luke's town was eventually known as **Luxton.**

Lydon is a variation of the Irish patronymic name **Leyden,** which is an Anglicized form of the Gaelic name *O'Loideain,* which means 'descendant of *Loidean,*' which is a given name of unknown origin. Another variation is **Leydon.**

Lynch is an Irish patronymic name, Anglicized from the Gaelic *O' Loingsigh,* meaning "descendant of *Loingseach"* which was originally a nickname meaning "mariner." It is also derived from the Gaelic *Linseach,* which was a Gaelic form of the Anglo-Norman-French **de Lench,** a local name of Norman origin. When derived of English origin, Lynch is a place name for the man who lived on a slope or hillside, from Old English *hlinc* = ridge, bank, rising ground. **O'Lynchy, O'Lynche, O"lensie, Linchey, Linchy,** are Irish variations. **Linch, Lince, Linck** are variations of de Lench. Diminutive forms are **O'Lyneseghane, Lynchahan, Lynchehan, O'Loingseachain.**

M

Mack is a Scottish patronymic name from an Old Norse given name *Makkr,* which was a form of *Magnus.* Occasionally, in the US, the name Mack is an shortened form of any of the many Scottish names that began with the patronymic designator Mc, or Mac. **Maccus** is a variation.

Mach is a Czech, German and Polish patronymic name, from the given name *Mach,* a pet form of the Czech name *Matej,* or the Polish name *Maciej.* **Macha, Machac, Machala, Machal, Machan, Machon** are Czech variations. **Machala, Machnicki, Machocki** are Polish variants. **Mache, Macha** are among the other forms found in Germany.

MacAulay is a spelling variant of **McAulay,** a Scottish patronymic name Anglicized from the Gaelic *Mac Amhalghaidh,* meaning son of *Amhalghadh.* **McAullay, McAuley, McAllay, McAlley, McCaulay, McCauley, McCally, Cawley,** and **Gawley** are among the other variations.

MacLeod is a Scottish patronymic name that is an Anglicicized form of the Gaelic name *Mac Leoid,* from the Old Norse nickname *Ljotr* = ugly. Beauty is in the eye of the beholder, though. **McCloud** is another form of the name. Actually, the word ugly is derived from Old English *uglike* which meant *fearful, dreadful*, and only evolved into "unpleasant to look at."

Madden and **O'Madden** are both Irish patronymic names, Anglicized from the Gaelic *O Madaidhin,* which meant 'descendant of *Madaidhin'* whose name was derived from *madadh* = hound, mastiff. Variations are **Madine, O'Madden, O'Maddane, O'Madagane, O'Madigane, Maddigan,** and **Madigan.**

Madera is a Czech cognate of the Hungarian name **Magyar,** which means literally "Hungarian." The Magyars originally came from the Ural Mountain area but occupied the Caucasus between the fifth and ninth centuries. Bulgarian expansionism forced them to move westward and were settled in their current location by the end of the ninth century.

Madura is the Polish nickname for the wise or learned man, one of the nicknames that actually had a positive connotation.

Maffin is likely an Americanized version of the Italian surname **Maffini,** which is a diminutive form of the Italian name **Maffii**, the cognate form of the English and Scottish name **Matthew**, which was derived originally from the Hebrew *Matityahu* = gift of God. Other Italian cognates are **Mattea, Mattia, Matteo, Mattei, Mattedi, Mattevi, Maffeo, Maffei, Maffia.**

Maheu is a French cognate of the English patronymic name, **Mayhew,** which was derived from the given name **Mahieu,** a variation of **Matthew.** Other French versions are **Mahieux, Mahieu, Maheu, Mahu, Maheo, Mehu** (Normandy), while English variations are **Mahew, Mehew, Mayo,** and **Mayow.**

Maier, Meyer, Meier, and **Myer:** were the principal officers in charge of large and important households in Germany, and often, an -s- was added as in **Meyers** and **Myers.** Later the term came to designate a sustantial farmer.

Malone: is an Irish Patronymic name from the given name Malone (servant of St. John).

Manke: Nicknames or descriptions of people often stuck as surnames, and many were none-too-politically-correct. Manke was what they called the man who was lame or crippled, and some wound up with it as a surname.

Maitland: was a lot like England: Mait and Eng being terms for a grassy field. Eng-land became the name of the realm, and Mait-land became the name of the family that made their home in Eng-land. It's an English Place name.

O'Mara is an Irish patronymic name, Anglicized from the Gaelic *O'Meadhra,* which meant "descendant of *Meadhra.*" That name came from Gaelic *meadhar* = mirth, joy. Variations are **Meara, O'Meara,** and as an aphetic form **Mara.** An Americanized O'Mara isn't to be confused with **Mára,** a variation of the Czech name **Marek,** from the given name *Marek,* which was the Czech form of Mark. **Mares, Mára** are variations. **Marecek, Marsik, Marik** are diminutive forms.

Markham is an English place name from the so-named place in Nottinghamshire derived from Old English *mearc* = boundary + *hám* = homestead. Occasionally, it is derived among the Irish as an Anglicized form of *Ó Marcacháin,* which means "descendant of *Marcach* " whose name meant "knight, horseman."

The name **Markowski** and many other versions are derived from the Latin *Marcus,* the given name of Mark the Evangelist, who authored the second Gospel. The etymology of Marcus is unknown, but it may come from the word Mars. It is an old and popular given name which constituted the origin of many surnames. **Markowski** is a Jewish version of the name, along with **Markewitz, Markovski, Markovitz,** and numerous others.

Mally is an Irish patronymic name, Anglicized from *O' Maille,* meaning 'descendant of the nobleman' from *mal* = prince, champion. Variations include **Malley, Mealley, Meally, Melly, Melia, O'Malley, O'Mally, O'Maillie,** and others.

Marsh is an English place name for the man who lived near or on a marsh or fen, and is derived from Old English *mersc* = marsh. During the period when surnames were adopted, -er was pronounced as -ar, and most surnames of the time retained the ancient pronunciation. Through later academic study of entymology, the correct pronunciation of -er was returned to the language and taught as vocabulary.

Marshall: originally cared for the lord's horses, and acted as an early vet and farrier. Later on, the term evolved to describe an official in a noble's household in charge of the military affairs. It's an English Occupational name, either way.

Marte is an Italian cognate form of the French and German matronymic name (from the name of the mother) **Marthe,** which is listed in the Greek New Testament as Martha, from Aramaic *Marta* = Lady, the sister of Lazarus. Other variations are **Morthe, Merta.** Other cognates are **Marte, Marti, Marta.** Diminutive forms include **Marton, Marthon, Martot, Marthelot.**

Marti, Marty are cognate forms of the name **Martin** found in Provencal. Martin is found as an English, French, Scottish, Irish, German, Czech, Flemish, Dutch, Danish, and Norwegian Patronymic surname -- derived from the ancient Latin given name *Martinus,* derived from *Mars/Martis,* the Roman god of fertility and war. A fourth-century saint had the name, and those early saints made for a lot of namesakes. Variations are **Marten, Martyn, Martine, Lamartine, Martijn** among others.

Martinez: Spanish Patronymic Name...St. Martin of Tours was the patron saint of France and made Martin the most common name in that country. As a saint (with a good festival, to boot) Martin was also popular around the world. In Spanish speaking countries, descendants of Martin were called Martinez.

Masters: a patronymic form of the English and Scottish nickname **Master,** which described the man who behaved in a masterful way, or as an occupational name for the master of a craft. It is derived from Middle English *maister* > Latin *magister.* The name was borne in early times by people who were freeholders of enough land that they had laborers who helped them work the land. In Scotland, the eldest sons of Barons held this title, and the name may have been an acquired nickname for the servant of the eldest son of a baron. **Meystre** is a variant.

There are numerous cognates in several languages in addition to patronymic and diminutive forms.

Matney is likely an English place name composed of the elements *Matt/Matta* (a medieval given name derived from Matthew) + Old English *eg* = island, raised land in a fen. It would describe the man who lived near Matta's homestead location.

Matthews/Mathis: English Patronymic Name...Matthew means 'gift of Yahweh' as does Matthias -- both were popular first names in early times, and it is almost impossible to determine which derivatives came from which name...at any rate, Matthews and **Mathews** are English Patronymic names (from the father) and Mathis is the German counterpart. Matthews with the double-t was more popular in Wales. **Matusek** is a spelling variation of **Matousek,** a diminutive Czechoslovakian form of **Matous** = Matthew. It's the equivalent of "Little Matthew."

Mattingly: is an English Place name from an Old English personal name *Matting* + *leah* (clearing in the woods) which is literally, Matting's clearing in the woods.

Maurer is a German occupational name for the builder of defensive walls, or the builder of walls of substantial buildings of brick or stone. It is derived from German *mauer* = wall. During the Middle Ages, the majority of walls were made of wood or lathe and plaster, so the maurer generally built public buildings and defensive walls. **Meurer, Mauer, Mauermann** are variations. **Mührer, Mührmann** are Low German cognate forms; **Mularski** is the Polish version, and **Mulyar** is found in the Ukraine.

Mayfield is an English place name from the so-named locale in Sussex which derived its name from Old English *mægðe* = mayweed + *feld* = pasture, open country. The man from that location was described by his new neighbors by their pointing out his place of origin. The surname is also common in Nottinghamshire, and an addition location with the name Mayfield may have been located there.

Mayor, see also: **Meyer/Meier:** English Occupational Name...The head of a village or town was the mayor, often a position held for life. Henry Fitz Ailwin was the first mayor of London in 1193.

McAllister is a Scottish and Irish patronymic form of the surname Alexander, from the popular given name from Greek *Alexandros* = defender of men. Other forms of McAllister are **McAlester, McAllester, McAlister, McAllaster, McCallister, Mac Alastair.**

McArdle/McArdell/McCardle: Scottish/English Patronymic Name...McArdle is an Anglicized version of gaelic *Mac Ardghail* which came from the given name *Ardghal.* That name is composed of *ard* = height + *gal* = valor, for high valor. Variations are **McArdell** and **McCardle.**

McCabe is a Scottish and Irish patronymic name, Anglicized from the Gaelic *Mac Caba,* from the name *Caba* = cape, which described the wearer of a distinctive cape.

McCann: Scottish Patronymic name for the 'son of Annadh' whose name means 'storm.'

McCarthy is an Irish patronymic name, Anglicized from the Gaelic *Mac Carthaigh,* meaning 'son of Carthach' whose name meant 'loving.' **Mccarty, McCartie, McCarhie, McCarha,** and **McArthy** are variations.

McCleaft: Possibly derived from **MacCleish,** which is Anglicized from *Mac Gill'losa* which meant `son of the servant of Jesus," and is documented in Dumfrieshire as early as 1376.

McClourghity: is an old Irish name, of which most have been Anglicized to one degree or another -- with McClourghity not quite as much as **McCafferty,** which is another version of *Mac Eachmhareaigh,* a patronymic surname from the given name *Eachmharcach.* If it wasn't Anglicized that way then his namesake son would have to sign his check: *Eachmharcach Mac Eachmhareaigh,* taking up so much space he could only write them for small amounts! Just kidding...

McClure is a Scottish patronymic name, Anglicized from the Gaelic *Mac Gille Uidhir,* which means 'son of the servant of St. Odhar.' Variations are **McCloor, McLure, McLeur, McAlear, McAleer.**

McCluskey is an Irish patronymic name, Anglicized from the Gaelic ' *Mac Bhloscaidhe* ' which meant 'son of *Bloscadh.'* The name probably derived from the Gaelic term *blosc* = loud noise. Variations are **McClusky, McCloskey, McClosky, McCluskie, McLusky,** and **McLuskie.**

McCollough is a variation of the Irish and Scottish name **McCulloch,** which is an Anglicized form of a Gaelic patronymic name **Cullach,** from *cullach* = wild boar. Some families translated the name as **Boar** rather than Culloch or McCulloch. There is also speculation that the name might be derived from *Cu-Uladh,* meaning 'Hound of Ulster.' Variations of the name are **McCullach, McCullagh, McCully, McCullie,** and **McCoulie.** Thomas Maculagh of Wigtonshire, noted in the year 1296 is the first known bearer of the name in Scotland.

McCallum is a Scottish patronymic name, Anglicized from the Gaelic *Mac Coluim,* which is a patronymic form of the name Columba. It is more frequently seen as **McCollum,** but also exists as variations **McAllum, McCollam.**

McConville is an Irish patronymic name Anglicized from Gaelic *Mac Conmhaoil,* a patronymic form of the given name *Conmhaol,* comprised of the elements *cu* = hound + *maol* = bald. **McConwell,** and **Conwell** are variations.

McConnell is a Scottish patronymic name, Anglicized from the Gaelic *Mac Dhomhnuill,* which meant "son of Domhnall" whose name came from Celtic elements *dubno* = world + *val* = might, rule. When the name is of known Irish origin, it is taken from the Anglicized form of the Gaelic name *Mac Conaill,* meaning "son of Conall" whose name was taken from Celtic elements *con*, *cu* = hound + *gal* = valor. Variations include **MacConnel, McConnal. Whannell** and **McWhannell** are Scottish variations.

McCormick is the patronymic form of the Scottish surname *Cormack,* an Anglicized form of the given name Cormac, from the elements *corb* = raven + *mac* = son. **Cormick** is a variant and **Cormican** is a diminutive form. **McCormack, McCormick,** and the Gaelic **Mac Cormaic** are patronymic forms; literally "son of raven's son."

McCracken: Irish Patronymic Name...An Irish sept or clan was a group of people living in the same area with the same surname, and most Irish names used the Mac or O' prefix, as well as the Norman inspired Fitz'. Most of the names were taken from the father's name (patronymic) although many dropped the prefix and most were Anglicized in America. Many Fitz prefixes were replaced with Mac. McCracken was the son of *Neachtan,* which meant 'pure one.'

McCrary is an Irish patronymic name Anglicized from the Gaelic *Mac Ruidhri,* from the given name *Ruaiddhri.* Other versions are **McCreery, McCreary, McCririe.**

McDonald and **McDonell** are variations of the same surname, both Scottish Patronymic names derived from the Gaelic -- *Mac Dhamhnuill,* which means 'son of *Domhnall,*' a given name from the Gaelic elements *dubno* =world + *val* =rule. Other variations are **McDonnell, McDonaill, McDonall,** and **McDaniel.**

MacEachern may be a slightly Anglicized version of ***Mac Eachain,*** a Scottish Patronymic name from the Gaelic given name *Eachan,* which means 'each horse.'

McElreavy is an Anglicized version of the Gaelic *Mac Giolla Riabhaich,* which means "son of the brindled lad" and is an Irish patronymic name. **McIlwraith** is the most commonly found Anglicized version, while other variations include **McIlravy, McIlrea, McElwreath, McElreath, McElreavy, McAreavey, McArevey, McGillereogh, McGilrae, Gallery, McCalreogh, McCalreaghe, McCallerie, Colreavy, Culreavy, Callery, Killery.** You may be interested to know the name McIlwraith is also found among the Scots as an Anglicized version of the Gaelic *Mac Gille Riabhaich,* with variants **McIlwrath, McIlaraith, McIlarith, McIlleriach, McIlreach, McIlurick, McIllrick, McGillreich,** among others.

McGary is a variation of **McGarry,** which is a variant of the Irish name **McAree.** That name is an Anglicized version of the Gaelic name *Mac Fhearadhaigh,* from the nickname *Fhearadhach* = manly, brave. Other variations are **McHarry, Mahorry, McKarrye, McKerry, McKeary, Mcgarry, Megarry, McFaree, McFarry, McVarry,** and **McVerry.**

McGilvray is a Scottish and/or Irish Patronymic name: It originates in both areas, from similar Gaelic forms. In Ireland, the Irish Gaelic version was *Mac Giolla Bhraith,* and the Scottish form was *Mac Gille Bhrath.* They both stem from a given name that means "Servant of Judgement," and Mac meaning "son of..." in the typical Gaelic fashion. The Anglicized version of the name most commonly found is **McGillivray,** and these other variations exist: **McGillvray, McGilvray, McGilvra, McGillavery, McGillivry, McGillivrie, McGillvary, McGilvary, McGilvery.**

McGinnis McEnnesse McEnnis McInnes Maguinness Magennis Guinness: Irish Patronymic Name...the *Mc* designates 'son of' and a literal meaning of "Son of *Guinness*" which is Anglicized. The Irish version was from the Gaelic *Mag Aonghuis* and the given name *Aonghuis* is anglicized to Angus.

Mc Gonigle is an Irish patronymic name, Anglicized from the Gaelic *Mac Congail,* a patronymic form of the name *Congal.* The given name Congal is comprised of Old Celtic elements that mean "high, valour," and Mac Congal is literally translated as "Son of Congal." The name is most often found as **McGonigle,** but **McGonagle** is a common variation.

McGowan is a Scottish and Irish Patronymic name from the Anglicized form of Gaelic *Mac Gobhann* (Scottish) and *Mac Gabhann* (Irish) both from occupational nicknames for the village smith. It is also occasionally derived in Scotland from *Mac Owein,* a patronymic form of the given name Owen or Ewen. Variations include **McGowing, McGowen, McGoune, Magowan, McAgown, McEgown, McIroine,** and **Gowans.**

McGrath is the normal Irish form of the name **McCrae,** which is a Scottish and Irish patronymic name, Anglicized from the Gaelic *Mag Raith,* from the name Rath (grace, prosperity). Variations are **McCray, McCrea, McCree, McCrie, McCraw, McCreagh, McCreath, McCraith, McCreith, McCreight, McGraw, McGra, McRay, McRea, McRee, McRie, McRaw, McRaith, McReath, McWray, Magraw, Magraph, Magrath, Megrath, Mackereth.**

McGuigan is a fine Irish name, and is actually an Anglicized form of the name *Mac Guagain,* which is in itself an altered form of *Mag Eochagain* -- a patronymic form (from the father's name) of the old Gaelic name *Eochagan,* from *eachadhe* = horseman. **Geoghegan** is another name that evolved from this given name. Variations of McGuigan (which is literally translated as "son of the horseman") are **McGougan, McGugan, McGuckian, McGuckin, McWiggan.**

McGrogan is a rare Anglicized form of the Irish patronymic name **Mac Gruagain,** that is normally found as **Grogan,** from **O' Gruagain** (descendant of *Gruagan,* whose name was a diminutive form of the word gruag = hair).

McGuire is an Irish patronymic name, Anglicized from the Gaelic *Mag Uidhir,* which meant "son of *Odhar"* whose name meant 'sallow.' St. Odhar was the charioteer of St. Patrick. Variations are **McGwire, McGwir, McGuiver, McGuier, Maguire,** and **Maguier.**

McIlwraith is a Scottish and Irish patronymic name, Anglicized from a Gaelic name -- McIlwraith is the most commonly found Anglicized version, while other variations include **McIlravy, McIlrea, McElwreath, McElreath, McElrath, McElreavy, McAreavey, McArevey, McGillereogh, McGilrae, Gallery, McCalreogh, McCalreaghe, McCallerie, Colreavy, Culreavy, Callery, Killery.** You may be interested to know the name McIlwraith is also found among the Scots as an Anglicized version of the Gaelic *Mac Gille Riabhaich,* with variants **McIlwrath, McIlaraith, McIlarith, McIlleriach, McIlreach, McIlurick, McIllrick, McGillreich,** among others.

McInch, McKinch, and **McHinch,** are among the similar Anglicized variations of the Gaelic name *Mag Aonghuis,* meaning "descendant of *Aonghus"* whose name was comprised of the Gaelic elements *aon* = one + *ghus* = choice. An 8th century Pictish king bore the name and he was popularly portrayed as being the son of Daghda, the chief god of the Irish, and Boann who have her name to the River Boyne. Angus was a county named for the king, and is still a popular name among Scots -- the early occurrences in honor of *Mag Aonghuis.* **McGuinness** is the most commonly found form of this Irish name, with variations **McGinnis, McEnnesse, McEnnis, McInnes, Maguinness, Maginness, Maginnis, Magennis, Meginniss,** and **Guiness, Guinness.**

McIntosh: is derived from MacIntosh, a Scottish occupational and patronymic name that means 'son of the chief or leader.'

McKaig (and the several spelling variations) is an Anglicized form of *Mac Thaidhg,* a Gaelic name found in Scotland and Ireland which means "son of Tadhg." Tadhg is an ancient given name that meant "Poet, Philosopher" in Gaelic. **McCaig** is the version most commonly found. Variations include **McKaig, McKaigue, McKag, McKaig, McKague, McKage, McKeige, McKeag, McKeague, Keag, Keague, McHaig, McHeigh, Heague, McAig, Keig, Kegg.**

McKeever: is a variation of **McIver** which is a Scottish version of an Old Norse given name *Ivarr* derived from *iw* = bow + *herr* = army. The name was adopted at an early date by the Scots, Welsh, and Irish, and most cases indicate Celtic ancestry. Other variations include **MacIvor, McIver, McEevor, McEever, McHeever,** and **McCure. Iverson** is the Danish and Norwegian version, while the Swedes opted for **Ivarsson** and **Iwarsson.**

McKie is a variation of the Scots and Irish patronymic name **McKay,** which itself is an Anglicized version of the Gaelic name *Mac Aodha,* from the personal name *Aodh* = Fire, which was originally from the pagan god of fire. Other variations are **McKoy, McKey, McKee, McKie, McCay, McCoy, McGhee, McGhie, McHugh, McCue, McEa, McAy, Magee, Quay, Quaye,** and **Key.** The McCoys were half of a legendary feud (with the Hatfields) and the "Real McCoy" was Norman Selby, who was a boxer in the late 1800's under the name 'Kid McCoy' and promoted himself as the genuine article as opposed to one of his contemporaries -- a boxer also named McCoy.

McKinley: derived from the given name *Finlay* a Gaelic tribal leader, whose name came from the given name, Fionnla 'fair hero.'

McLean: Scottish Patronymic from MacLean, 'son of the servant of St. John.'

McLaughlin is a Scottish patronymic name Anglicized from the Gaelic **Mac Lachlainn,** a patronymic form of the given name *Lachlann* which was a Gaelic term for "stranger" and was applied to the Vikings who had settled nearby. It is most often found as **McLachlan,** but other variations include **McLachlane, McLaughlane, McLauchlan, McLaughlin, McLaughlan, McLaughlane, McLaughlin, McLochlin, McLoughlin, McLoghlin, McGloughlin,** and **Chaplin** (Manx form).

McLucas is a Scottish patronymic form of the English, French, Spanish, Portuguese, and Flemish/Dutch patronymic name **Lucas,** derived from the given name Lucas, which has its origins in the Greek *Loucas,* meaning 'man from Loucania.' Loucania was a region of Southern Italy. Variations of Lucas include **Luke, Luck, Look, Lock, Lugg, Luc** (French), and **Lukas** (Flemish/Dutch). Cognate forms include **Luca, Lucchi, Lucco** (Italian); **Lluch** (Catalan); **Lucks, Laux, Lux, Lauks** (Low German); **Liksch, Lukesch** (Low German - Slav origin); **Lukáš, Lukeš, Káš** (Czech); **Lukasz, Lukos, Luczak** (Polish); **Lukash** (Ukranian); **Lukacs** (Hungarian). Diminutive forms include **Luckett, Lockett, Locket, Lockitt, Lockie, Lockey, Lucazeau, Luqueet, Lucot, Lugol, Lucchelli, Luchelli, Lucchetti, Luchetti, Luchini, Lucchini, Lucotti, Lauxmann, Lukascheck, Kaschke, Luasek, Kasek, Kasik, Lukasik, Lulka, Lukashenko, Lukashenya.** Patronymic forms include **Luckes, Looks, Loukes** (English); **McLucas, McLuguish, McLugush, McLugish, Mac Lucais** (Scottish); **De Luca, Di Lucca** (Italian); **Lukasen, Luxen** (Low German); **Lucassen** (Dutch); **Lukinov** (Russian); **Lukashevich** (Ukrainian); **Lukaszewicz** (Polish); **Lukanov** (Bulgarian).

McManus is an Irish patronymic name, Anglicized from the Gaelic *Mac Maghnuis,* a patronymic form of the given name Magnus. Variations include **McMannas, McMannes, Mayne, Maynes.**

McMath is the name for the Scottish number-cruncher -- just kidding! It's an Irish patronymic name Anglicized from the Gaelic *Mac Mathghamhna,* from the given name *Mathghamhain* = bear. **McMathghamhana, McMaghowney, McMahouna, McMann, McKaghone, McMaghon, McMachan, McMaghone, McMahon** are all versions of this name.

McMeeken is of itself altered from its origins -- the Gaelic name *Mac Miadhachain,* a patronymic form of the given name *Miadhachan* = honorable. **McMeeking, McMikin, McMicking, McMeekan, McMeickan, McMickan, McMeckan, McMeeken, McMiken, McMeechan, McMeecham, McMichan,** and **McMhychen** are all variations.

MacMullen is an Anglicized version of the Gaelic *Mac Maolain,* which means "son of Maolan." The name *Maolan* was a diminutive form of the Gaelic word *maol,* which meant "bald" but in most cases regarding the surname referred to "tonsured" as in, "one who wore a tonsure." It is considered an Ecclesiastical Highland clan. The more common Anglicized form of the name is **McMillan,** but it is also found as **McMillen, McMullan, McMullen, McMullin, McMullon, McMowlane, McMoylan.** (All of the Mc names began as Mac, the Gaelic term for "son of")

McMahon is an Irish patronymic name, Anglicized from the Gaelic *Mac Mathghamhna,* meaning 'son of *Mathghamhain* ' whose name meant 'bear.' **Mcmachon, McMachan, McMaghone, McMaghen, McKaghone,McMann, MacMahouna** are among the variations.

McMonagle is an Irish patronymic name, Anglicized from the Gaelic *Mac Maonghail,* from the given name *Maonghal,* which is comprised of the elements *maoin* = wealth + *gal* = valour. Listed variants are **McMunagle, McMenigall.**

McMullen is a variation of the Scottish name **McMillan,** which is an Anglicized version of the patronymic name *Mac Maolain,* from the given name *Maolan,* from *mao* = bald, tonsured. It generally described someone who wore a tonsure and in a transferred sense, to the devotee of a certain saint. Variations are **McMillen, McMullan, McMullen, McMullin, McMullon, McMowlane, McMoylan.**

McMurtry: possibly Irish Patronymic names, from Anglicized versions of the Gaelic given name *Muircheartach,* derived from *muir* = sea + *ceardach* = skilled, to mean 'skilled navigator of the sea.' The Patronymic forms are **McMoriertagh, McMurihertie, McMiritee, McMreaty,** and **McMearty.**

McNutt is an Ulster (Northern Ireland, settled by the Scots in 1610) variation of the Scottish patronymic name **McNaughton,** which is an Anglicized version of the Gaelic *Mac Neachdainn,* which means "son of Neachdan" whose name is of unknown origin. Other variations are **McNaughtan, McNaughten, McNauchton, McNauchtan, McNauton, McNachtan, McNaghten, McNaught, McNeight, McKnight, McNitt.**

McNeice (not spelled like niece) is an Anglicized form of the Gaelic patronymic name **Mac Naois,** a shortened form of *Mac Aonghuis,* which means 'son of Angus.' Variations are **McNeese, McNess, McNisse, McNeish, Mannish, Mannix, Minnish, Minch, McCreesh, Neison,** and **Neeson.**
McNeilly: Scottish Patronymic name from the 'son of Neil' whose name means 'champion.'

McNeilly and **McNeill** -- although they seem almost identical -- aren't. McNeilly is an Anglicized Gaelic name, while McNeill is standard patronymics from the given name Neil, although that name is of Gaelic origin *(Niall* = champion). It is a name common among the English, Scots and Irish. The Norsemen adopted the name as *Njall,* and Scandinavian settlers brought the name from Ireland to England. The double -L spelling is generally Northern Ireland and Scotland derived. Variations are

Neild, Neal, Neele, Neeld, Nel, Niall, Niell, Niel, Nihell, Neels, Niles, Nielson, Nielson, McNeil, McNeille, McNeall, O'Neil, O'Neill, O'Neal, and many others.

McNicol is a Scottish variation of the surname **Nicholas,** found mainly among the English and Welsh, derived from the Greek given name *Nikolaos,* from *nikan* = to conquer + *laos* = people. It was a popular given name throughout Christian Europe during the Middle Ages. The 4th century bishop Nicholas was venerated by both the Catholic and Orthodox Churches, and was the subject of many legends (remember **Santa** ? Klaus is an aphetic shortened form of Nicholas...). Variations of Nicholas are, **Nicolas, Niclas, Nickless, Nicholl, Nichol, Nicoll, Nickol, Nicol, Nickel, Nickell, Nickle.** Cognates include **Nicolas, Nicolau, Niclausse** (French); **Nicol, Nicoud, Nicoux** (Provencal); **Niccola, Niccoli, Nicolli** (Italy); **Niccolai** (Tuscany); **Nicolás** (Spanish); **Nicolau** (Catalan, Portugal); **Nicolaie** (Rumania); **Nickolaus, Niklaus, Nicklaus, Nicklas, Nücklaus** (German); **Mikulas, Mikula, Mikulanda** (Czech); **Mikula, Mikulski** (Polish). Other patronymic forms are **Nicholls, Nichols, Nicolls, Niccols, Nicholes, Nickoles, Nicholds, Nickolds, Nickalls, Nickells, Nickels, Nicholson, Nickleson** (English); **McNicholas, McNicol, McNichol, McNicoll, McNickle** (Scottish); **De Nicola** (Italian); **Nicolescu Niculescu** (Rumanian); **Nicolassen, Nicklassen, Nickelsen** (German). As a result of the variations, in Rumania the Christmas carole is sung --- Up on the rooftop, whoo, whoo, whoo! Down through the chimney with Nicolescu! (That part isn't true.)

McPherson is an Anglicized version of the Scottish Gaelic name *Mac an Phearsain,* which means "son of the parson." **McPerson** is a variation.

McQuaig, McQuade, MacQuaid, McQuoide: Scottish/Irish Patronymic Name... The Gaelic given name Wat (pronounced wait, and the same as Walter). The name Walter was brought by the Normans and derived from Wald, meaning rule, and theri, meaning army. ***Mac Uaid*** was the son of Wat (Walter). The Anglicized version took many forms, some of which dropped the Mac, and many of which arranged the vowels in combination. Many Gaelic consonants were used interchangeably.

MacQueen and **McQueen** are the same name, as "mac" is the Gaelic term for "son of" and abbreviations such as M' and Mc are simply shortened forms. McQueen is an Angliziced form of the Gaelic name *Mac Shuibhne,* a Scottish patronymic name that means "son of *Suibhne*" whose name meant "pleasant." After "the forty-five" the English tried to end the Highland clan system, and outlawed the use of Mac and tartans, although many just resurfaced later, when the troubles were past. Many Scot names were originally Mac-something, but were altered by dropping or shortening the Mac, leaving names such as Queen and Quaite (see above).

McShan is likely an Anglicized version of the Gaelic name *Mac Seain,* which meant 'son of Sean' a form of the name John. **Shane** is a popular Anglicization of *Mac Seain,* but it also appears as **McShane.**

McVie is another variation of the Scottish Patronymic name **McBeth,** from the Gaelic personal name *Mac Beatha* which meant 'son of life,' that is - man of religion. Other versions are **McBeath, McBeith, McBay, McVay, McVey, McVeagh, McVie, McAbee.**

Meacham: English occupational name from Machin, derived from Anglo-Norman French *machun,* which designated the stone mason.

Mearns is a Scottish place name from the place so-named in the former county of Renfrewshire, derived from Gaelic *maiorne* = office or province of the **Mair** (officer of the court). The man from there often derived that name as a way for neighbors to describe him after he moved to a new location.

Meeking is a diminutive form of the name **May,** which is a pet form of the given name **Matthew,** with **Makin** generally found in Northern England. Meeking is a patronymic form of the name, as are **Makins, Maykings, Meakings, Meakin** and **Makinson.** Variations of Makin are **Maykin, Meakin, Meaken,** and **Making.**

Mefford is likely an English place name derived from the Old English description for the crossing point of a stream of water, and may be from OE *maed* = meadow + *ford* = ford, crossing. The man who lived near the crossing place often became known by the name given the ford.

Mellanby is an English place name for the man who originally came from a settlement by that name (actually it was called Melmerby in Cumberlandshire and N. Yorkshire). It is derived from the Old Norse name *Melmore,* by way of Irish *Mael-Muire* (devotee of the Virgin Mary) and added to the Old Norse term *byr* = farm, settlement.

Mellow is the American nickname for the laid-back person (just kidding...) Actually, Mellow is a variation of the English place name **Mellor,** from the so-named locales in Lancashire, Derbyshire, and others, derived from ancient Briton words that evolved as Welsh *moel* = bare + *bre* = hill. **Mellors, Mellows** are other variations.

Menard is a variation of the French and English (Norman) patronymic name **Maynard,** derived from the Germanic given name *Mainard* and composed of the elements *magin* = strength + *hard* = hardy, brave. **Mainerd** is an English variation. **Meynard, Menard, Mesnard** are French versions. **Mainardi, Meinardi, Menardo, Minardi, Minardo** are Italian cognates. **Meinhardt** is the German version, while **Meiner, Meinert, Mehnert, Menthe** are Low German cognates. **Minnert** and **Mint** are Frisian forms.

Mercer: English Occupational Name...Mercer was the one who dealt in silks, velvet, and expensive materials, although the term was sometimes applied to merchants in general.

Merlo: derived from the Old French word merle = blackbird -- Merle was used as a French Nickname for simplicity, or for the catcher of blackbirds.

Merrill is an English matronymic name derived from the given name Muriel, which in itself came from Celtic *muir* = sea + *gael* = bright. **Muriel** was a popular name in East Anglia where it was introduced by Breton soldiers with William the Conqueror. Norsemen also brought the name to Northern England from Ireland. Variations include **Merril, Merrel, Merrall, Murril, Murrell, Murrills, Merrells, Merralls, Murrells, Mirralls.**

Metcaf is a variation of the English nickname **Metcalf,** from Middle English *metecalf* = meat calf, and was the name given the herdsman or slaughterer, or sometimes attached as a nickname to the sleek and plump person.

Middlesworth is an English place name that described the settlement located between two others, from Old English *midel* = middle + *worð* = settlement. The man who removed from that location to another settlement was sometimes described by his place of origin.

Miles: English Patronymic name by way of Old French and the given name Milo, or occasionally from the given name Michael. Miles is also infrequently derived as an occupational name from the servant or retainer called a miles in medieval times.

Mill: In Medieval times, an center in every village or settlement was the mill, where people took their corn to be ground into flour. The man who worked at the mill, and sometimes the miller himself, might come to be known as Mill, or a variant of the name. In fact, the most common form of Mill is **Mills.** It has cognative forms in almost every language.

Miller: English Occupational Name for the man who operated the mill from the Middle English term *mille.*

Mitchell is an English, Scot, and Irish Patronymic name from the given name Michel, the regular vernacular form of Michael. Variants are **Mitchel** and **Michell,** while the English patronymic version takes the form of **Mitchelson** or **Michelson.**

Mitter: German place name for the farmer whose land was in the middle of two other, particularly when the farmers had the same given name. It's from Middle High German, *mitte* = middle, and could be used as in Hans mitte, or the Hans in the middle.

Mixon/Mix/Mixson: English Patronymic Name...The archangel Michael was the patron of the 12th century Crusades, and the name Michael was a favorite as a result. 'Of Michael' or 'of Mich/Mick' denoted the son. Mix and Mixon/Mixson also denote son of Mick or Michael.

Moebeck is a Swedish ornamental name comprised of the elements *Mo* = sand dune + *back* = stream. The Swedes were among the last to adopt surnames in Europe and chose them strictly for their pleasing sound. Other Mo names are **Moberg** (dune hill), **Mogren** (dune branch). **Moe, Mohlen, Molen, Mohlin, Molin** are variations of the name **Mo** -- also found as a Swedish surname by itself.

Moen is a variation of the Irish patronymic name **Mohan,** which was Anglicized from the Gaelic *O'Mochain,* which means "descendant of Mochan." Mochan, the given name, was derived from Gaelic *moch* = early, timely. Sometimes the name was translated into English as Early. Other variations are **O'Mochaine, O'Moughane, O'Moghan, O'Moughan, O'Moghane, O'Moon, Moohan, Mowen, Moen, Moan.**

Moffatt is an English and Scottish Place name derived from a place so-named in the former county of Dumfries, from the Gaelic word *magh* = plain, field + *fada* = long. Variations are **Moffett, Moffitt, Muffatt, Muffett, Meffat,** and **Mefet.**

Mogk: English Patronymic Name from the Old English personal name Mawa, which was used to describe an important local personality in the settlement or village.

Monday is an English patronymic name derived from the Old Norse given name *Mundi,* a shortened form of several compound names with the element *mundr* = protection. Occasionally, it is a nickname for someone who had a particular association with that day of the week, such as having his feudal service due that day. Monday was considered a lucky day to be born, and some may have derived the nickname that way. Finally, Monday is sometimes of Irish origin, an Anglicized version of the Gaelic *Mac Giolla Eoin,* meaning "son of the servant of Eoin," and the confusion of the Irish in translating *Giolla Eoin* and *Luain* (the latter is Monday in Gaelic). **Mondy, Mundy, Munday** are variations.

Moneymaker is an English nickname for the rich man, or an English occupational name for the moneyer, similar to the name **Minter,** for the man who minted money. It is derived from Middle English *moneye* = money, from Old French *moneie* > Latin *moneta.*

Montecalvo is an Italian place name, comprised of two elements: *monte* is derived from Old French *mont* = hill + *calvo,* which is an Italian form of another Old French word, *chauf* = bald < Latin *calvus.* It may have been a town or settlement during Medieval times, and the name would have described the man who emigrated to his new location from the settlement called Montecalvo. The town would have gotten its name from its location near the "bald mountain" or "bald hill," which is a fairly common term regarding hilly geography, describing the hill which was covered by trees or grasses except at the top. The name Calvus was a given name (stemming from a nickname) among early Romans, and the name lingered as a given name among Medieval Italians, lending credence to the possibility that the name occasionally originated as a place name describing "Calvus's hill."

Moore is an English Place name for the man who lived on a moor, in a fen, or any of the various settlements with this name -- derived from their location near the moor or fen. It comes from the Old English *mor.* Occasionally, Moore is a nickname for the person with swarthy complexion, from Old French *more* = Moor/Negro, and sometimes Moore is derived from the Gaelic *O'Mordha* (descendant of *Mordha,* a name that meant 'great' or 'proud' in Gaelic) and Anglicized to Moore. Lastly, Moore can be a Scottish or Welsh Nickname for the big man, from Welsh *mawr* = big, great.

Moran is a variant of the English and French surname Morant, which is an old given name of unknown etymology, but believed to mean 'steadfast' or 'enduring.' When of Irish descent, Moran is derived by Anglicizing *O' Morain,* (descendant of *Moran*), which usually has its accent on the first syllable, as opposed to the English and French version's second syllable accent.

Morgan is a Patronymic name of Welsh, Scot, and Irish origin -- from an old Celtic given name (*Morien* in Wales) composed of elements meaning sea + bright. Morgan is one of the most common, and oldest of the Welsh names. There is a Scottish Clan Morgan established in medieval times with connections to the *McKays,* and was likely developed independently of the Welsh surname. The Irish version is from *O'Murchan* or *O'Morghane,* from the Gaelic *O'Murchain.*

Moriarty/Moirerdagh/Muirihertie: Irish Occupational Name...from very old Celtic terms *muir* =sea and *cheardach* =good navigator. Settled in County Kerry, on both sides of Castlemaine Harbor. The name is an anglicized version of *Muircheardach* or

O'Muircheardach, with a literal meaning of skilled navigator of the sea. Variations include **McMoirerdagh,** and **McMuirihertie.**

Morin: French surname for a dark complexion or dark-haired person; Moring may be a variation. The French Nickname Morin became Moreno in Italy and Spain.

Morris: Welsh/English/Scottish/Irish Patronymic name from the French given name Maurice which was introduced at the time of the Norman conquest.

Morrison is an English and Scottish patronymic form of the name **Morris,** an English, Welsh, Scottish, and Irish patronymic surname from the given name *Maurice.* It was introduced to the area by Billy and his conquering Normans in 1066. Maurice is taken from Latin *Mauritius,* and Maurice was the name borne by a number of early Christian saints. Variations are **Morriss, Morrish, Morrice, Maurice, Morse, Morce, Morss.** Cognate forms include **Maurice, Mauris, Maurisse, Maurize, Morice, Morisse, Morize, Meurice, Meurise** (French); **Maurizio, Maurizzi, Maurici, Maurigi** (Italian); **Mauricio** (Portugal); **Moriz, Moritz** (German); **Meuris, Risse** (Flemish/Dutch); **Moricz** (Hungarian). Other patronymic forms are **McMorris, MacMuiris, McVarish, Mac Mhuiris, McMorris, Fitzmorris, Moritzer, Moritzen, Morissen, Mouritsen, Mouritzen, Mauritzen.**

Mortley is an English place name comprised of the Old English elements Morta = OE personal name + *leah* = wood, clearing...which described the man who lived at or near the homestead of a man named Morta, whose location would have been well-known enough to use as a reference.

Morton is an English and Scottish Place name derived from several places called that, and originated in the Old English elements *mor* = marsh, fen, moor + *tun* = enclosure, settlement. It was a name to describe the man who lived at the settlement by the marsh or moor.

Actually, **Murrough** and **Morrow** are variations of the same name, and are Anglicized versions of the Gaelic given name *Murchadh,* composed of the elements *muir* = sea + *cadh* = warrior. Variations of Morrow, which is the most commonly found version of the Irish and Scottish name, are **Morrough, Murrow,** and **Murrough,** and **McMurrough** is a patronymic version.

Mosley is a variation of **Moseley,** an English place name for any of the several locations in Central, West, and Northwest England, derived from Old English *mos* = peat bog + *leah* = woods, clearing. The man who originated in that location was often described that way by his new neighbors after moving to their town or settlement.

Moss and **Moses** are derived from the Hebrew name *Moshe* > *Moses,* the Israelite leader in the Book of Exodus, and linked to the Hebrew word *msh* = to draw (from the water). **Mosse,** and **Mossman** are variations of Moss, which are similar in nature to **Moseman. Moosmann, Moser, Miester** and **Mosl** are cognates of Moss found in Germany.

Mulcaster is a place name in Northern England; Mulcaster (castle) (now Muncaster) near Ravenglas, belonged to the Pennington Family of Lancashire since the Conquest. Mulcaster is comprised of Celtic *mul* = bare hill, headland + Old English *ceaster* = Roman fort. David de Mulcaster the original of the family was son of Benedict Pennington who lived there in the time of King John and assumed the name from the place of nativity for distinction's sake.

Muldowney: Irish Patronymic name from the descendant of *Dunadhach,* the fortress holder, Gaelic *maol* = chief + *dun* = low hill.

Mulholland is an Irish patronymic name, Anglicized from the Gaelic *O Maolchalann,* which meant "descendant of the devotee of (St.) Calann."

Mullen is an Irish Patronymic name, an Anglicized form of the Gaelic name *O'Maolain,* which meant 'descendant of Maolan' whose name meant 'devotee' or 'tonsured one.' **O'Mullane** is a variation of Mullen, as are **Mullens, Mullin, Mullins, Millin, Mullings, Mullane, Mulhane, Mullon, Millens, Milling, Mollan,Moylan, Melane, O'Moylane, O'Mullane, O'Mollane, O'Melane.**

Muller is a cognate form of the English surname **Miller,** the occupational name for the man who operated the mill, one of the primary early occupations.

Millar is found in Scotland as a variation and **Milner** is the predominate form in Yorkshire. **Meller** is another English variation. Cognates include **Moulinier, Moliner, Meunier, Munier, Meunie, Mugnier, Mounier, Mounie, Maunier, Monnier, Lemeunier, Lemonnier, Meusnier, Millour, Millinaire** (French); **Molinaro, Molinari, Monari, Monaro, Munari, Mugnaro, Mugnai** (Italian); **Molinero** (Spain); **Moliner, Munne** (Catalan); **Moliero** (Portugal); **Morariu** (Rumania); **Müllner, Müller, Milner, Muller, Molner, Miller, Molitor** (German); **Möller, Moller** (Low German); **De Meulder, Mulder, DeMolder, Moller, Moolenaar** (Flemish, Dutch); **Mlynarski, Mlynski** (Polish); **Mlynar** (Czech); **Möller** (Swedish); **Molnar** (Hungarian); **Meuller, Muller, Miler, Miller** (Jewish Ashkenazik).

Muncy is generally derived from **Mounsey,** an English place name of Norman origin, from *Monceaux* or *Monchaux,* both in present-day France, and originating in the Old French word *moncel* = hillock. Variations are **Mouncey, Moncey, Munsey, Munchay, Mounsie, Muncie.**

Murdock: English Patronymic name derived from the old Irish name *Murdoch* (seaman) which was introduced into England before the Conquest.

Murgatroyd: English (Yorkshire) surname derived from the place of residence. In 1371 the records show that a *Johanus de Morgateroyde* was appointed the chief constable of Warley. The surname was derived from the area where the clan lived - *moor-gate-royd.* Literally the clearing by the gate to the moor. There are many variations on the spelling, **Murgitroyd, Morgatroyd** and **Margetroyd** being the commonest.

Myatt is an English patronymic name from the given name *Myat,* which was a truncated form of the given name *Mihel* (Michael in a vernacular form) + the diminutive suffix -at. **Miatt, Myott, Miot** are variations.

N

Nagel/Naher/Nager/Neher/Nader: German occupational name for the tailor. *Nahen* = to sew. Many of these names are also spelled with two dots over the first vowel. (umlaut)

Nations is a variation of the given name Nathan, which came from Hebrew *Natan* = "given (by God)." **Natan, Nusan, Nusen** are Jewish variations. **Natan, Nation** are English versions. Nation has its origin in the West Midlands of England with the alteration attributed to folk etymology. The addition of the -S at the end indicates a patronymic form of the name, as in "Nation's son, John."
Or –
"Whose boy is that?"
"Nation's."

Naude is a variation of the French surname **Naud,** which is taken from an aphetic form of several given names of Germanic origin that ended in *-wald* = rule; such as **Arnold** or **Reynold.** Cognates are **Noldt, Nolde, Nolte, Noll** (German); **Naldi** (Italian).

Neal is an English patronymic name, a variant of the name **Neil.** This is the way it is usually spelled in Southern and Central England, and is taken from the Middle English form of the name, *Neel.* **Neale** and **Neall** are variations.

Needham is an English place name comprised of the Old English elements *ned* > Middle English *nede* = poverty, hardship + *ham* = homestead. **Need** is an English nickname for an impoverished person, based on the same origin. Needham would be the homestead of the man nicknamed "Need" or it may have been the "poor homestead."

Negretti is an Italian diminutive of a cognate form of the French name **Noir.** Whew! It's not really that complicated. The

French name Noir is a nickname for the man with dark hair or complexion, from Old French *noir* = black > Latin *niger* = black. The Italian form of the name is **Negro, Nero, Negri, LoNero, Nigri, Nieddu.** Those names had variations (diminutive forms) that include **Negrelli, Negrello, Negrini, Negrino, Negrotto, Neretti, Nerucci, Nerozzi, Nigriello.**

Neil is a medieval given name which means "Champion" and evolved into an Irish, Scottish, and English surname. It is derived from the given name of Irish origin -- *Niall* -- and was brought to England by the Scandinavians. **Neill, Neild, Neele, Neel, Neeld, Niall, Niell, Nield, Niel, Nihell, Nihill** are variations.

Nelson is an English Patronymic name derived either from the given name Nell or Neil, both of which originated from the Irish given name *Niall.* It means literally -- Niall's son. It is believed to have meant 'champion' and was brought to England from Ireland by Scandinavian settlers where the 'son of Niall' became known as *Niall's son,* or Nelson.

Némecek and **Némec** are both Czechoslovakian nicknames, used to describe a man who came from another country and spoke a different language. The Russian form is **Nemchinov,** derived from *Nemchin* = German. In Old Slavic, this word denoted a foreigner and was derived from *nemoi* = dumb -- in the context of being unable to speak (the same language). **Nemtsev** is a Russian variation. Other cognates are **Nimchuk** (Ukraine); **Niemiec** (Polish); **Niemetz, Niemitz, Niembsh** (German of Slavic origin), **Niemiec, Niemic** (Ashkenazic Jewish); **Nemet, Nemeth** (Hungarian). Patronymic cognates are **Niemcewicz** (Polish); **Nimzowitz** (German/slavic origin); **Niemocow** (Jewish-A). Diminutive forms are **Nimchenko, Niemczyk, Nemecek, Niemtschke, Niemczyk, Niemtchik, Niemchenok.**

Ness is an English and Scottish place name that described the man who lived at a headland, or came from one of the many places by that name, from Middle English *ness* = headland.

Neufeld is a German place name comprised of the elements from Middle High German *niuwe* = new + *feld* = field, and is similar in nature to **Neuberg** and **Neuberger** (new town) which were often Americanized as **Newberg** and **Newberger.**

Newham is an English place name that described the man from the so-named locations in Northumberland and North Yorkshire, derived from Old English *neowe* = new + *ham* = homestead.

Newport is an English place name, from any of the so-named locations whose names were derived from Old English *neowe* = new + *port* = market town. The man who originated in that location would be known by that name when he moved to another locale, as in John-of-Newport > John Newport.

Niblett: English Nickname...Niblett comes from a Middle English word *nibbe* which meant 'beak,' and was a nickname for someone with a prominent nose. Some of the nicknames that stuck as surnames were none too kind, but by comparison, this is fairly mild.

Nickerson is an English patronymic name derived from a diminutive form of the name Nicholas, from Greek *nikan* = to conquer + *laos* = people. **Nicholetts, Nix, Nickes, Nickinson, Nickisson** are other patronymic forms derived from diminutives. **Nickerson** was predominately found in the Norfolk area.

Nigro: is a cognizant of **Noir,** a French nickname for someone with notably dark hair or complexion, from the Old French *noir* = black. **LeNoir** is a variant of the name as well.

Niziolek: Polish Nickname...The small or thin man often was referred to by a descriptive word that wound up as a surname -- Niziolek is the Polish version; **Littell, Lytle, Short,** and **Cline** are among the English counterparts.

Noble is an English, Scottish, and French nickname given to the man of lofty birth or high character -- or occasionally as an ironic reference to the man of low station and humble birth. It is derived from Old French *noble* = high born, distinguished. Among Jewish (Ashkenazic) heritage it is an Anglicized version of **Knobel,** or a similar surname. A French variation is **Lenoble.** Italian cognates are **Nobile, Nobili;** Portuguese call it **Nobre;** it is **De Nobele** among the Flemish and Dutch. **Nobles** and **Nobels** are patronymic forms of the name.

Noel is an English and French nickname for the man who had some connection with the Christmas season, such as owing some form of work or service (ie. providing a Yule log) as a feudal obligation at that time of year, or having performed in the Christmas pageant and doing a memorable job (it isn't uncommon to find surnames based on a part played in a pageant). Noel was also a given name used for children born at Christmas time. Variations are **Nowell, Nowill** (English); **Nouau, Nouhaud, Nouaud** (French).

The name **Nordmarken** is a compound name, and is among those taken by the Swedes when they were obliged to have a last name (their government required it in the 19th Century, among the last of the European societies to adopt surnames). Most of the Swedish names are simply compounds of nice-sounding elements. The government had a list of prefixes and suffixes that were acceptable -- they didn't want any double-entendre or risque last names, so they had an official list. *Nord* is the Swedish word for North, and *mark* means land. **Nordmark** would be north land. While there is a chance that it was a place name to describe a man from the north, most Swedish names are simply pleasant-sounding compounds. Other Nord names include **Nordberg, Norberg** = north hill; **Nordvall** = north bank; **Nordwall** = north bank/wall; **Nordlund** = north grove; **Nordahl** = north valley; **Nordgren** = north branch; **Nordquist** = north twig; **Nordstrom** = north river.

The man who came from the North-country during medieval times was described as *norð* or norðer (that -d like character is called eth, and pronounced like -th). **Norris** is an English descriptive name for people who lived originally in Scandinavia, Scotland, or sometimes -- just the north of England. Occasionally, Norris is derived from a compound, from Old English *norð* + hus = house. It described the man who lived in a house at the north end of the settlement. Sometimes Norris is taken from Old French *nurice* = nurse, and was an occupational name for a wetnurse or foster mother. Variations are **Noriss, Norrish, Norie, Norrie, Norreys.**

Most of the names beginning with NOR- are derived from the name **North,** which described the man who lived north of the main settlement, or in the north part of the village. Occasionally, it described the man who had emigrated from another land to the North. **Northe, Northern** are variations. Cognates include **Nordmann, Normann, Noroman, Van Norrden, Van den Noort, Nohr, Norring, Nordh, Norden, Nordin, Nordell, Norlin, Nordlin, Norling, Norelius, Norrman.**

Northrop/Northrup: English Place Name...An old Danish word termination was - *thorpe* which designated 'outlying farmstead or hamlet' was corrupted into - *throp* and - *thrup* in early England. North-thorpe -- the north farm -- became Northrop and Northrup as an English place name.

Novak is a Czechoslovakian nickname from the Czech word *novy* = new, which was used in reference to a newcomer to a place. It occasionally denotes a shoemaker who made new shoes (not a cobbler who repaired old ones) and is the third most common Czech surname. **Novotny, Novy** are variations. Cognates include **Nowak, Nowacki, Nowik, Nowicki** (Polish); **Nowack, Nowak, Naujock, Naucke** (German of

Slavic origin); **Novak, Nowak, Novik, Novick, Novic, Nowik, Noveck, Novicki, Novitzki** (Jewish); **Novak** (Hungarian). **Novacek, Nowaczyk, Novichenko** are diminutive forms.

Nuccio: The surname John is universally found, from the Hebrew name *Yochanan* which meant 'God has favored me with a son.' Each language had its own versions of John and the Italians used a good many, including **Giovannelli, Gianelli, Gianiello, Gianilli,** and **Giannucci,** among dozens of others. Giannucci often became **Nussi, Nuzzi,** and **Nucci,** to which the final -O- completed **Nuccio.**

Nuchols is a variation of **Nucklaus,** a German cognate of the English patronymic name **Nicholas** (also the basis for the similar name **Nichols**).

Nugent: Neugent is a variation of Nugent, which is a place name among the English and Irish derived from any of the several locations in Northern France called *Nogent,* or with *Nogent* as part of the name. It ultimately came from Latin *Novientum,* which was an altered form of a Gaulish term that meant "new settlement." It is a commonly found name in Ireland, and many of this name descend from Fulke de Bellesme, lord of Nogent, Normandy, who received land from William the Conqueror and settled near Winchester, England. It was his gr-grandson Hugh de Nugent who settled first in Ireland and lived there until his death in 1213.

There are a number of Swedish compound names that include the first element NY = new. One of them is **Nyberg** (new hill). The names are ornamental surnames taken by the Swedes in the 1800's when their government required that they do so. **Nyberger** or **Nybarger** would be likely variations.

O

Oak is an English place name that described the man who lived near a prominent oak tree or in an oak woods, from the Middle English word *oke* = oak. It may also have been a nickname for the man who was exceptionally strong, as the tree. Variations are **Oake, Oke, Oaks, Oakes, Oaker, Atrtock, Attoc, Attack, Atack, Aikman** (Scottish version).

O'Connell: Irish Patronymic Name...it originated with the grandson of *Conall,* whose name meant 'world mighty.'

O'Dungan is Anglicized from *O'Donnagain,* which mean 'descendant of *Donnagan* ' a diminutive form of a personal name that meant 'dark' or 'brown.' **Donegan** is the most common spelling, with variants **Dunnigan, Doonican, Dunegain, O'Donegan,** and **O'Donegaine.**

Olejnicazk/Olejniczak: Polish Patronymic/Occupational Name...There a few names that are patronymic (from the father's name) that originate from the father's occupation. The Polish name Olejnicazk/Olejniczak came from the 'son of the maker of oil from seeds for food purposes.'

Ohler is sometimes seen as **Öhler,** and is a German cognate of the English occupational name for the seller of oil, or the extractor of oil. It is derived from AngloNorman French *olier* < *oile* = oil < Latin *oleum* = (Olive) oil. Linseed oil was the predominate product in Northern England, extracted from locally grown flax. Variations include **Oyler, Olier** (English); **Ollier, Olier** (French); **Oliaria, Dell'Olio, Dall'Oglio** (Italian); **Ohleyler, Ohler, Ohler, Ohlmann** (German); **Oliemann, Olie, Olij** (Flemish/Dutch); **Olejnik, Volejnik** (Czech); **Ohlmacher** (Jewish).

Oliver: is both an English and a French surname, although the French version is often seen as Olivier. It's a Patronymic name from the given name Oliver, which means 'elf, host.'

Olney: is an English Place name derived from Old English ollaneg, which meant island of Olla.

Olzack: a variation of the Polish place name **Olszewski,** so-named from the Polish ' *olcha, olsza* = alder + *ew* = a possessive suffix + *-ski* = suffix of local surnames, to describe the man who lived by the alder, or who was from the settlement near the alder called by that name. Other variations are **Olszak, Olszacki, Olszycki, Olszanski, Olszynski, Olshevski, Olshevsky, Olchovski, Volchonsky, Olcha,** and **Olchik.**

Ortiz is a patronymic form of the Spanish surname **Fuerte** and **Fuertes** -- a name found among the English and French as **FORT,** a nickname derived from Old French *fort* = strong, brave -- that was given to the brave man. Occasionally, it was used as a place name for the man who lived near a fortified stronghold.

Oster is a Swedish name for "one from the East." **Oster** with an umlaut over the -O- is the German word for Easter.

O'Toole is a patronymic variation of the Irish surname **Toole,** which is an Anglicized version of the Gaelic name *O Tuathail,* which means "descendant of *Tuathal"* which was an old Celtic name meaning "people, tribe" + "rule." Other variations are **O'Tuale, O'Toughill, Toughill, Touhill, O'Twohill, Toohill, Tohill, Tohall, Toal,** and **Toale.**

Otter/Otterman: While many animal names derived from the pictures on the roadside inns during the Middle Ages, the surnames Otter and Otterman aren't among those. Otter is a corruption of the Old English names Otthar or Othere, which meant "terrible army." I don't know if that means 'terribly mean army' or just 'terribly bad army." Just kidding...I'm sure Otthar could throw a spear with the best of them!

An **Outlaw** is a man deprived of the benefit and protection of the law, and in medieval England it was legal to kill such a man...as a surname, it may have derived as a patronymic description of the son. As in John - *son of the Outlaw*...or John *of the Outlaw* -- most of which were condensed by dropping the "son of" or "of the." Remember, the son is not responsible for the sins of the father!

Owens is a patronymic variation of the Welsh surname **Owen,** from the Welsh personal name *Owain,* likely drawn from Latin *Eugenius.* **Bowen** is another patronymic form, a shortened version of **ap'Owen.**

Oxford is an English place name from a place in Oxfordshire, at a ford used by oxen. A ford is a crossing place at a river or stream, and a common surname element used to describe the medieval man who lived nearby.

P

Pagnozzi is an Italian diminutive form of the nickname **Compagni** or **Compagno,** which meant "good neighbor." **Compagnon** is the French version, and **Pagni** is another Italian form. Other diminutives are **Pagnotti, Pagnussi, Pagnutti.**

Palmer is an English nickname for the man who had been on a pilgramage to the Holy Land, from Middle English, Old French *palmer, paumer* (they generally brought back a palm branch as proof of the journey's success. Variations are **Palmar, Paumier, Palmes.** Cognates exist in several languages.

Pare is likely a version of the Scottish place name **Peart,** which is found throughout Northern England and Scotland, and derived from the place called Pert on the North Esk near Montrose, which was so-named for a Pictish/Celtic term for a woods or copse.

Paris/Parris: French Place Name...Paris is the name taken by many who originated in that French city.

Parrish is a variation of the English Place name **Parish** - the local name given to the man from Paris. The name of the French city came from a Gaulish tribe which was recorded in Latin sources as Parisii -- the original meaning of which was unfortunately lost along the way. Somewhat rarely - the name derived from Paris as a medieval given name, likely an Old French version of Patrick or associated with the Trojan prince *Paris* whose name has been speculated as having originated with the form Voltuparis or Assoparis (Hawk). The confusion over the -S- in Paris and the -SH- in Parish was compounded over folk etymological association with the church parish, which was a Middle English term. Foundlings left at the church for adoption were sometimes given Parish as a surname during the 17th and 18th centuries -- much later than most surnames were adopted in most of Europe. **Parris** is another variation found among the English -- cognates of the name appear in several other languages.

Parker: English Occupational name for the man who was the gamekeeper at the medieval park.

Parlee is an English place name derived from Old English *par* = pear + an atypical spelling of the Old English element *leah* = wood, clearing. The term *leah* came to mean meadow, so Parlee could be literally "pear meadow" or in the strict sense of the Old English translation "pear woods." The man who lived in the clearing where the pear trees grew could have been known as Parlee.

Parks: English Occupational name, along with Park, for the dweller in the enclosed woods which was stocked with game for royal use.

Parton, an English place name from several towns called that in medieval England whose names derived from Old English *peretun* = pear orchard, which was derived from OE *pere* = pear + *tun* = enclosure. The pronunciation of -er changed to -ar during the Middle Ages, although some words reverted back through etymological correction.

Patrick is an English patronymic name, from the given name derived from Latin *Patricius* = son of a noble father, member of the patrician class or aristocracy. **Pattrick** is a variation, and cognates include (French) **Patric, Patrice, Patris, Patrix, Patry;** (Portuguese) **Patricio.** Diminutive forms are **Padan, Padyn, Pedan, Patricot,** and **Patrigeon. McPhedric** is a Scottish Patronymic form.

Patton (not to be confused with Pattin, Patten) is a variation of the English and Scottish surname **Pate,** which is derived from Pat or Patt, a shortened form of Patrick. Patton is a diminutive form of Pate (which occasionally is a nickname for a man with a bald head); **Patey** is another diminutive form. **Pates, McPhaid,**

McPhade, McFade, McPhate, McFait, McFeate are all patronymic variations of Pate.

Paul is the English, French, German, and Flemish/Dutch patronymic name from the Latin name *Paulus* = small, a popular name throughout Christian Europe. It was the name adopted by Saul, a Pharisee of Tarsus, who converted to Christianity and was a industrious missionary during the Roman Empire. Numerous early saints bore the name as well, contributing to its popularity. English variations are **Paull, Paule, Pawle; Pol** is a French version; **Pahl, Pohl** and **Paulus** are found in German heritage, and the Flemish/Dutch were **Pauwel** or **Pauel.**

Pavey, an English matronymic name from the female given name *Pavia,* which is of unknown origin. Listed variations include **Pavy, Pavie,** and cognate forms include **Pavie, Pavy, Pavese. Pavett, Pavitt** are diminutive forms.

Payne: is a derivative of Pain, which is an English Patronymic name from the Middle English given name Pain. It comes from the Old French *Paien,* which came from Latin *Paganus* -- where *pagus* meant outlying village. To make the long story short (or to wrap up an already long explanation of its origin), Pain was a civilian instead of a soldier and lived in an outlying area. Derivatives include **Paine, Payne, Payen** and **Payan.**

Pawlik/Pawlicki/Pawlak/Pavlik: Polish Patronymic Name...derive from the given name Paul, which was a popular item around the surname-acquiring period. When the spelling used a V as in Pavlik -- the name has the same derivation, but its origin would be Ukrainian.

Payton is an English Place name from **Peyton** in Sussex, which got its name from the Old English given name *Poega* + *tun* = settlement, enclosure, meaning literally" Poega's settlement."

Pearce: and its variations: **Pearce, Pearse, Piers, Peers, Perce, Persse, Perris,** (and others) are derived from the English given name Piers, which is a form of the name Peter.

Pearsall /Piersol: (and its variations) refer to a medieval English place called Per's Valley and one who lived there or nearby often became known as Pearsall.

Peeler is generally a variation of the English nickname **Peel,** which described the tall, thin man, from Anglo-Norman-French *pel* = stake, pole. **Peele, Peale, Piele, Pelle** are variations.

Pendley, Penley, Penly, Pendly are spelling variations of the English place name derived from Old English elements *penn* = hill, head + *leah* = wood, clearing. It described the location where those who came to bear the name made their home.

Pennebaker/Pennebakker/Pannebakker: Dutch Occupational Name. Pennebaker evolved from the Dutch *penne* = tile + *bakker* = baker; literally tile-baker. The Pannebakker family shield motto is: *Mein Siegel ist ein Ziegel* - "My Seal is a Tile." September 15, 1463 an edict in Holland forbade thatch and straw roofing and required tiles, making the tile-making a busy trade.

The name **Pennock** is an English place name that is synonymous with the word hillock, which described the man who lived at the small hill. The name is comprised of the elements *penn* + *ock;* penn was a Breton word meaning hill that was absorbed into Old English -- *ock* is a suffix added to words to create a diminutive form. Pennock is literally "hill little" or "small hill" and would have described a recognizable location to describe the man who lived at that place.

Perham is an English place name for the man from any of the several locations by that name, which received their name from Old English *peru* = pear + *ham* = homestead. Perram is a variant, and several of the locations are now called Parham as a result of Middle English pronunciation development.

Perkins: is a Welsh Patronymic name derived from the given name Peter, which was introduced into the area with William the Conqueror. There were many other varieties in England, but Perkins was most popular in Wales.

Perry: Henry was a popular name during the Middle Ages when surnames were adopted, and one of its pet forms was Harry. To point out a lad who was the 'son of Harry' a person might say "Yon is ap Harry." As a result, ap Harry eventually evolved into Perry for some who adopted the surname. It's an English Patronymic name.

Persch is a diminutive form of **Petren,** which is the German form of Peter, a name derived from the Greek *petros* = rock, stone. **Perschke, Persicke, Perscke, Persich, Persian, Pichan, Pecht, Peche, Peschmann** are among the many diminutive German forms of Slavic origin.

One of the most popular given names throughout Christian Europe during the Middle Ages was **Peter.** It appeared in numerous languages and in numerous forms. **Pietrzak** is a Polish patronymic form of the name which was derived from Greek *petros* = rock, stone.

Petrie: Scottish Patronymic name that is derived from the given name Peter. As a given name, Peter became popular after the Norman conquest of England, and Peter was often used as a surname by itself. Petrie is a dimunitive form of Peter, that was more popular in Scotland.

Phelps: In the 11th, 12th, and 13th centuries were French kings named Philip, which helped to popularize the name. Among the English variations of Philip, which means 'lover of horses' is Phelps.

Phillips/Philips: Philip was an extremely popular name in medieval times -- Philip was one of the apostles, and four French kings were named Philip from the 11th to the 13th century. The name -- which means 'lover of horses' -- came into England from France at the time of the conquest. Philips is patronymic (named after the father Philip, whose sons would be referred to as Philip's sons). The common Welsh and English version of the surname is spelled with two l's, giving the descendants the surname Phillips. **Phillips** is a variation of the English, French, Dutch/Flemish, and Danish/Norwegian Patronymic name Phillip/Philip from the Greek name *Philippos* and elements *philein* = to love + *hippos* = horse. Its popularity seems to have been due to medieval stories about Alexander the Great, whose father was Philip of Macedon. Variations are **Philipp, Phillip, Philp, Phelp, Phalp** (English); **Philippe, Phelip, Felip, Phelit, Philip, Phalip** (French); **Filip** (Flemish/Dutch). There are numerous other diminutive, patronymic, and cognative forms.

Pian is an Italian cognate form of the French place name **Plain,** which described the man who lived on a plateau or plain, derived from Old French *plan* > Latin *planum, plannus* = flat, level. Variations of Plain are **Plan, Plaine, Duplain, Duplan, Duplant.** Other cognates are **Plane** (English); **Plana, Planas, Planaz** (Provencal); **La Piana, Piana, Lo Piano, Pian, Piani, Del Piano, Delle Piane, Pianese** (Italian); **Piangiani** (Tuscany); **Llano, Llanos** (Spain); **Planas, Plana** (Catalan). Diminutive forms include **Planet, Planeix, Pianelle, Pianel, Pianeau** (French); **Pianella, Pianelli, Pianetti** (Italian).

Pickard is an English place name that described the man from Picardy in Northern France, which adjoins Normandy, where William the Conqueror left to take on the English, and where many English surnames are derived. **Picard** (as in Capt. Jean-Luc Picard of the Starship Enterprise, quoth he, "Engage!") is a French cognate, as are **Piccard, Piquard, Picart, Piquart, Lepicard.** Italian cognates are **Piccardi, Piccardo;** German versions are **Pikhardt, Pikhart.**

Piercy: a variation of the English (from the Normans) place name Percy, from any of the several places called that in Northern France, from the Gallo-Roman given name *Persius* + the local suffix *-acum,* and was given to the man who emigrated from there, likely as one of the followers of William the Conqueror. Other variants are **Percey, Persay, Pearcey, Pearsey, Piercey, Piercy, Pericey,** and **Pursey.** William de Percy (1030-1096) was one such follower -- he accompanied William the Conqueror and settled in the Northumbrian area, where his family was instrumental in holding the English border against the Scots.

Pillsbury: English place name and refers to Pil's fort, a place of safety during medieval times.

Pine is the English place name that described the man who lived near a conspicuous pine tree, or grove of pines, from Old English *pin* = pine > Latin *pinus.* Occasionally, it may have been a nickname for the tall, thin man who resembled such a tree (those green arms may have had something to do with that -- *kidding...*) **Pyne** is a variation. Cognates and Diminutive forms also exist for the name.

Pingree --according to Hanks & Hodges -- is the French nickname for the man who was fond of playing the old game of *cockles.* In that game, the blindfolded player extended a hand behind the back, which other players touched or slapped. The blindfolded player attempted to guess who did the touching. It was considered a game of flirtation.

Pinson: It's an English nickname based on an Old French word -- *pinson* -- which meant finch, and was used to describe a cheerful person.

Pinter is listed among the variations of the Spanish, Portuguese, Italian, and Sefardic Jewish nickname **Pinto,** for the person with a blotchy complexion, or salt-and-pepper hair. It is derived from the *pinto* = mottled, from Latin *pingere* = to paint. **Pintado** is a Spanish variation; **Pinta** is found in Portugal, **Pintus, Lo Pinto, LaPinta** are Italian, **Pinter** is an Anglicized version of the Jewish version of the name.

Pitt: English Place name...OE *pytt;* a pit, hollow, or low valley

The place name for the man who lived near a quick-set fence was **Place,** derived from Old French *pleis* > Latin *plectere* = to plait, interweave. **Plex, Plez, Plesse, Play, Place, Leplay, Deplaix, Duplaix, Duplay, Dupleix, Plessis Plessix, Plessy, Platzmann, Plazman, Van der Plaetse** are all versions. Place was also the name for the man who lived near the English main market square, and occasionally, the name for the fishseller or the thin man (thin as a fish).

Poe: is a variant of the English nickname **Peacock,** which described the man who seemed to strut about, or was brightly fashioned. The Flemish version is **DePauw/Depaeuw,** and the Dutch version is **DePaauw.**

Poisson is a French diminutive version of an Italian Occupational name (**Pesce**) which was given to the fisherman, or fish seller. **Peschi** is a variation of **Pesce,** and other French versions include **Poisson, Poissonnet, Poissenot, Poyssenot.**

Poll: is an ancient Gaelic word that means 'pool, pit' and the name Poll would describe the man who lived near the deep pool of water. It's a Place name of Gaelic origin.

Pollard: derived from two sources: the Englishman with a closely-cropped or shorn head was described as 'pollard' and for some the name stuck as an English Descriptive name. Other Pollard families were those who lived near the head or the end of the lake, and wound up with an English Place name.

Pollina is an Italian diminutive cognate of the French occupational name **Poule,** the name that described the breeder of chickens or -- occasionally -- a nickname for a timid person, from Old French *poule* = chicken > Latin *pulla* = young bird. Italian cognate forms are **Pollo, Pudda, Puddu;** the English cognate is **Poulter.** French variations are **Poul, Poulle.** Other diminutive forms are **Poulin, Poulet, Poullet, Poulot, Poullot, Pouleteau** (French); **Polini, Puddinu** (Italian).

Pomeroy is a French Place name given to the person from any of the several locations in France by that name, generally spelled similar to *pomeroie,* which was Old French for 'apple orchard.' The Pomeroy family of Devon can trace their heritage to a close associate of William the Conqueror, Ralph de la Pomerai, whose descendants lived for over 500 years in a castle near Totnes, Devon.

Pooler is likely an Anglicized spelling of the German **Pfuhler,** or a variation of the English surname **Pool.** Pfuhler is the Germanic version of Pool, which is a place name that described the man who lived by a pool of water, or pond. Among the Dutch, Pool is an ethnic name that described the man from Poland. English variations are **Poole, Poolman, Polman.** Cognates are **Pfuhl, Pfuhlmann, Pfuhler** (German); **Pohl, Pohlmann, Puhlmann, Puhl, Pohler** (Low German); **Van de Poel, Van der Poel, Peolman** (Flemish/Dutch).

Poncelet is a French diminutive cognate form of the English (of Norman origin) name **Points,** which comes from the Medieval given name *Ponche.* That name can be traced back to Latin *Pontius,* which may have come from an Italian cognate of *Quintus* (fifth-born). Variations of Points are **Poyntz, Punch.** Other cognate forms are **Pons, Ponce, Point** (French); **Ponzi, Ponzio, Ponzo, Punzi, Punzio, Punzo** (Italian); **Ponce** (Spain); **Poms** (Dutch). Other diminutive forms include **Pointel** (English); **Ponci, Poncin, Poncet, Punchet, Punchon** (French); **Ponzetti, Punzetti, Punzetto** (Italian).

Poulain is a French cognate of the English occupational name **Pullen,** which described the horse-breeder or sometimes -- a nickname for the frisky person. It is derived from Old French *poulain* = colt > Late Latin *pullamen,* derived from *pullus* = young animal. **Pulleine, Pulleyn, Pullin, Pullan** are variations. **Poullain, Poulan, Poulenc** are other French cognates.

Poulin is a variation of the French occupational name **Poule,** which described the breeder or keeper of chickens (although it was also known as a nickname for the timid person). It is derived from Old French *poule* = chicken > Late Latin *pullis* = young bird. **Poule, Poulle** are variations. Cognates include **Pollo, Pudda, Puddu** (Italian); **Poulter** (English). Diminutive forms are **Poulin, Poullet, Poulet, Poullot, Poulot, Pouleteau** (French); **Pollini, Puddini** (Italian). **Poulat, Poulas, Polloni, Poulard, Poulastre** are other forms.

Poyner is an English nickname for the man who was good with his fists when involved in an argument, from the Old French *poigneor* = fighter, from Latin *pugnator,* from *pugnare* = to fight. Occasionally, the name is of Welsh origin, and is an aphetic form of the patronymic name *ap'Ynyr* (the Welsh used ap in the same fashion the Scots used Mc to indicate 'son of'). Variations are **Poynor, Punyer. Bonner** and **Bunner** are variants of the Welsh version.

Powers: English Descriptive name for the man who had little money. There were many more Powers and Poors in early times, than Richs.

Pratt: English Place name derived from the word used to describe a grassy field during early times. The man who lived there was sometimes referred to as Pratt.

Preston is a Northern English Place name from the numerous locations, including Lancashire) derived from Old English *preost* = Priest + *tun* = enclosure, used to described a village held by the church or village with a priest.

Prestridge is an English place name derived from the elements *preost* = priest + *hrycg* = ridge, which would have described a location such as "ridge where the priest lives" or "ridge near the priest."

Pritchett is a diminutive variation of the English occupational name **Pryke,** which was the medieval term for the maker of pointed instruments, or occasionally, the nickname for the tall, thin man. It is derived from Middle English *prike, prich* = point. Diminutive forms include **Prickett, Pritchet, Pritchett, Pritchatt.**

Prochazka: is a Czech Occupational name for the travelling tradesman, especially the travelling butcher. It is derived from Czech *prochazet* =to walk, stroll, or saunter. It is among the most common Czech surnames.

Proctor is an English occupational name that described the steward, and is a contracted form of the Old French word *procurateour* < Latin *procurator* = agent. The term was used for solicitors, and officials such as collectors of taxes, and agents licensed to collect alms for lepers and monks. **Procktor, Procter, Prockter** are variations.

The root for **Prosser** was the given name *Rhosier,* which was the Welsh form of the name Roger (they called it Rosser). Roger is derived of Germanic elements *hrod* = reknown + *geri* = spear, and was introduced to the islands by the invading Normans. The Welsh patronymic designator was ap, and *ap'Rhosier* and *ap'Rosser* became Prosser, the reduced form of the name the same way as did many of the Welsh names beginning with -P-.

Prout is a variation of the English nickname **Proud,** which described the man considered to be vain, or haughty-acting. It is derived from Middle English *prod, prud* = proud. **Proude** is another variation.

Provost: English Occupational name...During the Middle Ages serfs elected one of their own to oversee the work on their lord's manor. One title for the position was Provost. It's considered an Occupational name.

Among the Welsh, *ap* is the patronymic designator similar to Mac, Fitz, and O' among other nationalities. **Pugh** is the reduced form of *ap Hugh,* meaning "son of Hugh" in the same fashion as many of the Welsh names beginning with the letter -P-. Hugh was a Norman name introduced into England by followers of William the Conqueror. It is actually a shortened form of several Germanic names with the initial element *hug* = heart, mind, spirit. St. Hugh of Lincoln, who died in the year 1200, founded the first Carthusian monastery in England and helped popularize the name.

Pruitt: English Descriptive Name...Pruitt is a diminutive derivative of an old English term meaning bold, impetuous, brave, soldier.

Punnett: One version is that it comes from Pugnator or a person who is a fist fighter or boxer.

Purcell is an English occupational name for the man who herded pigs, or occasionally, an affectionate nickname derived from Old French *pourcel* = piglet. In France it is **Pourcel, Pourceau;** in Italy it is **Porciello, Porcelli, Purcelli. Purcel** (Rumanian). Diminutive forms are **Porcellino, Porcellini, Porcellotto, Porcelletti.**

Putnam: English Place Name...Many English villages were described by attributes, and some surnames were adaptations of those locales. Putta's Homestead was one such settlement and some residents described themselves as being Putnam.

Pye is indeed an English surname, primarily found in the Lancashire and E. Anglia areas. It is a nickname given to the man who was especially talkative, or occasionally, given to the man who was prone to pilfering things, as in magpie/magpye. Pye was also occasionally the name given to the baker who specialized in pies. In Italy, the name was known as **Pica.**

Q

Quaite, Quate, Quade, McQuade, MacQuaid, McQuoide: Scottish/Irish Patronymic Name...The Gaelic given name Wat (pronounced wait, and the same as Walter). The name Walter was brought by the Normans and derived from *Wald,* meaning rule, and *theri,* meaning army. ***Mac Uaid*** was the son of Wat (Walter). The Anglicized version took many forms, some of which dropped the Mac, and many of which arranged the vowels in combination.

Queen: See McQueen.

Quigg/Quigley/Quigley/Quick/Quickley: English Nickname for an agile person, from Middle English *quik* or Old English *cwic* = lively. The surname is also sometimes derived from the place where cinch grass grew – it was a quick-growing grass. Quick and its variations were also derived occasionally from Old English *cu* = cow + *wic* = outlying settlement, for the man at the dairy farm.

Quinton: English Place Name...Quinton was the name given to several locations in Gloucester, Northants, and Birmingham that derived from Old English *cwen* = queen + *tun* = enclosure, settlement. The name is patronymic when derived from the Old French given name Quentin (Quintin) from Latin Quninus and Quintus meaning fifth(born). The name was introduced by the Normans but never really caught on. Finally, Quinton sometimes derived from a Norman location named for St. Quentin of Amiens, a third Century Roman missionary.

R

Rabinovich and Ravinovitch are versions of the Jewish Status name Rabin from the Polish rabin = rabbi. Variations include Rabinerson, Rabinsohn, Robinsohn, Robinzon, Rabinow, Robinov, Rabinowicz and others.

Ragsdale: is an English Place name comprised of the elements *rag* = rough + *dale* = valley, for a literal translation of 'rough valley.' The letter -S- is added to many names and elements to make them easier to pronounce.

Ralph: Ralf de Tankerville was the chamberlain for William the Conqueror, and from his name, a number of given names were derived. From Ralf came: **Raff, Ralph, Rand, Randall, Randolph, Rankin, Ransom, Ranson, Rawlings, Rawson,** and **Rawle.**

Ramey is a variation of the name **Ram,** which -- as a French name -- described the man who lived in a thickly wooded area, from the Old French term *raim* = branch. Ramey is considered a "diminutive" term -- somewhat like "little ram." **Ramel, Ramelet, Rameaux, Rameau, Ramelot, Ramlot, Ramet** are other variations of the French version of the surname Ram.

Ramirez: is a Spanish cognizant of Reinmar, a German Patronymic name from *ragin* = counsel + *meri* = fame. The Spanish version was **Ramiro,** from which the patronymic derivative Ramirez evolved.

Ramsey: is a Scottish place name in Essex and Huntingdonshire from Old English *hramsa* =wild garlic + *eg* =island or low land, for a literal meaning of 'wild garlic island.' Someone who lived near the spot where the wild garlic grew became known as Ramsey.

Randall/Randolph: English Patronymic name from the early given name Raedwulf, which means 'shield wolf.' It was popular in England before the Norman Conquest. The name eventually became *Radulf* and Randolph and Randall are among the derivatives.

Ray/Rey/Wray: English Nickname/Place Name...Ray is polygenetic in that it has several sources. One version is an English nickname from Old French rey or roy meaning king, to designate someone who had regal airs (not necessarily regal heirs!). It was also from the Middle English word *ray* which meant female deer (Ray -- a deer, a female deer...) and was given as a nickname to one who was timid. It also derived from the places *Rye* and *Wray* -- for people who were from there.

Rayfield is an English place name derived from Old English *ryge* = rye + *feld* = pasture, open country. It described the man who lived near the field where rye was grown.

Rayner/Raynor: French Patronymic name, from the Norman given name Rainer, which was derived from *ragin* = counsel + *hari* = army.

Ready/Reed: Scottish Patronymic Name...of the Scotsman Reedie in Angus. Also, in some cases, a Descriptive English name, as in -- always ready. Sometimes, meaning the descendent of Little Read (red), the nickname for a redhead, or the pet form of Redmond "counsel, protection."

Regarding **Reavey:** it is an Irish name, derived from the Gaelic *Riabhach,* a nickname meaning 'grizzled.' Other forms of the name are **McReavy, McCreavy, McCreevy, McCrevey, McKrevie, McGreavy, McGreevy, McGrievy, McGrevye, McGreave, Magreavy,** and **Magreevy.**

Redman is polygenetic, derived independantly from surnames **Read** and **Roth.** When arriving from the former it originates from the Old English *read* = red and designated the man with the red hair or ruddy complexion. The softening of the -E- sound in OE read to modern English red is not well-explained. Variations of Read are **Reade, Reed, Redd, Reid, Redman, Readman, Ride, Ryde, and Ryder.** Roth is the German Nickname and Jewish Assumed Ornamental Name for the person with red hair, derived from German *rot* = red. Variants are **Rothe, Rother,** and the Jewish variations are **Roter, Roiter, Royter,** among others.

Reidenbach is a German and Jewish (Ashkenazic) place name derived from Old High German elements that include *bah* = stream. The *-en* is a weak dative ending using after prepositions and definitive articles in Old High German. The "reid" part is likely a variant pronunciation of of OHG *rot* = red, and may be indicative of a Jewish ornamental surname combining the elements *rot* = red + *en* = dative ending + *bah* = stream. It may also have been a purely geographic related name that referred to the "red stream" however unlikely that may seem.

Reece: There was a family in the south of Wales that favored the given name Rhys: one was Rhys ap Tudor (Rhys the son of Tudor) who led men in stopping the advance of the Normans into South Wales. His grandson was Rhys ap Gruffydd (Rhys of Gruffydd) who became so powerful that he was appointed King's Judiciar for Wales by King Henry II of England. As heroes, they were responsible for a lot of given names, of which some translated into surnames. **Reece, Reese,** and **Rice** were all derived as Welsh Patronymic names from the given name *Rhys.*

Reedy is likely a spelling variation of **Reedie,** a Scottish place name for the so-named location in the former county of Angus, the name of which has uncertain origins. **Readie, Ready, Reidie, Reidy** are other spelling variations.

Reichenberg is a Ashkenazic Jewish ornamental surname derived of the elements *reich(en)* = rich + *berg* = hill -- literally 'rich hill.' Ornamental surnames were taken for their pleasing sound rather than any significant meaning, and occured when nationalities such as the European Jews and the Swedes adopted surnames in the 1800's.

Reichert is a variation of the patronymic name Richard, found among the English, French, German, Flemish, Dutch, and derived from a Germanic given name of the elements *ric* = power + *hard* = hardy, brave. Variations of Richard are **Ritchard, Ricard, Riccard, Rickard, Rickerd, Rickert** (English); **Ricard, Riguard, Rigard** (French); **Reichhardt, Reichardt, Reichert, Richardt** (German); **Rickaert, Rykert** (Flemish).

Reid/Reed: Scottish Patronymic Name...English nickname from OE *read* (red) for red hair or complexion.

Renfro is a Scottish place name from the so named location that was named with Gaelic elements that meant "flowing stream." The man who emigrated from there to a new location was sometimes called that as a way to differentiate him from others in his new town who had the same first name.

Reismann is a variation of **Reis,** the German place name for the man who lived in an overgrown area, from Middle High German *rís* = undergrowth, brushwood.

Remington is an English place name from Rimington in Yorkshire, which was name as "settlement on the rim, or border." The man who moved away from a location was often known to his new neighbors by his place of origin.

Renaud is a variation of the English patronymic name **Reynold,** deriving from a Germanic based given name composed of the elements *ragin* = counsel + *wald* = rule. Scandinavian settlers first brought the name to England in the Old Norse form that evolved into **Ronald,** but the French version was reinforced with William the Conqueror. Variations of the English form are **Reynell, Rennell, Rennoll, Rennold, Renaud,** and **Renaut.** French Cognates are **Reynaud,**

raynaud, Rainaud, Reynal, Reinaud, Regnault, Reneaud, Reneaultr, Renaut, Rigneault, Renaux. There are numerous other forms and variations.

Reyes: is from the Old French rey=king, and is a nickname for the man who carried himself in a regal fashion, or sometimes - a timid person.

Rheinecker is a German place name derived from the Germanic elements *Rhein* = Rhine + *ecke* = corner. The name **Eck** or **Ecker** generally describes the man who lived at the corner of two streets in town, or the corner of an area of land. **Rhein** described the man who lived on the Rhine River. Rheinecker would be the man who lived at a corner, or bend, of the Rhine.

Richey, Richie, and **Rich** (when not a nickname for the man with money, or ironically for the poor man) are diminutive forms of the English patronymic name **Richard;** found among the English, French, German, Flemish, Dutch, and derived from a Germanic given name of the elements *ric* = power + *hard* = hardy, brave. Variations of Richard are **Ritchard, Ricard, Riccard, Rickard, Rickerd, Rickert, Rickett, Ricket** (all English versions). There are cognates and patronymic forms as well, in several languages.

Richmond: English Place Name. William the Conqueror brought many French names with him, including Richemont "lofty mountain" which was Anglicized to Richmond.

Riddle is a spelling variation of **Riddell,** the Scottish and North English place name for the man from Ryedale in North Yorkshire, in the valley (dale) of the river Rye. **Riddel, Riddle, Riddall, Ridal, Rideal** are variations.

Rideout is a variation of the English surname **Ridout** - which is of uncertain origin, but discussed as an occupational nickname for a rider, from Middle English *riden* = to ride + *out* = out, forth; on the other hand, that could be fancied folklore! **Ridoutt** is a variation.

Ries is a German nickname for the man who was short and stocky, one of many Germany surnames that evolved from such personal descriptions.

Rigg/Riggs/Ridge/Ruge English Place Name...The person who lived at the ridge or at a range of hills was known in England by various names, including: Rigg, Riggs, Ruge, and Ridge. These names also derive from small settlements by these names within the British Isles.

The name **Rind** is a Scottish place name that described the man who lived during medieval times near a minor location in the former county of Perthshire, Scotland called *Rhynd,* which came from the Gaelic term *roinn* = point of land. As with most names taken from Gaelic origins, the spellings vary widely, but Rhynd, Rhind, Rhyne, are common variations.

Roach: an English place name for the man who lived by a rocky crag or outcropping. **Roche** is an Irish variation. Cognate forms are **Roche, Roc, Laroche, Desroches** (French); **Roca, Rocques, Larocque, Larroque** (Provencal); **Roca, Rocha** (Spanish).

The Normans brought the French given name **Robert** to England at the time of the Conquest. It means 'fame, bright' and was derived from the Old German *Hrodebert.* Rob, Hob, and Dob were pet forms of the name, and from Rob a number of surnames were derived. The patronymic forms of the name include **Roberts** and **Robertson.**

The Normans brought the French given name **Robert** to England at the time of the Conquest. It means 'fame, bright' and was derived from the Old German *Hrodebert.* Rob, Hob, and Dob were pet forms of the name, and from Rob a number of surnames were derived -- including the English Patronymic name **Robinson.** Other versions are **Robart** (English), **Robart, Robard, Rebert, Rospars** (French), **Ropartz** (Brittany), **Flobert, Flaubert** (also French from a variation), **Robbert, Rubbert, Ropert, Ruppert** (Low German). Cognates include **Roubert, Roubeix** (Provencal), **Roberti, Roberto, Ruberti, Ruberto, Ruperto, Luberti, Luberto Luparti, Luparto** (Italian), **Roberto** (Portuguese), **Rupprecht, Rupprecht, Rauprich** (German), and **Robberecht** (Flemish).

McCroan is likely derived as a Scottish patronymic name, Anglicized from the Gaelic *Ruadhan,* which was a diminutive form of *ruadh* = red. Mac, of course, is the Gaelic term for "son of" and in a number of cases the spellings of the names carried the "c" from Mac into the base name. **Ruane** is found as an Irish name as well, with other Anglicized versions from Gaelic that include **O'Ruane, O'Rowane, Roan, Rowan, O'Roan, Rouane, Roane, Rewan, Ryoan, Raun, Roon.**

Roch: a French patronymic name from a Germanic given name which may have originally meant 'crow' or may have come from Old English *hroc* = rest.. Variations are **Roz, Rose.** Cognates are **Ruocco, Rocchi, Roque, Rochus, Ruocco, Rocci Roque** is the Portuguese version. **Roch** and **Rochus** are found among Low German surnames.

Rodney was first recorded as *Rodenye,* and was a medieval settlement in the marshes of England near Markham. The man who emigrated from there to a new location was sometimes described by the name of his former home. Rodenye was named from an Old English given name -- *Hroda* -- with the suffix *eg* = island, or dry land. It is literally translated as "Hroda's island."

Rodriguez is a Spanish version of the given name Hrodrick, comprised of the Germanic elements *hrod* = reknown + *ric* = power. The Spanish form of the given name is **Rodrigo,** and the Patronymic form is Rodriguez, meaning 'son of Rodrigo.'

The name *Rogier* was introduced into England by followers of William the Conqueror and the name **Roger** developed as a surname among the English, French, Catalan, and Low Germans. Variations include **Rodgier, Rogger** (English); **Rodger** (Scottish); **Rosser** (Wales); **Rogier, Rogez** (French); **Rogger, Rottger, Rottcher, Rodinger** (Low German). Numerous cognate forms exist, as do patronymics, which include **Rodgers, Rogers, Rogerson, Rodgerson,** and many others.

Rogers: English/French Patronymic name from the given name Roger which was brought to England by the Normans as Rogier. Its elements are *hrod* = renown + *geri* = spear, or `reknowned spearman.'

Roke is an English place name, derived from the Middle English phrase "atter oke" which meant, "at the oak." A misdivision of the phrase sent the -r- to the second syllable, resulting in Roke, often spelled **Rock** or **Roake.** The addition of the -er generally designates an occupational name, and the **Roker, Rocker, Rooker, Rucker** (various spellings) was the spinner of wool or maker of distaffs, from the Middle English word roc = *distaff* > Old Norse *rokkr.*

Rollins is a patronymic (from a diminutive form)version of the name Rollo, which is a Latinized form of the name *Rou* or *Roul,* which was a Norman form of Rolf. Rolf has its origin in Germanic elements *hrod* = renown + *wulf* = wolf. When written in official documents in Medieval times, Rou/Roul was commonly Latinized. **Roll, Rolle** are variations. **Rollin** is a diminutive form, and Rollins describe the son of Rollin.

Romaine is a variation of the English, French, Rumanian, Catalan, Polish, Ekrainian, and Belorussian surname **Roman,** from the Latin given name *Romanus,* which was the name of several early saints and contributed to its early popularity. Occasionally, it is found as a place name for the man from Rome. Variations are **Romain, Romaine, Romayne, Romayn**

(English), **Romain** (French for the place name), **Roma** (Catalan), **Romanski** (Poland). For the place name, **Rome, Roome, Room** are English variations. **Romano, Romani** are Italian cognates; **Romeign, Romign, Romeyn** are the Dutch forms.

Roncin, a French occupational name for the man in charge of horses used as pack animals, from Old French *roncin* = workhorse.

If **Rone** is of Irish heritage, it is likely another Anglicized version of the Gaelic *O'Ruadhain,* which meant "descendant of *Ruadhan* " which was a given name that meant "red." **Ruane** is the commonly found version, with variations **O'Ruane, O'Rowane, O'Roan, Roan, Roane, Rouane, Rowan, Rewan, Royan, Raun, Roon.**

Rosine is a variation of the English, French, and German surname **Rose,** from the name of the flower, and as a place name for the man who lived near where they grew, or in the town, for the man who lived at the house with the sign of the rose. Numerous variations exist, as do patronymic, and diminutive forms.

Ross is an English and Scots place name from a place near Caen in Normandy, which was the original home of the family 'de Ros' who were located in Kent by the year 1130. Some names have more than one origin depending on the family, and Ross is one of those. Occasionally, it comes from a Gaelic word *ros* that meant 'promontory' or 'upland' and there were several locales named with this meaning in mind. Also, somes **Ross** families are descended from an ancestor who bore the Germanic given name **Rozzo,** which meant 'reknown' in its original sense. Finally, the German breeder or keeper of horses was sometimes called Ross, from the Southern German word *ross* = horse, or the man who lived at the house displaying the sign of the horse might also come to bear this name.

Rostan is likely a variation of the French surname **Rostaing,** from a Germanic personal name composed of the elements *hrod* = reknown + *stan* = stone. Variations of the name include **Roustaing, Rostang, Rostand, Roustan.**

Round/Rounds: When surnames were adopted, sometimes nicknames stuck as in the case of Round and Rounds, which were English Descriptive surnames for the person who was about as wide as he was tall.

Rowell is a variation of the English place name **Rothwell,** which described the man who emigrated from any of the several so-named locations (there were Rothwell settlements in Lincolnshire and Northamptonshire, among others). Rowell is occasionally derived from a location in Devonshire called Rowell, from Old English *ruh* = rough, overgrown + *hyll* = hill. It would have described the man who came from that village. Sometimes, Rowell is simply a variation of the given name Rowe, a shortened form of Rowland. It would have described the son of a man by that name.

Rucker is a variation of the English occupational name **Rock,** for the man who spun wool or made distaffs, from the Middle English term *rok* = distaff, from Old Norse *rokr.* Other variations include **Rocker** and **Rooker.** The name Rock is generally a place name for the man who lived by a notable boulder or outcrop, from Middle English *rocc* = rock, or a place name for the man who lived at a settlement by that name. **Rocke,** and **Rocks** are variations of the place name.

Rudderham, as an English name, contains the suffix *-ham* that is taken from Old English *'holm'* meaning island, or 'dry place in a fen.' It is used in the case of Place names, which are drawn from a specific locations. The Middle English word *'rudde'* meant 'red' or 'ruddy,' which could easily have **Rudderham** as a description for the man who lived at the 'red island.'

Rummler is a variation of the Low German, Dutch, and Flemish nickname **Rommel,** from Middle Low German *rummeln* = to make a noise or create a disturbance. It was used to describe the obstreperous person. Variations are **Rommele, Rommler, Rummel, Rummele, Rummler.**

Rundle: In the Middle Ages, when surnames were being adopted, some were Nicknames that neighbors or relatives pinned on a man to help identify him from others with the same first name. Sometimes they were cruel, sometimes not too bad. Rundle is a diminutive form of the Middle English *rund* which meant 'round' and was used to describe the man who was slightly round at the middle. Occasionally, Rundle identified the man who was from Rundale, in Shoreham parish, Kent, which derived its name from Old English *rumig* = roomy. Variants are **Rundell,** and **Rundall.**

Rush is an English place name that described the man who lived near a clump of rushes, from the Middle English word for that plant. When it is derived from Irish ancestry, Rush is an Anglicized form of the Gaelic O' Ruis, which meant "descendant of Ros" which is a given name from the word 'ros' = wood. In Ulster (the Northern counties of Ireland that were colonized by the Scots in 1610) the name was a translation of O'Fuada or O'Luachara, which are Anglicized as Foody and Loughrey. Variations are **Rusher, Rischer;** cognates are **Risch, Rische, Roschen, Roschman,** and **Ruys.**

Russell is an English, Scottish, and Irish patronymic name from the given name *Rousel,* which was a common Anglo-Norman-French nickname for someone with red hair. Variations are **Russel, Roussell, Rowsell, Russill.** Cognates include **Roussel, Rouxel, Leroussel, Rousseaux, Lerousseau** (French); **Rosselli, Rossiello, Russello** (Italian); **Rossell** (Catalan); **Rouselet, Rousselin, Rousselot, Rosselini** are patronymic variations.

Rutledge is a variation of **Routledge,** an English and Scottish name of unknown origin. It is likely a place name, but the specific place has been lost to history. The locale *Routledge Burn* in Cambridgeshire received its name from a man, rather than the other way around. **Rutledge, Rudledge, Rookledge, Rucklidge** are known variations.

Rycenga: Dutch surname derived from German town of Rysum combined with Dutch *ga* = from to designate the man from Rysum, Germany. Variations include **Rycenga, Rycinga, Ryzenga, Rijzinga, Rijzenga, Rijsinga, Rijsenga.**

S

Sablun/Sabluns: Italian Place name, for the man from the place settled by the ancient Italic people of Central Italy.

Sadler: aptly described the Englishman who was the maker of saddles and is derived from the Old English *sadol.* Varieties include **Saddler** and **Sadlier,** among others.

Sagle is likely a spelling variation of the surname **Sagel,** a French diminutive form of the English and French name **Sage,** derived from Old French *sage* = learned, sensible. **Lesage** is a French variation. Cognate forms include **Saiave, Save** (Provencal); **Saggio, Savi, Savio, Lo Savio, Sapio** (Italy). Diminutive forms include **Sagel, Saget, Sageon, Sageot, Saivet, Saviotti, Savioli, Saviozzi.**

Salisbury/Saluisbury/Saulsbury: English Place Name...Saulsbury is a variation of Salisbury (pronounced the same way as Saulsbury) which was an English city in Wiltshire that was derived from *searu* = armour and *burh* which meant town -- for a literal meaning of armour-town. People from their would sometimes use it as a surname.

Salvoto is likely a variation of the Italian patronymic name *Salvi,* from the name *Salvius* = safe, from Latin *salvus* = safe, and borne by a number of early saints. Variations are **Salvy, Sauvy, Salvo, Salvio.** Diminutive forms include **Salvetti, Savlinellli, Salvini, Salvinello, Salvioli, Salvucci, Salvioni, Salvione.** A patronymic form is **Di Salvo.**

Samuel, which is an English, French, German, and Jewish patronymic name, from the given name Samuel, dertive from Hebrew *Shemuel* = name of God. **Samwell** is an English variation. **Samel** is found in Germany. **Schmuel, Samuel, Shmil, Schmueli, Schmuely, Shmouel,** and **Schmoueli** are among the Jewish variations. Diminutive and patronymic forms exist in many languages.

Samson is an English, French, German, Jewish, and Flemish/Dutch name derived from the Hebrew *Shimshon* < *shemesh* = sun, and derived from the bible as Samson. Generally the name was given during medieval times to honor the 6th Century Welsh bishop of that name who was venerated greatly across Europe, including those followers of William the Conqueror who popularized the name among the Bretons. English variations are **Sampson, Samsin, Sansom, Sansome, Sansum, Sansam.** Other variations include **Sainson, Sanson** (French); **Simson** (German), **Shimshon, Shimsoni, Shimsony** (Jewish); Cognate forms include **Sansone, Sansoni, Sanson, Sanzone, Sanzonio, Sanzogno** (Italian); **Samso** (Catalan).

Sanders is derived the long way around from the popular given name Alexander. An aphetic version is one where the initial syllable is lost through poor or lazy pronunciation, as in *squire* evolving from *esquire.* Alexander became **Sander** in parts of England, Scotland, and Germany, and the addition of the -S at the end denotes a Patronymic name, as in "son of."

Sandis/Sandison/Sandys/Sand: English/Scottish, German, Danish, Norwegian or Swedish place name for the man who lived near the sandy soil...and occasionally, the son of Alexander.

Sanks may be derived from **Sankey:** an English place name derived from a so-named location in Lancashire named for a river, which may have been named from elements meaning "sacred, holy." **Sankey** is also derived from Irish heritage, when Anglicized from the Gaelic *Mac Seanchaidhe* (son of the Chronicler). **Sanky** is a variation. **Sanks** could be a patronymic form, meaning "son of Sankey."

Sanguino/Sanguinetti: Spanish/Italian Nickname...Both Sanguino and Sanguinetti have as their root -- *sanguinis* -- the Latin word for blood. The word was also appropriated by

Medieval English and Medieval French as a root for words with blood as a reference. The Italians often placed diminutive suffixes on names, which would create "little blood" Sanguinetti. Descriptive names are somewhat rare among the Spanish-speaking languages, and those taken from colors are even more rare; Blanco (white), Castano, Moreno (brown), and Pardo (gray) are the only ones among the top one-thousand Latin American names.

Santi: English and French nickname derived from the word saint, which described a pious person.

Santiago is a Spanish and Portuguese place name that described the man who emigrated from any of the several locations so-named, which got their names from the dedication of their church to St. James, the patron saint of Spain. **Tiago** is an aphetic variation found in Portugal, arrived at by misdivision of the two parts of Santiago.

Sarsfield is an English place name as determined by the suffix -*field.* The identifying portion of the name may be derived from Old French *saracen* in the context of "the east, or toward the sunrise," or from the medieval given name *Saher,* which would have the name mean the "field in the east" or "Saher's field."

Satterfield is an English Place name for the man who lived in a hut in the open field.

Sauer: German Nickname...In England there were several names for the grave or austere man, including **Sterne** and **Stark.** Sauer is the German and Jewish (Ashkenazic) nickname for the cross or cantankerous person, and is derived from the German *sauer* = sour, from Middle High German *sur,* a cognate of English sour. Mental and moral qualities were often ascribed to people during Medieval times, with the differences in spelling and pronunciation due to the varying dialects and languages. Sauer and **Wunderlich** both designated the morose or moody man in Germany. Variants are **Sauermann** and **Sauerman,** as well as the Jewish variant **Zoyer. Suhrmann** and **Suhr** are both Low German cognate forms, while the Danish and Norwegian version is **Suhr. Sauerle** and **Seyerlin** are German diminutive forms.

Saunders: Scottish Patronymic name derived from the popular name Alexander. Three Scottish kings bore the name during Medieval times and there are a large number of variations taken from its pet forms. Sanders and Saunders are among those well represented in Scotland.

Savage is an English nickname for a 'wild or uncouth person,' derived from a Middle English version of Old French *salvage, sauvage* = untamed. Variants include **Sauvage, Salvage, Savidge, Savege.** French congitives are **Lesauvage** and **Sauvage;** Italian = **Salvaggi, Selvaggio, Salvatici,** and French diminutive versions are **Sauvageon, Sauvageau,** and **Sauvageot.**

Schachet: a variation of **Shoikhet,** a Jewish (Southern Ashkenazic) name for the ritual slaughterer, from Yiddish *shoykhet,* with variants: **Shoichet, Schochet, Shohet, Szoachet,** and **Schauchet.**

Schechter: The Jewish (Ashkenazic) Occupational name for a ritual slaughterer is **Schechter,** of which there are a number of variations, derived from German **Schachter** (agent deriv. of *schachten,* from the Yid. verb *shekhtn,* whose stem is from Hebrew *shachat* - to slaughter. Variations include **Schachter, Schaechter, Schacter, Schechter, Schecter, Szechter, Scherchner,** and **Schechterman.**

Scheidtz/Sheets: German place name used to describe the man who lived by a boundary or a watershed.

Schneider is a German and Jewish (Ashkenazic) occupational name for the tailor, from the German word *Schneider,* from Old German *sniden* = to cut. As a Jewish name it comes from the

Yiddish *shnayder* from the same origins. It has roots in Old French *tailleur* as a translated version. Variations include **Schneidermann** (German); **Snider, Snyder** (which are Anglicized Jewish); **Schneidman, Schneiderman** (Jewish); **Sznajderman** (Jewish with Polish Spelling). Cognate forms are **Snider, Sniderman, Snyder** (English); **Schniedr, Schnieder** (Lowlands German); **Sneyder, Snyder, Snieder** (Flemish); **Sneider, Sniyder** (Dutch); **Snajdr** (Czech); **Sznajder** (Polish). Those names with an -S added are generally patronymic forms.

Schoff: German Occupational Name...German occupational name for a shepherd and derived from the element *schaf* = sheep

Schoener is a variation of **Schön,** the German nickname for the handsome man, from German *schön* = fine, beautiful, bright, refined. There are numerous variations including **Schöne, Schöner, Schönert, Schönemann, Schönherr, Schon, Shon, Schoen, Scheiner, Scheyn, Shain, Szejn, Szajner.** In addition, there are dozens of compound names taken up by the Ashkenzac Jewish families when the government began requiring the use of surnames. They are in this form: **Schoenbach** (lovely stream); **Schoenbaum** (lovely tree); **Schoenbrot** (lovely bread); **Schoenherz** (lovely heart) -- you get the idea.

Schreiber is the German occupational name for the clerk, from the German word *schreiben* = to write. Occasionally, it is found as a Jewish (Ashkenazic) name from Yiddish *shrayber* = writer, adapted from Hebrew *Sofer* = scribe. A variation of the German form is **Schreber,** and **Szreiber, Schreibman, Schreibmann** are Jewish variations. **Schriever** is a Low German cognate as are **Schriever, Schriefer, Schriwer. Schrijver** is the Dutch version, and **Skriver** is found among the Danes and Norwegians.

Schroeder: In Germany, the Schroeder drove a dray, which was a low, wheeled cart with detachable sides -- the drayman, or *schroeder,* was the driver.

Schwalb is usually a German nickname for the man who resembled (presumably in grace or swiftness, -- those crazy medieval namers!) the swallow. Back/Bach is the German reference to the man who lived by the stream so **Schwalbach** would be literally, "swallow stream" and could be a reference to a small river or stream named Schwalb (such a stream is located in England, known by the English term Swallow).

Schwertz is from *schwert,* a German Occupational name from the word for sword, which described the man who worked as an armourer for soldiers.

Scott is an English and Scottish ethnic name that was used to identify the man from Scotland, or the man who spoke Gaelic within Scotland. Cognate forms include **Escot, Lescot, Lecot, Lescaut, Lescaux** (French); **Scoto, Scoti, Scuotto** (Italian); **Schotte, Schott** (German); **Schot** (Flemish/Dutch); **Skotte** (Norwegian/Danish). **Schottle** is a German diminutive form and **Scotts, Scotson** are English patronymic versions.

Seigneur was an unflattering nickname given to the peasant man who gave himself airs, or carried himself above his station. Occasionally, it described the man who worked for a great lord. As an Italian cognate, it evolved into a title of respect for professional men such as notaries. **Signorella** is a diminutive form of the Italian versions, which include **Signori, Signore, Sire,** and **Seri.** Variations of the French form are **Sieru, Lesieur, Lesieux, Sire,** and **Lesire.**

Seal/Seale/Seales: English place name from Sale in Manchester, or as an occupational name for the maker of seals or saddles. It was also occasionally used as a nickname for a plump person.

Sells: English Place Name given to the man who lived in the rough hut that was designed for animals – that person was usually the herdsman who was in there watching over the animals.

Saverance: Likely derived from the same origin as **Severn,** one of Britain's most ancient river names, which flows from Wales through W. England to the Bristol Channel. The man who lived on the banks of the river was identified as Severn or **Severne. Severence** and **Saverence** may have indicated someone from there who emigrated to another area, in the sense of "from Severn." The river's name, by the way, means "slow-moving."

Scarisbrick is an English place name derived from the place near Liverpool that bears the name, which came to be called that through a combination of the Old Norse given name *Skar* added to the Old Norse vocabulary word *brekka* = slope, hill. The settlement at that location was literally "Skar's hill" or "Scar's brekka." Any man who formerly lived at that settlement, but moved to a new village could be described by his new neighbors by the reference to his former place of residence (to differentiate him from others already in the village with the same given name). Variations are **Sizebrick, Siosbrick.** Most who bear the name today are descended from Gilbert de Scaresbrec, who was lord of the manor of Scarisbrick in the 1200's.

Scull is an English nickname for the bald-headed man, from Middle English *scholle* = skull. **Scullard** as a name of English derivation would be a variation on that surname.

Sewell is polygenetic, in that it was derived from separate sources at the time names were being acquired. Some Sewells are wearing an English Patronymic name, and are descended from Sewel (victory, strength) and others have an English Place name, from an ancestor who lived near Bedfordshire or Oxfordshire -- both had places called Sewell, which designated 'seven wells.'

Sexton is an English occupational name for the sexton or church maintainer, who also cared for the cemetery and dug the graves, from Old English *sexteyn,* derived through Old French from Latin *sacristanus.* When of known Irish origin, it is an Anglicized form of the Gaelic name *O Seastnain,* meaning descendant of *Seastnan,* whose name is of unknown origin. **Sexten, Sexston, Sexon, Seckerson, Secretan, Saxton, Saxon** are variations. Cognate forms include **Sagreestain, Segrestan, Segreta, Segretain, Segretin, Secretain** (French); **Sacriste, Sacreste** (Provencal); **Sacristan** (Spanish); **Siegrist, Sigrist, Siegerist** (German).

Shand is a Scottish name, **Shands** is the Patronymic version of the name, that is, the equivalent of "son of Shand." The origin of Shand itself is uncertain, but may be a shortened form of Alexander. It may also be a Place name from Chandai, located in Orne, and recorded in the 12th century. A rare but old surname in Scotland. The surname of Shand seems originally to have been confined to the north-eastern counties, particularly Aberdeenshire, and in that county more especially to the districts comprising the parishes of Turriff, Forgue, Drumblade, Auchterless, Culsalmond, Fyvie, King-Edward, and Gamrie. In old times it was variously spelled Schawand, Schaand (1696), Schande, Schand (1528), and Shand. Magister Robert Schawnd was prebendary of Arnaldston, 1522. Probably French, Philibert de Shaunde was created earl of Bath in 1485; but nothing is known of him, except that he was a native of Brittany, according to *The Surnames of Scotland* by George F. Black, 1946.

Sharma: in sanskrit means brahmin or uppercaste men. The caste system in ancient India consisted of Brahmin, Kshatryas, Vaishyas and Shudras. Brahmin = priestly or educated class, Kshatryas = kingly/warrior, vaishyas = business class, and Shudras = untouchables.

Sharp is an English Nickname given to the man who was keen, active, and quick; derived from the Middle English term *scharp*. Variations include **Sharpe,** and **Shairp** (the second of which is primarily Scottish). **Scharff** and **Scharfe** had the same meaning in Germany, while **Scherpe** is the Flemish and Dutch version.

Schaub is a shortened form of **Schauber,** which in itself is a variation of the German occupational name **Schauer,** the name given the official inspector -- of a market, for example, from the Middle High German *schouwer* > *schouwen* = to look, inspect. Other variations are **Schauert, Schauber.**

Schimmel is a German and Dutch nickname for the man with the grey or white hair, from Middle High German and Middle Dutch *schimel,* which denoted both 'mildew' and 'white horse.' Occasionally, when of Jewish heritage, it was assigned as a surname by a non-Jewish government official as an unflattering nickname.

Sevigny is a spelling variant of **Sevigne** (with apostrophe marks over both -e's) which is a French place name that described the man from Ille-et-Vilaine and the place in that location called *Sevigne.*

Shaffer is a variation of **Schaffer,** the German occupational name for a steward or bailiff, from German *schaffen* = go manage, run. **Schaffner, Scheffner, Schaffer, Schofer** are other variants.

Shaid is likely a spelling variation of **Shade,** the Scottish and English place name for the man who lived near a boundary, from Old English *scead,* from *sceadan* = to divide. **Schade** is another version.

Shank when a variation of **Schenck** is derived from **Schenke,** the German occupational name for the man who served as a cup-bearer, or server of wine, from Middle High German *Scenko,* from *scenken* = to pour out. The vocabulary word *schenke* came to be used as an occupational name for the innkeeper, and later it was used as an honorary title for a high court official. Variations are **Shenk, Schenke, Schenker** (tavern keeper). **Shenker, Schenker, Sheinker, Sheinkar, Szenkier** are all Ashkenazic Jewish versions (a common name, as at one time only Jews were allowed to sell alcohol in the Russian Empire).

Shanks is an English (primarily Northern England) and Scottish nickname for the man with the long legs, or strident gait, derived from Old English *sceanca* = shin-bone, leg. In Scotland, the word survived as a vocabulary word, but was replaced in the English standard by Old Norse *leggr.* **Cruikshank** was crooked legs, **Longshanks** was somewhat redundant, **Sheepshanks** was the man with the odd gait or walk. **Shank** is a variation of Shanks.

Shaulis is likely a variation of the English, French, German, and Italian patronymic name *Saul,* which is Hebrew for "asked for" (in the context of child, as in -- the child who was prayed for). Saul was the name of the first king of Israel, but was not a particularly common given name during medieval times -- likely due to the nature of his reign (somewhat troubled). Also, the name was somewhat stigmatized by the story of St. Paul who was originally named Saul, but changed his name when he converted and ended his persecution of Christians. As a result, the surname is comparatively rare. Variations include **Sauil, Sawle, Saulle, Saule, Saulli, Saullo, Shaul, Shauli, Shauly, Shaulsky, Saulino, Shaulick, Shaulson, Shaulov, Shauloff.**

Shaw: English place name for a copse or thicket, and would have been given to someone living near the thicket.

Sheffield and **Shaffield** are English Place names from Sheffield in South Yorkshire, so called from the river Sheaf, meaning 'boundary.'

Shelanskey the -skey, -sky, -ski suffix is indicative of Eastern European place names, and generally found in Poland, where first uses were descriptive place names as in Zukowski = from Zukow. Later, the suffix was attached to many names as a status indicator, such as the prefix "Von" was used in Germany to indicate higher status. The name is likely Americanized from a name similar to **Szellenski,** derived from *szell* = wind, a place name that described the man who lived in a place that was habitually windy -- or **Szczcinsky,** which described the man from the seaport of *Szczecin* in NW Poland.

Shelley is an English place name that described the man from any of the so-named locations in Sussex, Essex, Suffolk, Yorkshire -- derived from Old English *scylf* = shelf + *leah* = wood, clearing. **Shelly** is a variation.

Sheridan is a fain Irish name, Anglicized from the Gaelic *O' Sirideain,* which meant "descendant of Siridean" whose name was of uncertain origin. **Sherridan, O'Sheridane, O'Shiridane** are variations.

Sherrer: Variation of **Scheuer,** a German Place name for the man who lived near the tithe-barn, or an Occupational name for the official who was responsible for collecting the tithes of the farmers, derived from Middle High German *schiur* (barn, granary). Versions include **Scheurer, Scheurermann, Scheuerman, Scheier,** and **Schaier. Sherrer** is likely an Americanized version, which was a common practice among immigrants.

Shields is a Patronymnic version of **Shield,** an English Occupational name for an armourer, the man who provided arms and implements to the soldiers. It is occasionally derived as a place name from a locale in Northumberland called Shields, and more infrequently is from the Old English term *scieldu,* which designated the shallow part of the river, and denoted the man who lived near there. Also, somewhat less frequently than all of the above, Shields can be an Anglicized version of *O'Siaghail,* which means "descendant of *Siadhal* " a Gaelic personal name of unknown meaning.

Shireman is an English occupational name for the man of authority in the county, derived from Old English *scir* = office, charge, authority + *mann* = man.

Shirer, Sherer, and others are variants of **Shearer,** the man who used scissors to trim finished cloth, or the sheep-shearer.

Shirley is an English place name from any of the so-named locations in Surrey, Derbyshire, and others, derived from Old English *scir* = bright + *leah* = wood, clearing.

Shoffner is derived from **Schaffner,** which is a variation of **Schaffer,** the German occupation name for the bailiff or steward, and derived from German *schaffen* = to manage, run. Variations are **Schaffner, Scheffner, Schaffer, Schofer.** The Czech cognate form is **Safar.** Diminutive forms include **Schafferlin, Safarik. Scheffers** is the Low German patronymic form.

Short is an English nickname derived from Middle English *schort* and Old English *sceort* = short...which described the man of non-basketball-playing stature. When of Irish origin, it is derived from Gaelic *Mac an Ghirr,* which means "son of the short man" and was often translated to Short, when Anglicized. **Shortman, Shortt** are variations.

Shultz is likely an Americanized version of **Schultz,** the title given to a German village headman who collected dues or rents and paying them to the lord of the manor, from Middle High German *schultheize* > *sulca* = debt, due + *heiz* = to command.

Sicilia: (which also appears as **Sciliani** and **Sciliano**) is an Italian/Spanish Place name for the man who was from Sicily, which was part of Aragon from 1282 to 1713.

Silkstone is an English place name from a so-named place in South Yorkshire, from the Old English name *Sigelac* (victory, play-sport) + *tun* = enclosure, settlement.

Silvester is an English and German patronymic name, from the Latin Silvester > *silva* = wood and a name borne by three popes, which added to its early popularity. **Selvester, Sylvester, Siviter, Seveter** and English variations; **Vehster, Vester, Fehster,** and **Fester** are German variants.

Simson: is an English Patronymic name derived from the Medieval given name Sim. It has a number of variations that include: **Simson, Simms, Symms,** and **Symes.**

Simpson: English Patronymic from the popular given name Simon (gracious hearing) from which evolved many surnames, including the two most popular versions: **Simmons** and **Simpson.**

Sigmund/Siegmund: and other variants are German patronymic names from *sigi* = victory + *mund* = protection **Siemund** and **Seemund** are among the other versions.

Silver and **Silber** are cognates of the same name, the first an English nickname for the rich man, or the man with silvery-gray hair. Occasionally, it comes from the occupation of silversmith. Silber is the German version of the name, with variations **Silbert** and **Silbermann,** among others.

Sisson is one of the somewhat uncommon matronymic names, taken from the name of the mother -- Sisley, Cecilie -- from Latin *Caecilia.* It was the name of a Roman virgin martyr of the 2nd or 3rd century who was regarded as the patron saint of music. **Sisley** is the most common form of the name, and **Sicely** is a variation. **Sisson** is a diminutive form. Cognates include **Cecille, Cecile, Cicile, Cicille** (French) and **Cacilie** (German).

Skipper was derived chiefly in the Norfolk area of England as an Occupational name for the master of a ship, although occasionally it originated from the Middle English term *skip(en)* which meant to 'jump' or 'spring' and described an acrobat or professional tumbler. **Skepper** and **Skipp** are variations.

Sladden is also an English place name, but the original location has been lost to history, although its elements are derived from Old English *sloh* = slough + *denu* = valley.

Slaughter: English occupational name for the man who slaughtered the animals for the butcher, and also a place name for the person who lived by the muddy spot, or the sloe tree.

Slight/Slightam: Scottish Descriptive name from Middle English *sleght* = smooth or slim.

Sloan: Scottish/Northern Irish patronymic name from the Anglicized version of the Gaelic *Sluaghadhan,* a diminutive form of *Sluaghadh.* The family emigrated from Scotland to Northern Ireland during `Great Plantation' of Ulster during the reign of King James I. Sir Hans Sloan (1660-1753) a collector of papers, manuscripts and curios, donated his holdings to the government, and they became the basis for the British Museum.

Smalley is an English place name that described the man from Smalley in Derbyshire or Smalley in Lancashire -- both of which derived their names from the Old English words *smoel* = narrow + *leah* = wood, clearing. **Smally** is a variation of the name.

Smallwood is an English place name from the so-named location in Cheshire comprised of the Old English elements *smæl* = narrow + *wudu* = wood.

Smart is an English nickname for the brisk or active person, stemming from the Middle English word *smart* = quick, prompt -- which came from Old English *smeart* = stinging, painful. **Smartman** is a variation. Sir John Smart was a Garter Knight during the reign of King Edward IV (1461-1483).

Smedley is an English Place name from Old English *smede* = smooth + *leah* = clearing, for a literal translation of "smooth clearing" in the woods.

Smith: is an English Occupational name for man who works with metal, one of the earliest jobs for which specialist skills were required. It is a craft that was practiced in all countries, making the surname and its cognizants the most widely found of all occupational names in Europe. Medieval Smiths made horseshoes, plows, and items for the house. English variations are **Smyth,** and **Smither;** German = **Schmidt;** Flemish = **De Smid;** Dutch = **Smit;** Norwegian = **Smidth;** Polish = **Szmyt;** Czechoslovakian = **Smid;** Jewish = **Schmieder.** Even the gypsies had the name: the Romany **Petulengro** translates to Smith.

Snyder: Dutch form of Taylor, an occupational name for the person who stitched coats and clothing.

Sobek is a Polish diminutive form of the Czech surname **Sobota,** derived from the given name *Soběslav,* from the elements "take for oneself" + "glory". **Sobiech Sobieski, Sobanski, Sobinski, Sobalski** are Polish cognates. Diminutive forms include **Sobotka** (Czech); **Sobek, Sobczyk, Sobieszek** (Polish). Occasionally, Sobota is derived from the Polish and Czech word *Sobota* = Saturday, the name given to the man who was born, baptized, or converted on a Saturday.

Sokalofsky is one of the many variations derived from the Czech word *sokol* = falcon, which was the occupational name for the man who trained and hunted with falcons. Occasionally, it was used as a nickname in a transferred sense. When of known Jewish heritage, it is one of the many ornamental names taken when so ordered by the government -- animal names being among the many sorts that were adopted. **Sokol** is the Czech form; **Sokoll, Sokole, Socol, Sokolski, Sokolsky** are Jewish variations. **Sokol, Sokolski, Sokalski, Sokal** are Polish cognate forms. **Sokolik** is a diminutive Jewish form. **Sokolov** is a Russian patronymic form of Sokol, while **Sokolowicz,** is the Polish patronymic form. **Sokolowsky** and **Sokalofsky** are also found as place names of Polish origin.

Solis is an English surname taken from a medieval given name bestowed on a child born after the death of a sibling, from the Middle English term *solace* = comfort, consolation. **Soliss** and **Solass** are variations, **Soulas** is the French version.

Solis/Soltis: Polish occupational name for the magistrate or the mayor of the town.

Sommerfeld is a Jewish compound ornamental name comprised of the Germanic elements *sommer* = summer + *feldt* = field. **Summer** is an English nickname for the person with a warm personality, or the man who was associated with the season in some fashion. Occasionally, Summer is a variant of **Sumner** (the summoner) or **Sumpter** (the carrier). Other Jewish compounds are **Somerfreund** (summer friend), **Somerschein** (summer sunshine), **Somerstein** (summer stone). These ornamental names were chosen for their pleasing sound when surnames were bestowed on the Jews by government officials in central Europe. Variations of Summer are **Somer, Sommer, Simmer;** cognates of the English Summer are **Sommer** (German), **De Somer** (Dutch/Flemish); **Sommer** (Danish/Norwegian).

Sorenson means "son of Sorin." It is a Jewish name that comes from the Yiddish female given name Sore (Sarah), which comes from Hebrew Sara = princess. Sorenson is actally a double-suffix, since the name Sorin itself is an indicator of descendancy from Sore (Sarah). **Surin, Suris, Surizon** are other variations.

Sorrell is a variation of the English place name **Soar,** which described the man who lived near the river *Soar,* which was name from Breton *sar* = to flow. Occasionally, Soar derived as a nickname for the man with reddish hair, from Anglo-Norman-French *sor* = chestnut (as in the color of dried leaves). **Sor, Saur, Saura** are cognates. Diminutive forms are **Sorrel, Sorrell, Sorrill, Sorel, Soreau, Saurel, Soret, Sauret, Saurin, Saury.**

Southworth is an English place name, from the location in Cheshire (formerly South Lancashire) so named, and comprised of the Old English elements *suod* = south + *worod* = enclosure, originally to identify the enclosed settlement lying in the south.

Speakman is an English nickname (or occupational name) given to the man who acted as a spokesman for the settlement in dealing with outsiders. It is derived from Middle English *spekeman* = advocate, spokesman. **Spackman** is a variation.

Spears: is among the many variations of the English Nickname for the tall, thin person, or for the man who used the spear with great skill. It derives from Old English *spere* = spear. It occasionally is derived from the maker of spears. Variations include: **Spear, Speir, Spier** (Scotland) and **Speer** (N. Ireland). When the -S- is present at the end of the name, it generally denotes a Patronymic version, as in the 'son of Spear.'

Spence/Spencer: English Occupational name for the person at the manor who dispensed the lord's provisions to those who lived on his land and worked at his estate.

Spires is a patronymic variant of the surname **Spire** (that is, one would have identified the son of Spire by saying he was Spire's...). Spire is an English Nickname from the Middle English word *spir* = stalk or stem, and was used to describe the tall, thin man. By the way, church steeples, sometimes called spires, were not known as such until the 1500's, well after the surname was established.

Springer, Weller, and **Wilder** are examples of names that end in -er that are NOT occupational names. Most that do -- are. These three surnames are English Place names derived from colloquialisms at the time for a woods or forest, and the man designated as Springer lived nearby.

Stafford: is an English Place name that was adopted by the man who lived near a river or creek at a crossing point -- which was called a ford. The particular crossing point was a 'stony ford, or ford by a landing place.'

Stanbrook is an English place name -- it is derived from *stan* = stone + brook, and the man who lived near the stony stream was described by that name.

Stancil (also **Stansell, Stansill**): When English, of joint Saxon-Viking origin with links to a farmstead and Roman villa of the same name in SouthYorkshire. The name refers to a stone chamber, or stane-sell, possibly within a church in the village of Stancil. In antiquity, the name is most often found in Yorkshire near the village of Doncaster, as well as in Berkshire and Kent.

Standen is the English place name derived from Old English *stan* = stone + *denu* = valley (which described the man who lived in the stony valley). **Standing** is a variation of Standen.

Standish: is an English Place name for the location in Lancashire (now Greater Manchester) from OE *stan* =stone + *edisc* =pasture, for a literal meaning of 'stone pasture.'

Stanier/Stonyer/Stanyer/Stonier: English Occupational Name...for stone cutter. Old English *stan* =stone. A stan sawyer or stan'yer was a cutter of stone.

Stanley is an English place name derived from the Old English elements *stan* = stone + *leah* = wood, clearing, and described the man who lived at the stony clearing in the woods, or a similar known geographic location.

Stanton is an English place name, from Old English *stan* = stone + *tun* = settlement, enclosure. The man from the "settlement on stony ground" was described as "stan-tun." There are numerous locations throughout England with the name, and the man who left one of those locations for a new settlement would also be referred to in that fashion by his new neighbors, to designate him as the new guy from that town.

Starnes is a regional variation of **Stearnes,** a patronymic variation of **Stern,** the English nickname for the severe person, from Middle English *sterne* = strict, austere. The son the the man they nicknamed Stern was Stern's boy, or Stern's son, or simply -- **Sterns.** The spelling variations are common -- surname spellings were not standardized until well after the American Civil War. **Sterne, Stearne, Stearn** are also common variations.

Staron is a Polish cognate of the Russian patronymic name **Starikov,** from the nickname Starik (Old Man) derived from *stary* = old. Other cognate forms include **Starski, Starzycki, Staron** (Polish); **Stary** (Czech); **Starik, Starski** (Jewish). Patronymic cognates include **Starov** (Bulgarian); **Starikov, Staricoff** (Jewish Ashkenazic). Diminutive forms are **Starek, Starzyk, Starczyk** (Polish); **Starek** (Czech) **Starshenko** (Ukrainian); **Starcevic** (Croatian). **Starzynski, Starczewski** are Polish place names with the same origin that served as origins for some surnames.

Starr: English Place name... Many surnames derived from the signs at the roadside inns during early times, when people didn't read signs as much as they looked at the pictures – and innkeepers sometimes took their sign's picture as a surname. Most were animals, birds or fish, but occasionally the innkeeper displayed other signs, such as the star, by which they became known.

Starrett, Sterritt, etc are among the variations of the English and Irish place name **Start,** derived from Old English *steort* = tail, and used in a transferred sense to describe the spur of a hill. The man who lived at that location would have been the first to be known by that name. Cognates are **Stertz** (German), **Sterdt, Stert, Steert** (Low German), **Stertzel** (Low German diminutive form). **Starte, Stert, Sturt** are other English versions, and **Sterritt** is the form chiefly found in Northern Ireland (the land originally settled by the Scotsmen who came to be known as Scotch-Irish).

Steele: English Place name, from 'stile' or a place of steep ascent.

The suffix is actually - *ski,* or - *sky* -- which was originally associated with names in the same fashion the English suffix - *ish* was associated with nouns, ie. bookish, pertaining or related to books. The - *ski* suffix is found among the Polish and Ashkenazic Jewish, and later came to be associated with status in the same fashion that *de* - and *von* - were used among the French and Germans, respectively, to indicate gentry status

Sterba (**štérba** is close...the -e should actually have the same mark above it as the -s) is a Czech nickname for someone with a tooth missing, from the Czech word *štérba* = gap. Many of the Czech surnames had suffixes or other alterations that weren't literal variations.

Sterling is a variation of the Scottish place name **Stirling,** from the city in central Scotland which was recorded as early as the 12th century, and may have been derived from the name of a river, although it's origin is unclear. The name described the man who emigrated from that city during Medieval times.

Stevenson is a variation of the English Patronymic name Stephen/Steven, which originated in the Greek given name *Stephanos,* meaning 'crown.' Stephen was the first Christian martyr, stoned to death three years after the death of Christ, and his name was widely adopted throughout the Christian countries in the Middle Ages. Among the numerous variations are **Stephenson, Stevenson, Steven, Stiven, Steffen, Steffan.** French cognates are **Stephan, Stephane, Estienne, Etienne.** Other cognates include **Estievan, Etievant, Tievant, Thevand** (Provencal), **Stefano, Stifano, Stephano, Stievano, Steffani** (Italian), **Esteban** (Spanish), **Esteva, Esteve** (Portuguese), **Stefan** (Rumanian), **Stoffen** (Bavaria), **Stevaen** (Flemish), **Schippang, Zschepang, Schoppan** (German of Slav origin), and many, many others.

Stiehr, Stier, Steer: German occupational names for the man who watched the livestock.

The Old English word *stille* = quiet + *burna* = brook, stream -- *stille burna* would easily evolve into **Stilborn** and its variants, to describe the man who lived by the quiet stream.

Stilling is likely a diminutive form of the English and German nickname **Still,** given to the placid person, from Middle English and Middle High German *still* = calm, quiet. The "little placid one" would be a stilling.

Strickland is an English place name, from the so-named location in Cumberland and derived from Old English *styric* = bullock + *land* = pasture.

Stirland is a variation. In the year 1230, Sir Walter de Stirkeland was the holder of Stirkland Manor in Cumberland.

Stoddard is a variation of the English occupational name **Stoddart,** who was the keeper and breeder of horses. The name derived from Old English *stod* = place where horses were kept for breeding + *hierde* = herdsman, keeper. Variations are **Stodhart, Stoddard, Studart, Studdeard, Studdert, Stiddard, Stothard, Stothart, Stothert, Stuttard.**

Stokes is a patronymic form of the name **Stoke,** an English place name derived from the numerous places thoughout England by that name. They were named from Old English *stoc* = "place, house, dwelling" and generally referred to an outlying settlement away from a larger one. Variations are **Stokes, Stoak, Stook, Stookes, Stoker.**

Stonham is a variation of the English place name **Stoneham,** the names of two villages in Hampshire which got their names from Old English *stan* = stone + *ham* = homestead. Stonham is also a place is Sussex that would serve as an place of origin for many with this name.

Stout is an English nickname for the brave or steadfast man, from the Middle English term *stout* = steadfast. Occasionally, it is derived from Old Norse *Stutr* = gnat, which is just the opposite of the English term. **Stoute, Stoutt, Stutt** are variations.

Strobel: German nickname that is derived from **Straub**, which comes from Middle High German *strup* = rough, and was given to the "shock-headed man" for his hair style.

Stroman is a variation of the German cognate of **Straw,** the English occupational name for the man who dealt in straw, from Old English *streaw* = straw, or occasionally, a nickname for the man with the straw-colored hair. Other German forms of the name are **Stroh, Strohmann, Stroman, Strohman.** Jewish versions are **Shtroy, Shtroi** (from the Yiddish pronunciation of straw).

Stroud is an English place name from the so-named locations in Gloucester and Middlesex derived from Old English *strod* = ground overgrown with brushwood. The man who emigrated from one location to another was often referred to by his place of origin, and thereby adopted the surname. **Strood** and **Strode** are variations.

Stroupe: comes from the Middle High German word *strup,* which means 'rough, unkempt' and is a German Descriptive name for the 'shock-headed' man.

The German name **Stucker** is a place name for the man who lived near the prominent tree stump, while the German name **Stuck** is a place name from the so-named town whose name origin means "plot of land."

Stukeley: Stukley, Stucley, and **Stukeley** are variations of a habitation name from a place in the county of Huntingdonshire (now Cambridgeshire) which got its name from Old English *styfic* = stump + *leah* = wood. A family by the name of Stucley can be traced to Richard Stucley (died 1441) who is also recorded as Richard Styuecle.

Sullivan/Sullivant: Anglicized form of the Gaelic *O'Suileabhain,* descendant of *Suileabhan,* a given name composed of the elements *suil* = eye + *dubh* = black, dark + the diminutive suffix -an.

Susko is a variation of **Zisin,** a Jewish metronymic name derived from Zise, a Yiddish female name that meant "sweet" + the suffix -in. **Zissin, Susin, Zisovich, Ziszovics** are variations. Diminutive forms include **Ziske, Ziskis, Ziskin, Zyskin, Siskin, Suskin, Susskin, Ziskovitch, Ziskovich, Ziskovitz, Zuscovitch, Susskovich, Suskovich, Susko, Zislis, Zislin, Sislin, Zisslowicz.**

Sutherland is a Scottish regional name that described the man who came from the former county by this name, which got its name from Old Norse *suðroen* = southern + *land* = land. It was called the South land because it was south of Scandinavia and south of the Norse colonies of Orkney and Shetland Islands. The man who came from that area of Scotland was referred to by his former place of residence.

Sweeny is an Irish patronymic name, from an Anglicized form of *Mac Suibhne,* which meant 'son of *Suibhne'* whose name was a nickname meaning 'pleasant.' Variations include **McSeveny, McSween, McSweeney, McSwiney, McSwine, McQueenie, McQueen, McQueyn McQuine, Magueen, McWhin,** and **McWhan.**

Swann/Swan: English Nickname for a person noted for purity of excellence (attributes of the swan, supposedly), from Old English *swan.* Some Swan surnames derived from the signs at the roadside inns during early times, when people didn't read signs as much as they looked at the pictures – and innkeepers sometimes took their sign's picture as a surname. (Most were animals, birds or fish.) Occasionally, Swan is derived as an

Occupational name for the servant or retainer as a variant of **Swain.** Cognates include **Schwan** (German), **De Swaen** (Flemish), **De Swaan, Van den Swaan, Van den Zwaan** (Dutch), **Svane** (Norwegian), and **Svahn, Swahn** (Swedish).

Sweet: Swett is a variation of Sweet, an English Nickname for a popular person, derived from Old English *swete.* Given names Swet(a) -- masculine, and Swete -- feminine, were derived from this word, and survived into the early Middle Ages, and may be the source of the surname. Swett isn't the only variant: **Swetman, Sweetman, Sweatman, and Swatman** are among the English varieties. There are cognative versions many countries including **Sussman** (German), **DeZoete** (Flemish), and **Susser** (Jewish).

Syri: English Patronymic Name... from given name Syred and elements *sige* = victory + *roed* = counsel

Szczepanski is a Polish cognate of the patronymic surname **Stephen,** which has its origins in the Greek *Stephanos* = crown, and was a popular name throughout the Christian countries in Medieval times. **Stefanski** is another Polish form. Polish patronymics (that is, "son of Stephen or Stefanski") are **Stefanek, Stefanczyk, Szczepanik, Szczepanek.**

Szymczyk/Szymczak: Polish Patronymic Name...from the popular name Simon, which means 'gracious hearing' and was common during the Middle Ages. It was due to affection for Simon Bar-Jonah surnamed Peter, rather than to Simeon -- the second son of Jacob by Leah. (from Elsdon Smith)

T

Taber/Tabor: was the man who beat the tabor, a small drum. It's an English Occupational name.

Taylor is an English occupational name for the tailor, from Old French *tailleur* < late Latin *taliare* = to cut. It is among the most commonly found surnames, due to its popularity as a medieval occupation. Variations are **Tayler, Tailour, Taylour.** Cognate forms include **Tailleur, Letailleur, Taillandier, Tallendier. Taylorson, Taylerson** are patronymic forms of the name.

Tasker is an English occupational name for the man who did piece-work, especially in reference to the man who threshed corn with a flail. It is derived from Anglo-Norman-French *tasque* = task, from Old French *tasche* = task. **Tascher** is the French version of the name, and **Taschereau** is a French diminutive form.

Tartarka is a cognate form of the Russian patronymic name **Tatarinov,** derived from the name *Tatarin, Tatar* = stammerer (the word is actually of Turkish origin). It was used as a nickname among the Czechs, Italians, and others, as a reference to an uncontrollable person, or a wild-acting person. **Tatarintsev** is a Russian variant. **Tatarski, Tatar, Tartari, Tartaro, Tatarowicz, Tatarkiewicz, Tatarewicz, Tatarek, Tartarini, Tartarino, Taterini, Tartarelli, Tartaroni** are other Czech, Polish, and Italian forms.

Teal is an English nickname for the man who was said to somehow resemble the so-named bird in some way, from Middle English *tele* = teal. Teale is the most common version, while **Teall** is a variation.

Tello is a Spanish patronymic name from a medieval given name which was similar to the Germanic given name *Tila* (as represented in Old English).

Tellez is a patronymic form and **Tesles** is a Portuguese patronymic form. It is also found among Italians in this way **DeTello, D'Tello** and is a place name meaning "from *Tello* " or some location similar to that spelling.

Templeton is a Scottish place name from Templeton near Dundonald in the former county Ayreshire, now part of Strathclyde. It was so-named for Middle English *temple* = house of the Knights Templar + *toun* = settlement. There are also places named Templeton in Wales and other locations, but likely derived their names from someone with the surname, rather than the other way around.

Tenberg was originally **Ten Berge,** which is a Dutch form of the name **Berg,** which is a place name for the medieval man who lived by a hill or mountain. It comes from an Old Norse word *bjarg* which means "hill" or "mountain." Different cultures used various means to say "from the mountain" or "from the town of Paris" and so on. The Germans used the prefix -von, and the French used the prefix "de." John de'Paris would be "John from Paris." Erik von Berlin would be "Erik from Berlin." The Dutch used several prefixes, including Van den; Van der; Van -- which meant "from" or "from the." Andy Van den Berg would be "Andy from the hill." Another prefix used was "tot" -- which meant "of." "Andy tot den berg" -- means "Andy of the hill." The "tot" and the "den" were said so quickly that they became a single word -- "ten." It is sort of like a contraction, where "can not" becomes "can't."

Terrell: is an English Patronymic name, with a little Nordic influence. (remember, they invaded early on...) Thurold or Thorold were given names that mean 'Thor, strong' and have lapsed into disuse these days...but during the Middle Ages there were enough that their sons were sometimes known as Terrell, meaning the 'son of Thurold' or 'son of Thorold.'

Terry: is derived from the pet form of the given name Terence, which means 'smooth, tender.' It's an English Patronymic name from a Latin given name.

Testa is a variation of **Teste,** a French nickname for someone with a large head, (or something distinctive about their head) derived from Old French *teste* = head < Late Latin *testa* = head. Variations are **Tete, Testu, Tetu.** Cognate forms include **Testa, Testi** (Italian). Diminutive forms are **Testot, Tetot, Teston** (French); **Testini, Tesetino** (Italian). Other forms include **Testoni, Testone** (Italian augmentive); **Testard, Teetard, Testart, Tetart, Testaud, Tetaud** (French pejoratives); **Tester, Testar** (English pejoratives).

Tew: English Place name from the Old English word *tiewe* which meant row, or ridge, and the person living near the ridge became known as Tew.

Theodore is a French patronymic name, derived from Greek Theodoros, and the elements *theos* = God + *doron* = gift, and was a popular Middle Ages given name. The Russian version of the name is **Fyodor.** Cognates are **Tudor** (Welsh); **Teodori, Teodoro, Toderi, Todeo** (Italian); **Teodoro** (Portuguese); **Joder** (German/Swiss); **Teodorski, Fedorski, Fedynski** (Polish). Diminutive forms include **Doret, Dorin** (French); **Toderini, Todarini** (Italian); **Tedorenko, Fedoronko, Fedorchenko, Fedorchik, Fedorchak, Fesenko** (Ukranian). Other patronymic forms and diminutive forms exist as well.

Thiele is a Low German diminutive form of the surname **Terry** from the Norman given name Terry from Old French *Thierri*, derived from Germanic elements *þeudo* = race, people + *ric* = power. Variations are **Terrey, Tarry, Torrey, Torrie, Todrick**; cognates include **Thierry, Thiery, Thery, Thiry, Tery** (French); **Tiark, Tjark, Jark, Jarck** (Frisian). Diminutive forms include **Thiriet, Thiriez, Theuriet, Thiriot, Theriot, Thriion, Thirieau** (French); **Tietzel, Tietze, Thielsch, Tilke, Tillich** (German); **Thiede, Tiedmann, Thiedemann, Theimann,**

Thede, Thieke, Tiecke, Theeck, Tietze, Tietzmann, Titze, Tetze, Thiele, Thiel, Tiel (Low German). Many other forms exist as patronymic, pejorative, and diminutive cognates.

Thomas is one of the most common given names, and as a result, it created a HUGE number of surnames found throughout Europe. See the definition under Thompson for more info on its origins...Cognates of Thomas are **Tomas** (Spanish); **Tome** (Portugal); **Tomas** (Catalan); **Toma** (Rumania); **Tuma, Toman, Tomas, Tomes, Tomsa** (Czech); **Tomasz, Toma** (Poland); **Tamaasi** (Hungarian). Diminutive forms are **Thomazin, Thompsett, Thom, Tomalin, Tomabling, Tamblyn, Tompkin, Tonkin** (English); **Thomasset, Thomazet, Thome, Thomassin, Thomelin, Thoumasson, Thomazon, Thomesson, Thomasseau, Thomazeau** (French); **Tomassini, Tommasini, Tommasino, Tomadini, Tomaini, Tomaino, Tumini, Tummaselli, Tommasetti, Tumiotto** (Italian); **Thomel, Domel, Theml, Teml, Dehmel, Demelt, Thamel, Thamelt, Dahmel, Thumnel** (German); **Thoma, Thomann, Dohmann, Themann, Demann, Thumann, Thomke, Domke, Demke, Demchenm, Dumke** (Low German); **Tomasek, Demaschek, Tomaschke, Domaschke, Damaschke** (German/Slavic influence).

There are countess variations of Thomas, and **Tompkins** is a diminutive of the English form, along with **Tomazin, Thompsett, Tompsett, Thom, Tomalin, Tombling, Tombin, Tomkin, Tonkin.**

Thomasson: English Patronymic name derived from the given name Thomas, which was the preferred usage in Wales, while in England the Patronymic surname evolved as **Thoma, Thomasson, Thompkins, Tomlinson, and Toombs.**

Thompson: English and Scottish Patronymic name from Thomas (twin) which was a popular name in the Middle Ages (and still is...). The name Thomas comes from an Aramaic term for "twin." It was one of the really popular given names at a very early time, which led to people who bore the name achieving some renown, leading to an increased popularity. The first letter of the name was originally the Greek "theta" which accounts for the TH spelling -- the pronunciation of which was lost due to the French influence in the earliest stages of the name. As with many of the early popular given names, they became the subject of variations due to familiarity or fondness -- pet names, if you will -- in the same fashion that William Clinton is called Bill, or William Mayes was called Willie. Several of the pet forms of Thomas (there are loads of them, like Tom, Tommy, etc.) did not carry on as given names to modern times, and involved the letter -p, which was generally added as a pronunciation aid to make a pet form. For example, from Thomas came the pet form Thompkin, similar to Thumbkin being a "little thumb" (a nursery rhyme). Thompkin was "little Tom" and when someone described his son, they might say William -- Thompkin's son. They also contracted names or dropped the diminutive (or pet) form, which would cause Thompkin as an adult to be known as Thom or Thomp, for short. His son might be described as William -- Thomp's son. And that is what Thompson means -- son of the man known as Thom, Thomp, or Thompkin, or other diminutive form of Thomas.

Thomson: Thomas was a popular given name in the Middle Ages, and it has endured through the years. Thom is a pet form and the man who had Thom for a Dad, was Thom'son. It's an English Patronymic name.

Thurman: Thor was the ancient god of thunder, and was known in Old Norse as *Porr* (not exactly the correct P as the Norse wrote it, but it's the best this keyboard will do). *Porr + mundr* = Thor's protection, and that became a given name in Old Norse -- *Pormundr,* which evolved into the Middle English version Thurmond. Thurman is an English Patronymic Name derived from Thurmond as a given name.

Tipton: English Place name from Staffordshire which described Tibba's homestead.

Todd: English Occupational Name...In the north of England, a fox was commonly referred to as a 'todd' and the picture of the fox or todd often appeared on the sign outside a roadside inn. (Many couldn't read and the signs used pictures instead.) The animal on the signs often were adopted as surnames by those who lived there.

Surnames ending in the suffix *-land* generally are place names referencing a field or part of a field. The Old English word *toll* = tribute, tax gatherer (the meaning carried through to modern English fairly clearly). The toll-land would be the field where the tax collector lived, and **Toland** would identify a man who lived nearby.

Tolbert is a French and Norman patronymic name from the Germanic personal name derived from *Tol* = (meaning unclear) + *behrt* = bright, famous.
Tomlin: English Patronymic name...another derivative of the given name Thomas. Thomas was the preferred usage in Wales, while in England the Patronymic surname evolved as **Tomlin, Thoma, Thomasson, Thompkins, Tomlinson, and Toombs.**

Tonin is a variation of the surname **Toney,** from the medieval given name *Toney* (Tony), an aphetic form of Anthony. Cognates are **Thoine, Toin, Thoin** (French); **Toni** (Catalan); **Togni, Ton** (Italy); **Thon** (Germany). There are numerous diminutive forms as well.

Toomey, O'Toomey and **Twomey** are Anglicized versions of the Gaelic *O'Tuama* (descendant of Tuama) with Tuama being a personal name derived from *tuaim* 'which meant "small hill." Other variations are **Twoomy, Tuomy, Towmey, O'Twomey, and O'Toomey.**

Tourneur is the French version of the English and Scottish occupational name **Turner,** which was the name for the man who made small objects from wood or metal by turning them on a lathe, from Old French *tornier* = turn. Variations of the French form are **Tornier, Tournier, Tourneux, Letourneur, Letourneux. Tornadou, Tornadour, Tournadre** are Provencal cognates.

Towery is likely a variation of the English place name **Tower,** for the man who lived near a tower or defensive watchtower. It is derived from Middle English *tur* > Latin *turris* = tower. Cognates are **Tour, Latour, Delatour** (French); **Torres** (Provencal); **La Torre, Torri, Turri, Della Torre, Torrese, Torrese, Torrisi, Turrisi** (Italian); **Torre, Torra** (Catalan).

Townsend is nearly a literally vocabulary expression for the man who lived at the "town's end" and is derived from Middle English *tun,tone* = village, settlement + *end* = end. Variations are **Townhend, Townend, Townen.**

Tracy: English Place name based on a French town called Tracy, which meant 'terrace.' Many English surnames were those based on the name of the former home of those who emigrated with William the Conqueror or soon after.

Traube is the German occupational name for the grower of grapes for winemaking, from German *traube* = grape > Middle High German *trube* = bunch of grapes. In some cases, in may have come from the sign at the inn displaying a bunch of grapes, where the keeper of the house would become known by that name. Variations are **Traube, Trubner, Traubner, Traubmann, Traubel, Treibel, Trauble.**

Travere is a variation of **Travers,** the English and French place name that described the man who lived near a bridge or ford, or occasionally as an occupational name for the collector of tolls at such a location. It is derived from Old French *traverser* = to cross > Late Latin *transversare.* English variations are T **raves, Travis,**

Traviss, Trevis; French versions include **Traverse, Traver, Travert.** Cognate forms include **Traversa, Traverso, Traversi** (Italian); **Travieso** (Spain); **Traversini** is a diminutive Italian form.

Treat: The surname Treat is an English descriptive name that originated with a 'friendly, beloved person' whose company was well-enjoyed, as any treat today would be!

Tremble, Trumble, and **Tromble** were all descended of men named *Trumbold,* from elements meaning "strong, bold" and are English patronymic names.

Tricker is a variation of the English nickname **Trick,** which was given to the crafty or cunning person, from the Middle English word *trick* = strategem, device. **Trickett** is a diminutive form.

Trotter is an English and Scottish occupational name for a messenger, from Middle English *troten* = to walk fast. When of German heritage, Trotter is the occupational name for the grape-treader, from Middle High German *trotte* = winepress. **Trott** and **Trotman** are variants of the messenger, while **Trott, Trottmann** and **Trotmann** are versions of the German name.

Trowbridge is an English place name from the so-named location in Wiltshire, derived from Old English *treow* = tree + *brycg* = bridge, which referenced a fallen tree serving as a bridge. **Troubridge, Trobridge, Trubridge** are variations.

Troy: French Place name from Troyes, a place known for "the Gaulish tribe, the Tricassii."

True is a variation of the English nickname **Trow,** which is derived from Old English *trowe* = faithful -- and described the man who was trustworthy and steadfast. Variations are **Trew, True, Trueman.** Cognate forms include **Treu, Treue** (German); **Treu, Treumann Treiman, Getreuer, Getroir, Getrouer** (Jewish Ashkenazic).

Trussell is an English name that is either a diminutive form of the Middle English word *truss* = bundle or package, which would describe a peddler, or it may be a variant of the English Nickname **Thrussell,** which described a happy, singing person, from a word used to describe a songbird -- throstle. **Trussel** and **Truswell** are variations.

Although the origin of **Tyrer** isn't absolutely certain, it is believed to have come from the Middle English word *tiren* = to equip, dress -- from Old French *atirier,* which came from the phrase " *a tire* " meaning "in order." In that context it would be an occupational name for the man in charge of the wardrobe of an important person of that medieval time and specific location.

Tull is an English patronymic name, believed to have originated in the Old English given name *Tula,* whose name is of uncertain origin.

Tullos/Tulloh/Tulloch/Tullock: Scottish Place Name near Dingwall on the Firth of Cromarty which got its name from the Gaelic *tulach* = hillock, or hill.

Tune is a variation of the English place name **Toner,** which described the person who lived in a village, as opposed to an outlying area like a farm or family settlement. It comes from the Middle English word *tune* / *tone* from Old English *tun,* which meant fence at the time, but came to mean "enclosure" from its usage as a description of primative settlements. When of known Irish heritage, however, it is an Anglicized version of the Gaelic name *O'Tombrair,* meaning descendant of *Tombrar,* whose name meant "protection." Variations are **Town, Towne, Toon, Toone, Tune, Townee, Towne, Towning.** Cognate forms include **Van den Tuin** (Dutch), **Tuijnman, Tuynman. Zauner** is a German cognate form that retained its original meaning of "fence."

Turnbull: Some names are derived from descriptions of their originators...like the Englishman strong enough to 'turn a bull.'

Turner: English/Scottish Occupational Name...from the French *turnier* = turn for the man who used a lathe to turn objects from wood or metal.

Turvey: English Place name from a place by that name whose elements are comprised of OE *turf* = grassy + *eg* '= island.

Tutt is generally an English patronymic name from the Old English given name *Tutta,* which can be found among some surviving place names, but isn't all that popular as a name for boys any longer. **Tutnall,** and **Tuttington** are among place names derived from *Tutta,* which died out as a given name in the Middle Ages.

Tweedy/Tweedie: English Place Name...traced back to the Scotsman who came from the land of Tweedie (which means 'hemming in') in Stonehouse parish, Lanarkshire.

Twigg is an English nickname that described the thin man, and is derived from the Old English word *twigge* = twig, shoot. It is believed to have been borrowed from Old Norse, since the word occurs late in the Old English period and was confined to the Northern dialects. **Twigge** is a variation. **Zweig** is a German cognate, **Cwaig, Zeigenhaft, Cwaigenhaft** are Jewish Ashkenazic versions, and **Tweig, Zweigle,** and **Zweigel** are Jewish versions of Polish origin

Tyler is a spelling variation of the English occupational name **Tiler,** the man who made and laid tiles, derived from Middle English *tile* = tile > Old English *tigele* > Latin *tegula, tegere* = cover. Tiles were used in floors and pavements in the Middle Ages, but the roof aspect came in the 1500's. **Tyler, Tylor** are variations. Cognate forms include **Thuiller, Tuilier, Thuillier, Tivolier, Tivollier, Thiolier, Thioller, Theolier, Teulier, Teulie, Tullier, Tulliez** (French); **Tejero** (Spain); **Ziegler** (German and Jewish); **Tegler, Tegeler, Tiegeler** (Low German); **Tichelaar** (Dutch).

Tyrrell as a surname is of unclear origin, but it is believed to have derived from Old French *tirer* = to pull, which when used in the context of an animal and reins and applied to a person, was intended to mean stubborn.' Other variations of the name include **Tyrell, Tirrell, Terrill, Terrell, Terrall, Turrell, Tearall, Tirial.** Cognates are **Tirand, Tirant,** and **Tirard** (French).

U

Uberuaga: originates from Bizkaia, the Basque Country, Spain, and means Hot Springs in English, derived from the elements *ur* = water + *bero* = hot + *aga* = place of.

Ulmer: Von Ulm is a Place designation that references Ulm, a city in Baden-Wurttemberg, Germany.

Underwood is a Scottish and English place name that described the man who lived at the edge of the woods, from Middle English *under* + *wood* (both terms survived to modern day with the same meanings). It is also a place name that described the man who left any of the several settlements (later towns) by that name, to settle in a new location.

Ungerleider is a variation of the German, Czech, and Jewish ethnic name **Unger,** which described the Magyar or the man from Hungary. In some instances, it denoted a man who had trade connections in Hungary. Variations include **Ungar, Hunger, Hungar, Ungerer, Ungermann, Ungerland, Ungerman, Hungerer, Hungerland.** There are many cognate forms in other languages as well.

Uusimake: Finnish Acquired/ornamental Name... Like many other nationalities, the Finnish people often constructed surnames that pleased the ear; maki = hill.

V

Valdez/Valdes: Spanish Place Name...The Spanish and Portugese were fond of bestowing as a surname, the name of the place from which the person had departed. Valdez ends in -ez, so it is Spanish rather than Portuguese where -es is preferred. Valdes was the name of the town that gave its name to those who came to be known as Valdez.

Vail is a variation of the English place name **Vale,** which described the man who lived in a valley from Old French *val* and ultimately Latin *vallis.* Cognates are **Val, Vaux, Lavalle, Lavaud, Lavault, Leval, Leveau, Delaval, Deveaux** (French) **Valle, Valli, Valla, La Valle, Da Valle** (Italian); **Valles** (Spanish); **Valeano** (Rumanian). Several diminutive forms also exist.

Valentine: means 'vigorous or healthy' and was originally a Latin given name that found its way to various countries. Valentino was a derivative in a number of countries. It's Patronymic in that it was derived from the father's name.

Valerio is an Italian patronymic name, from the medieval given name *Valerius* (Latin origin) which was the name of several minor Christian saints in the 4th and 5th centuries. **Valeri, Valleri Valier, Valer** are variations. Cognates include **Valere Valeri, Valery** (French); **Vallier, Valier** (Provencal); **Valero** (Catalan); **Valério** (Portuguese); **Valerius** (German).

Dutchmen whose names were those of cities, towns, or districts were identified by the prefix Van- which means "from" or "of the," which also was used in reference to nicknames. **VanCuren** means literally "from Curen" or "of the curen" and would identify the man who originated in that locale. If Curen is not an existing Dutch locale, it may be a vocabulary word used as a nickname.

Van den is 'of the' - so if Abbeele is a type of tree, then **Van den Abbeele** is "of the poplar tree (or whatever type tree it translates to).

The name **van der Grinten** is Dutch. A *grint* is a river wash where fine gravel which was washed up has built an island or low-land, for example, Valkengrind, near Roermond, Holland. Contributed by Wolfgang van der Grinten.

Van is a prefix that means "from the" or "of the" and is used in such names as **Van Geest,** a Dutch name for the man who lived by the barren sandy soil -- literally, "of the sandy soil."

Van Horn is a Dutch place name for the man who lived at the horn-shaped spur of a hill. *Van* is a prefix that denotes "of" or "from."

Varn: Variation of Fern, an English Place name for someone who lived in a place where many ferns were growing, derived from Old English *fearn* = fern. Variations include **Fearn, Fairn, Feirn, Fearne, Ferns, Farnes, Vern, Verne, Varn, Varne,** and **Varnes.**

Varner is a French version of the German patronymic name **Warner,** comprised of Germanic elements *warin* = guard + *heri* = army. The name was introduced into England by the conquering Normans. **Garnier, Gasnier, Guernier, Vernier** are other French versions.

Vass/Voss: English Occupational name... OE *vassus* = serf, Gaelic *foss* = servant.

Veale/Veal: English Nickname...Veale is a name that was influenced by the Normans. Old French *viel* meant old, and the nickname referred to an old man or the elder of two brothers that had the same given name American heavyweight boxer George Foreman named several of his sons George, so it still happens!).

Veitch/Veach/Vetch/Veath: Veitch is a Norman (Old French) cognitive of the name **Veath/Vacca** (Italian) which described 'one who herds cows.'

Verdon is predominately derived from **Vardon,** a Norman name brought to England with William the Conquerer. Verdun is a name held by several locations in France, and is of Gaulic origin, deriving from the elements *vern* = alder + *dun* = hill, fortress. Many of the men bearing the name originated from La Manche, and the village called Verdun in that area. During the middle ages there was a dialectic change in which -er was pronounced as if -ar; for example, the cloth-seller was called a marchant, which meant merchant. Later, the erroneous pronunciation was corrected by scholars. Vardon has remained as the predominant version of Verdun, which was corrected in the case of Verdon. Variations of the name are V **arden, Derdon Verden, Verduin, Verdin, Verduyn.** The French form of the name is **Verdu/Verdun.** In Catalan it was called **Verdu** (accent over the -u). The name can also be a French form of the Italian name **Verde,** from the Italian word *verde* = green. It is presumed to have been a nickname for someone who always dressed in green. The diminutive form of the French version was often Verdon. Variations of Verde are **Verdi, Virde, Virdi, Lo Verde.** French forms of Verde are **Vert, Vert, Ver, Levert.** Other diminutive forms of the name (as in Little Green, Greenie, Greenette, etc.) are **Verdelli, Verdini, Verdicchio,** (all Italian); **Verdel, Verdelet, Verdet, Verdon, Verdonnet** (French).

Verdoorn / VanDoorn / Van den Doorne / Doorneman: Dutch Place / Patronymic. A version of the English name THORN; a person living by the thorn bush/hedge, or from the Danish version of "tower". With the prefix Van it becomes "the son of Thorn/Tower" and Ver would denote "from Doorn," a place of thorns.

Vermillion is likely a Dutch place name from *van der million* in a collapsed form, and meaning "from the mill" or a town named in that sense.

The German nickname **Vetter** is derived from *fater* = father, by way of Old High German *fetiro,* which was a generic term for male relatives. The modern German word vetter means 'cousin.' The surname evolved from Middle High German *vetere* = uncle, nephew - in the sense of father's brother, or brother's son. In Northern Germany, it was also used as a given name. **Votter** is a variation found in Bavaria; **Vetterle, Votterl** are diminutive forms.

Vick is derived from separate sources (polygenetic, as it is called). Frederick is an English patronymic name from a Germanic given name composed of the elements *frid* = peace + *ric* = power, which was introduced into England by the invading Normans. (Actually, they introduced the name after the invasion, when the fighting settled down.) Vick is a Frisian diminutive form of the name, as are **Freddercke, Fedde, Feck,** and **Fick.** If the heritage is known to be English, the name is an English nickname, drawn from the Anglo-Norman-French word *l'eveske,* which means 'the bishop.' The phrase was erroneously divided as though 'le vick' and the Vick retained, although technically, it should have been *Evick*. Variations of the English version are **Livick, Livock, Leffeck, Veck, and Vick.**

Vidal: Italian Patronymic name from Vitale, a name derived from the Latin *Vitalis* and its root *vita* which means life. It was a popular name among Italians professing their early Christian faith.

Vinzenz is the German cognate of the English and French patronymic name **Vincent** from a medieval given name, derived from Latin *vincere* = to conquer. **Vienzenz** is another German form, and other German diminutives are **Vinz, Vinzel, Finzel, Zentz, Vietze, Fietz, Fietze, Wientzek, Fietzek, Fietzke.**

Virgin is a variation of the English surname **Virgo,** of uncertain origin, but believed to have derived from Latin *virgo* = maiden, and used as a nickname to describe the man who played the part of the Virgin Mary in the medieval pageant, or simply, nicknames for shy men. Other variations are **Virgoe, Vergo, Virgine, Verge.**

W

Wachsmann is the German occupational name for the collector of beeswax, which was used in candle making and in document seals. **Vaks, Vaksman, Vacksman, Vax, Vaxman** are cognate forms of Yiddish origin.

Waddell is a Scottish place name from Wedale, near Edinburgh. The exact meaning of the town's name isn't clear, but the surname arrived as a way to identify a man who hailed from there. In Scotland, the emphasis is placed on the first syllable, but elsewhere it is generally emphasized on the second to avoid confusion with waddle. **Waddel, Waddle, Weddell, Woddell,** and **Weddle** are among the variations. Hugh Waddell was an early American who served in the North Carolina militia and defended the western frontier of that colony during the French and Indian War.

Wadsworth and **Wordsworth** both derived from the settlement called Wadsworth near Halifax in West Yorkshire, which got its name from the Old English elements *Woeddi* (a Medieval given name) + *worð* = enclosure. It described an enclosed settlement headed by a man named Woeddi. A man who removed from there and relocated somewhere else might be described by his new neighbors by pointing out where his place of origin.

Wagner/Waggoner: German/English Occupation Name...One who drove the high-sided carts or wagons carrying produce between manors was called the Waggoner in England, and the German counterpart is Wagner. Among the Pennsylvania Germans who were among the first non-English settlers of the American colony, Wagner also denoted a wagon-maker. According to one survey, Wagner is 116th on the list of most-frequently found surnames in America.

Wahl is an Ashkenazic Jewish name that is taken from the German word *wahl* = election, from Old High German *wala* =

choice. It was taken as a name by the descendants of Saul Katzenellenbogen, who was born in 1541 and died circa 1617. According to a Jewish legend, he was elected King of Poland for a single day during a period when Poland was an elective monarchy.

Walker is the English and Scottish occupational name for the fuller (also a surname) from the Old English elements *wealcere/wealcan* = to walk, tread. The fuller was the dresser of cloth, which was readied by beating it, or soaking it in water and trampling, or walking on it. Walker is sometimes derived also from a place in Northumberland by that name from Middle English *wall* = Roman wall + *kerr* = marsh.

Wall/Walls/Waller: English Place and Occupational Name...one who lived by the wall (medieval towns always used them for protection) was Wall/Walls/Waller, and the name was also used to designate the one who did the repair.

Walsh: English/Welsh place name. In England, the man from Wales would be described as **Walsh, Welsh, Wallace,** or **Welch** -- that is, foreigner or stranger.

Walt: Walter means "rule, army" and has been a popular name since the Middle Ages. There were a number of surnames derived from the given name -- including the pet form Walt. The son of Walt was **Walts.** It's an English Patronymic name.

Walton: The ending -ton comes from the Old English/Norse -*tun* which designated a town or settlement. Walton was the 'walled' town or the 'wood' town and is an English Place name.

Wankel is likely a diminutive form of the Low German (of Slavic origin) name **Wanke,** which is a cognate of the English name John. One of the earliest first names was John, derived from Hebrew *Yochanan* (gift of God), which in the 17th century replaced William as the most popular name for a male child. Low German cognates of Slavic origin are **Wanka, Wahncke,**

Wancke, Wahnke, Gentzsch, Geniscke, Jentzsch, Jenicke, Janoscheck, Jahncke, Jahnisch, among others.

Wantz is likely a variation of the German (of Slavic origin) patronymic name **Wenzel,** from that given name, which was a diminutive form of the name **Wenze,** wilth the diminutive suffix -el added. It was a shortened form of the Old Czech given name *Vececlav* and was borrowed before the Czech language lost their nasal vowels. Variations are **Wentzel, Wanzel, Fenslein, Wetzel, Wodtzel, Watzold, Wentzke, Wenzke, Wentzig, Wetsig.** Dimutive German forms are **Wenz, Wach, Fach, Feche,** among others.

Ward is an English occupational name for the watchman or guard, from Old English *weard* = guard. It is occasionally derived as an Anglicized version of the Irish (Gaelic) patronymic name *Mac an Bhaird.* Variations are **Warde, Wardman,** and **Wordman. Wards** is a patronymic form.

Ward is the English occupational name for the watchman or guard, from the Old English term *weard* = guard. Occasionally, it is derived as an Irish patronymic name, as an Anglicized form of the Gaelic name *Mac an Bhaird,* or as an Anglicization of the Jewish surname **Warszawczyk.** Variations of the occupational name are **Warde, Wardman,** and **Wordman. Wards** is a patronymic form.

Warf: is taken from the Old English word *hwearf* =shipyard and as an English name would designate a man who works at the docks, and the word evolved into our lexicon as wharf. The Dutch equivalent is *Van Der Werf.*

Warner/Warren: both names were derived from the job of the man who watched over the wildlife at a park. They are both English Occupational names.

Waterhouse is an English place name that described the man who lived in a house by a body of water. The name was found primarily in the Yorkshire, Lancashire, and Midlands areas of England as the geographic location of its origin.

Waters is a patronymic variation of the English surname **Water,** which in itself is a variation of the name Walter -- actually it is the way Walter was pronounced in medieval times. Occasionally it is derived as a place name for the man who lived near a body of water, or from the Irish as an Anglicized version of the Gaelic name *O Fuarisce* and associated with the word *fouran* = water, spring. **Wasser** is the German version, **Van den Water** is found among the Flemish and Dutch. **Watters, Warters, Worters, Watterson, Fitzwater** are all patronymic forms in addition to Waters.

Warren: English Place Name...(Norman) from La Varrenne in Seine-Maritime which means sandy soil.

Waterworth is an English occupational name that described the 'water bailiff' or the overseer at the water, collector of fees at the water's edge. The name was found primarily in the area of the banks of the now drained freshwater lake *Martin Mere* in West Lancashire, and was derived from *Waterward,* from the Middle English elements *water* + *ward* = bailiff, guard > Old English *woerd* = watchman, guard.

Watson is a patronymic form of the English and Scottish name **Watt,** which came from the extremely popular Middle English given name *Wat* or *Watt,* which was a pet form of the name Walter. Diminutive forms of Watt are **Watkin, Watking, Watling, Whatling;** patronymic forms are **Wattis, Watts, Watson;** patronymics from diminutives are **Whatkins, Watkiss, Watkeys, Gwatkins** (Wales) **Swatkins** (Gloucester), and **Watkinson.**

The name **Wayne** is actually a spelling variation on one of the oldest professions, that of a wheelwright, or " **Wain** " wright, as they were called. They were also called Cartwrights (as in Bonanza, the TV show...), from the Middle English word *wain* =

cart, wagon (from Old English *woegen*). Sometimes Wain was a place name that described the man who lived at the house that bore a sign of the astronomical constellation of the Plough, which was known in medieval times as Charles' Wain (Charles being short for Charlemagne) -- but that was the exception to the naming rule. Variations include **Wayne, Wane, Waine, Waines, Wainman, Whenman, Wenman.** In Germany, the man of that profession was called **Wegenmann.**

Webster is a variation of te English occupational name **Webb,** who was a weaver, from early Middle English *webbe* > Old English *webba* = to weave. By the time the name was adopted, the word webbe was almost obsolete, and the -ster and -er suffixes had found their place in the language, which led to Webster. **Webbe, Webber,** and **Web** are variations. Noah Webster was the man behind the book where suffixes and prefixes are readily available, and was a descendant of John Webster, the governor of Conn (1656).

Weeks is a patronymic form of the name **Week,** which is an English place name that described the man who lived in an outlying village or settlement, removed from the main town or village of the area -- from Old English *wic* = outlying settlement, farm. In that sense, Week is a variation of the surname **Wick,** which has the same meaning. Occasionally, Week is a nickname that described the man in poor shape, from Middle English *wayke* = weak, feeble. Variations are **Weake** (the more commonly found version), **Week, Weekes, Wheeker.**

Weiler is polygenetic...one form is the German cognate of the English (Norman) name **Villiers,** a place name that described the man from any of the so-named locations. The Germans called the same man Weiler. **Villers, Villars, Villis,** are English variations. **Villers, Devilliers, Deviller, Divillier** are French versions. Weiler is also a Jewish (Ashkenasic) place name for the man from any of the locations name **Weil,** in Baden, Wurttemberg, or Bavaria.

Wells is a patronymic form of the English place name **Well,** which described the man who lived by the spring or stream, and derived from the Old English term *wella* = well, spring. Variations of Well include: **Wells, Weller, Welling, Wellings, Wellman, Welman, Wall, Will, Wool.** Cognate forms include **Weller, Welle, Wellman** (Low German); **Van der Wel, Van Wel, Van Wells, Welman** (Dutch).

Welter is a Low German cognate of the name **Walter,** which is derived from Germanic elements *wald* = rule + *heri* = army. **Wolter, Wolder, Wohlder, Wohldert, Wohlert, Wohler** are other Low German versions. **Gaultier, Galtier, Galtie, Gauthier, Gautier** are among the many French variations; **Gualtieri, Gualtiero, Gualdieri** (Italian); **Walther, Waldherr** (German); **Wauter, Wouter** (Flemish/Dutch).

Wessel: is a Frisian cognative of the name Warner. The Frisian Islands are in the North Sea off the coast of the Netherlands and near Denmark. It's a patronymic name from the given name Warner (guard).

Westcott is an English place name from any of several so-named locations in Surrey, Berkshire, and others, named from the Old English elements *west* = west + *cot* = cottage, shelter. A man who came from that location would be identified by his new neighbors as the man from the "west-cot" ie. John Westcott.

Westmoreland is a spelling derivation of **Westmorland,** the English place name that described someone from the former county by that name, which was originally called *Westmoringaland* in Old English, and described the "territory of the people living west of the moors.'

Westwick is an English place name composed of the Old English *west* = west + *wic* = outlying settlement. It described the man who lived in the smaller, outlying settlement that depended on a nearby larger settlement (like a suburb, of sorts).

Whaley: English Place Name for the meadow by the road or hill.

Wheeldon is an English place name derived from Old English elements *hweol* = Wheel + *dun* = hill, and described the man who lived by the rounded hill.

Whetstone: normally whet is a derivative of white, and white stone would be a place name for one who lived near a prominent white stone...but the Old English word *whetten* = to make keen + *ston* = stone --combine for whetstone, an abrasive stone for sharpening tools, which could have been adopted as a surname by the man who used it.

In the Middle Ages, the word *-cock-* was a generic term for a young man. It originally was used to applied to the young man who strutted proudly about (like the rooster), or was cock-sure of himself, but came to be applied to any young man who was self-assured, or a leader of his peers. As a result, it was applied to several names as a suffix that better-defined the youngish man by his personality. The name **Wilcox** is a compound name with the elements *Will* = pet form of William + *cock* = self-assured young man. Variations are **Wilcock, Wilcocke;** Patronymic forms are **Wilcocks, Willcocks, Wilcox, Willcox, Willcockson,** and **Willcoxon.**

Whitt is a variation of the Scottish, English, and Irish nickname **White,** which described the man with white hair, or a pale complexion. There was also a Middle Ages given name *Whita,* which bore the same meaning (pale complexion), and the name is sometimes a patronymic identifier from that given name. **Whyte, Whitte, Witte, Witt** are other variations. Cognate forms exist such as **Weiss, Weisse, Weisser, Weissert, Wyss** (German); **Weissmann** (Switzerland); **Witte, Witt** (Low German); **DeWitt, DeWitte, DeWit** (Flemish, Dutch); **Wajs, Wajsowski** (Polish). There are also a number of compound surnames among the Jewish (Ashkenazic) names that use Weis or Weiss as the first element of an ornamental surname.

Whitfield is an English place name that describes the man who originally lived in any of the settlements known by that name, found in Kent, Derbyshire, Northumberland, and other locations. The settlements got their names from Old English *hwit* = white + *feld* = pasture, open country...and were described that way because of the chalky soil. **Whitefield** is a variation.

Whitehead is an old English and Scottish nickname, that described the man with the fully grey (white) hair, particularly when it was on the head of a man considered too young to be that way. It is derived from Middle English *whit* = white + *heved* = head. Occasionally, it is derived as a mistaken translation of the Irish Gaelic name Canavan, incorrectly using the terms *ceann* = head + *ban* = white. **Whytehead** is a variation of the English and Scottish name.

Wilkerson is a variation of the English patronymic name **Wilkin,** which was taken from a medieval given name, Wilkin, derived from a shortened form of William (Will) with the addition of a suffix -kin to form a diminutive or pet form of the name. **Wilken** is a variation; other patronymic forms are **Wilkins, Wilkens, Wilkinson, Wilkenson, Wilkerson.**

William is among the most commonly found Medieval given names, and as a result, is among the most common surnames. **Williams** is a patronymic form. William is derived from an Old French given name with Germanic elements *wil* = desire, will + *helm* = helmet, protection. It was introduced by followers of William the Conqueror and became in short order one of the most popular given names in England. Bill the Conqueror may have had an influence there... Variations are **Welliam, Gilliam, Gillam, Gilham, Gillham Gillum.** Cognate, diminutive, and other forms exist in great number.

Winegardner is likely an Americanized form of an occupational surname found in many countries -- although it may be a simple spelling variation. In Germany, the man who lived by the vineyard, or who worked in the vineyard, was known as **Weingardt, Weingartz, Wingert, Weingartner, Weingarter.** In England, (where wine production was more common in medieval times than today) the man was called **Winyard, Wynyard, Wingard,** and **Winnard.** The Flemish form is **Wijnyaerd** or **Van de Wijngaerden.** The Dutch is **Wijngaard** or **Van Wijngaarden,** and the Ashkenazic Jewish form is **Weingarten.** In Denmark and Norway the name is spelled **Wiingard** and **Wiingaard.**

Winrow is an English surname of uncertain origin found chiefly in Lancashire, possibly a place name from the Old Norse elements *hvin* = whin, gorse + *vra* = nook, corner. Variations are **Whinrow, Whinwray, Whineray, Whinnerah.**

White: English/Scottish/Irish Nickname for the man with white hair, or pale skin, from the Middle English *whit* = white.

Whitehead: is an English Nickname that described the man with the fair hair, or the prematurely white hair. It's from the Old English *whit* =white + *heved* =head.

Whitelock/Whitlock/Whitlatch: English Descriptive name for the man who had an especially white head of hair.

Whitmer/Whitemore: English Place name derived from Whitemore, in county Staffordshire. It was a white barren ground, and the man who lived near could easily be identified by his dwelling's location.

Wien: German/Jewish Place Name for a city in Vienna of Celtic origin. There was a large Jewish population in Vienna previous to the Holocaust.

Wiesenhunt: German place name from Middle High German *wise* = meadow.

Wiesner is a variation of the German place name **Wiese** which described the man who lived near a patch of meadowland, from the Old High German *wisa* = meadow. **Wieser, Wiesener, Wiesemann** are other variations. **Iterwies** is found among the Lowland Germans, while **Wiesner** and **Wiesen** are variations found among Jewish ancestries (Wiesner is polygenetic, in that it has multiple origins).

Wiggins is a patronymic variation of the English name **Wiggin,** derived from the Breton given name *Wiucon,* with elements meaning worthy + high, noble. The name was brought to England by followers of William the Conqueror. Occasionally, the name is derived from the given name **Wigant,** which originally was a nickname meaning 'warrior' and also introduced during the Conquest. Variations are **Wigin, Wigan,** and **Wigand.** Cognates in Germany are **Weigand, Weigang, Weigt, Weicht, Wiegandt,** and **Wiegank.** Other patronymic versions are **Wiggans** and **Wigens.**

Willmon is a diminutive variation of the English patronymic name William, from the Norman form of an Old French given name composed of the Germanic elements *will* = will, desire + *helm* = helmet, protection. The name was introduced into England with William the Conqueror. Other diminutive variants among the English are **Willmett, Wilmot, Willimott, Willmin, Wilmin, Willimont.**

Wilcynski: is a Polish Place name and is derived from the Polish *wilk* which means wolf. Wilk was generally used to describe someone wolf-like -- but in the case of Wilcynski, it indicates a place name, and could be for the man who lived near the wolves.

Wiley: Some names were taken from the places where the home was kept...in the case of the man who became known as Wiley, he lived near the Wiley River in England, which was so-called as a "tricky" river.

Wilson/Willson/Will: Scottish/N.English Patronymic name derived from the given name William. It was also sometimes an English Place name for the person who lived by the stream or well from the Saxon *wiell* = well.

Wimberly is an English place name that described the man who lived near the windy wood or clearing, and is comprised of the Old English elements *windbaere* = windy + *leah* = woods, clearing. Settlements found at the "leah" were often described by the man who headed the settlement, as in "Wilmoer's leah" which is the origin for the surname **Womersley.** It may be possible that the name Wimberly corresponds to a given name that is now lost. There other names, though, that reflect a continually windy area.

Windt is a variation of the English place name **Wind,** which described the man who lived near a path or alley, or particular road. It is derived from Old English *gewind* > *windan* = to go, proceed. Occasionally it was the nickname for a swift runner. **Winde** is another variation. If it is from German origin, it is likely a variation of **Wendt,** from **Wend,** an ethnic name for the people who once occupied a large section of Northern Germany and contributed greatly to the names of the locale.

Winter is found among the English, German, and Danish/Norwegian names that are derived as a nickname for the man with the gloomy or cold personality, from the Middle English vocabulary word that survived to present day. Occasionally it is drawn as a Jewish ornamental name, taken -- or distributed at random -- at the government's order. Also, Winter is occasionally an Anglicized version of *Mac Giolla-Gheimhridh,* which translated as "son of the servant of Winter," or something similar. Patronymic forms include **Winters, Wynters, Winterson.** Variations include **Wynter, Wintour** (English); **Vinter** (Norwegian/Danish). **De Winter** is a Flemish and Dutch cognate form. **Winterl, Winterle, Winterlein** are German diminutive forms.

Wlodylo is a Polish cognate variation of the Russian and Bulgarian patronymic surname *Vladimirov,* from the given name Vladimir, comprised of the Slavic elements *vlad* = wealth, rule + *mer* = famous, glorious. St. Vladimir was extremely popular during his time (died 1015) and as a result Vladimir was one of the few Slavic names that were accepted for Orthodox baptisms. **Volodimerov** is a Russian variation. Polish cognates include **Wlodzimirski, Wlodzimierski;** Jewish cognates are **Vladimirski, Vladimirsky;** Rumanian cognates (patronymic) are **Vladimiresco, Vladimirescu;** Other diminutives are **Volodko** (Ukraine); **Volodzhko** (Belorussian); **Wlodek, Wolodko** (Polish), **Wlodasch, Wlotska, Wlotzke** (German of Slavic origin).

Wingate: English Place Name...taken from the Wingate, Durham area of England. Wingate was the 'pass where the wind blows.'

Wirth is the German and Ashkenzic Jewish occupational name for the innkeeper, from the German word *Wirt* = host, and occasionally is found as a German status name for the head of the household, in the sense of "provider." **Wurth** is a variation; **Wurthle, Wirthgen** are diminutive forms. **Wirtz, Wirths** are patronymic versions.

Wöhrlein is derived from Germanic elements *warin* = guard + *heri, hari* = army and is a patronymic cognate of Warner. Low German patronymic forms include **Werning, Wereking, Warnkonig, Warnkes, Warnken, Warning. Warner** is English of Norman import, with cognates in several languages.
Womack: English Place name that designated a 'hollow or crooked oak' tree. The person who wound up with the surname was the one who lived nearby.
Normally, the name **Wood** described the man who lived in or near a wood, but it sometimes was used as an occupational name

for the woodcutter. It is derived from the Middle English word *wode* = wood, from Old English *wudu* = wood. Variations are **Woode, Woods, Wooder, Wooding, Woodings, Wooddin, Woodin, Attwood, Bywood.** Cognate forms are idde, **Wehde, Wede, Wehe, Weh, Wedemann, Wehmann** (Low German); **Wedin, Vedin** (Swedish). **Wedberg** is a Swedish compound ornamental name that is literally translated as "wood hill."

The standard Place-name suffix *-ford* (occasionally spelled *- forde*) was sometimes corrupted into *- fork,* as a result of colloquial dialect, misunderstanding, or just 'fooling around.' At any rate, the root name of **Woodfork** is **Woodford,** which is an English and Scottish Place name that described a man who came from any of the so-named settlements, found in Essex, Wiltshire, Cornwall, Northampton, and other areas of medieval England and Scotland. Woodford is comprised of the Old English elements *wudu* meaning wood + *ford.* A ford is a place of crossing at a stream or river. The wood-ford was the stream or river crossing near the woods, which is what the settlements that were established there became known as, and a number of the inhabitants of the settlement became known as, when surnames helped identify a particular person. Other variations of Woodford are **Woodforde, Woodfords,** and **Woodforks.**

Wooster is an English place name from Worcester, derived from Old English *ceaster* = roman fort, which was added to a now-unrecognized tribal name. **Wostear, Worcester, Worster** are variations.

Wojcik/Wojtas: Polish Patronymic Name...The Czech missionary who converted Poland to Christianity was Voitech, which meant 'noble, bright.' The Polish version of the name was **Wojciech** which became a family name in Poland, and another form of the name was **Wojcik,** as was **Wojtas.**

Word: is an English (and German) place name for the man who lived near the thicket. Or near a winding brook. Or the man who inhabited an open place in a village. Or the man who had an ancestor named Werdo, which was a pet form of the name Werdmann or Werdheri. In the case of the latter, it's a Patronymic name.

Wyatt: the word *wido* was Old German for 'wood' and was brought to England with the Normans as the given name Guy. Diminutive forms include Wyatt which was adopted as a Patronymic surname.

Wyles is a variation of the English occupational name **Wileman,** which described the man who trapped or hunted for a living. It was derived from Middle English *wile* = trap, snare – Old English *mann* = man. **Wiles** is another variation.

X,Y,Z

Xavier is a variation of the name **Javier**, a Spanish given name that honors St. Francis Xavier, a Jesuit missionary (1506-52). He was born into nobility that took the name from the castle of Javier, in Navarre, and is of Basque origin.

Xemenez is a variation of Jimeno, which may be a form of Simon, although its exact origin is unknown. During medieval times, the name was Ximenus, and variations are **Gimeno**, **Jinenez**, **Gimenez**, and **Ximenez**.

Nearly every name that begins with Yak is a form of the name Jacob, and the -son suffix is a patronymic indicator, which would indicate "son of Jacob" for **Yakerson,** and is similar in form to the many Jewish patronymic names of the same order, such as; **Yakoboff, Yakubov, Jakubowski, Yakubowski, Yakobovitch,** etc.

Yates is a patronymic form of **Yate,** the North English place name for the man who lived near a gate, or occasionally an occupational name for a gatekeeper, from Old English *geat* = gate. **Yeats, Yeates, Yetts, Yeatman, Yetman** are variations.

Yisek is a variation of the Jewish, English, and French name Isaac, derived from the given name *Yitschak,* derived from Hebrew *tsachak* = to laugh. **Isaac** has always been a popular name among Jews but was widely used by Christians as well during medieval times, and as a result, gentile families bear the last name as well. Variations are **Isac, Isaak, Issac, Issak, Izac, Izak, Itshak, Itzshak, Yitzhak, Yitzhok, Jzak, Eisik, Eisig, Aizik, Aizic, Aysik, Ajsik, Ishaki, Izchaki, Izhaki, Izhaky, Yitschaky, Yitshaki, Yitzchaki, Yizhaki, Yithaky, Jizhaki, Itzchaki.** Numerous patronymic forms exist as well.

Young: Comparitive age was an easy way to reference men with a common name -- for example, John, the young -- as opposite to John, the elder. It is sometimes found with the old spelling Yong, and is found in other languages. Jung is the version found in Germany, and Jaros is the Polish variety.

Youngblood is an English nickname, a compound name derived from the words Old English *geong* = young + *blód* = blood, which meant "young relative." Young generally designated one of two men with the same given name, and blood was an affectionate term for a blood relative.

Zappa is of Italian origin, and describes an agricultural worker, from the Italian word *zappa* = mattock. Variations are **Zappi, Zappell, Zappellini, Zappelli, Zappetta, Zappettini, Zappetti, Zappino, Zapparoli, Zappoli, Zapulla, Zappulli.**

When of English origin, the name **Zell** is a variation of the place name **Sell,** derived from Old English *(ge)sell,* which described the man who lived in a rough hut generally occupied by animals - many times the man living there was the herdsman. **Selle, Sells,** and **Zelle** are other variants.

Zillwood is derived from a forest on the Somerset / Wiltshire border in the southern UK, "Sellwood Forest". The first reference to the forest was in 878AD as *Selewudu,* meaning Sallow Wood or Willow Forest. The sallow part seems to originate from the latin for "aspirin like effect" of the under layer of the willow bark, salicylates (Latin *Salix* = willow) The Wessex dialect and the inability of the majority of its people to read or write led to the Parish Priest or Recorder spelling the name phonetically and changing it over time from Sel(l)wood to Zillwood.

Zimmerman is the German form of the occupational name Carpenter, derived from Middle High German *zimbermann,* formed from *zimber, zimmer* = timber, wood + *mann* = man. **Zimmerer, Zimmer, Zimerman, Cimerman, Cymerman Cymmermann, Cimermann, Timmerman, Timmermann** are variations.

Susko/Zisin, a Jewish metronymic name derived from **Zise,** a Yiddish female name that meant "sweet" + the suffix -in. **Zissin, Susin, Zisovich, Ziszovics** are variations. Diminutive forms include **Ziske, Ziskis, Ziskin, Zyskin, Siskin, Suskin, Susskin, Ziskovitch, Ziskovich, Ziskovitz, Zuscovitch, Susskovich, Suskovich, Susko, Zislis, Zislin, Sislin, Zisslowicz.**

Among the Slavic countries, the names **Ziv, Zivin,** and **Zivney** are nicknames for the "vigorous, alert" man.

Zumberge is a variation of the Germanic place name **Berg,** with addition of the prefix -zum (at the) generally found among the Lowland Germans, Swiss, and Dutch. Berg comes from Old High German *berg* and Old Norse *bjarg* -- and both meant "hill" or "mountain."

Zumwalt/Zumwald: The prefix -zum is the German indicator for "at the" or "of" and Zumwalt and Zumwald are "at the woods," or "of the woods."

Zweiacker: is two German words, Zwei and Acker, Zwei is the number 2 and Acker means field.

Index